NIRVANA
A TOUR DIARY

Andy Bollen played in bands from the age of 15. His friends needed a drummer in an emergency so he helped out Captain America and ended up touring with the hottest band on the planet, purely by accident. Since then, he has worked in comedy for 20 years, mostly with the BBC. He has written topical gags and sketch-based comedy for network BBC TV as well as BBC Scotland TV, Radio Scotland and BBC Radio 5 Live. He has been a columnist for the *Sunday Mail*, as well as contributing to such diverse publications as the *Glasgow Herald*, *Scotland on Sunday* and *The New York Times*. He plays drums when the neighbours are out, DJs, has a dog called Bonnie and walks around the park most days thinking about funny things.

NIRVANA

A TOUR DIARY

**MY LIFE ON THE ROAD WITH ONE OF
THE GREATEST BANDS OF ALL TIME**

ANDY BOLLEN

metro

Published by Metro Publishing,
an imprint of John Blake Publishing,
3 Bramber Court, 2 Bramber Road,
London W14 9PB, England

www.johnblakepublishing.co.uk

www.facebook.com/Johnblakepub   facebook

twitter.com/johnblakepub   twitter

First published in paperback in 2013

ISBN: 978 1 85782 875 7

British Library Cataloguing-in-Publication Data:

A catalogue record for this book is available from the British Library.

Design by www.envydesign.co.uk

Printed and bound in Great Britain by CPI Group (UK) Ltd

5 7 9 10 8 6

Papers used by John Blake Publishing are natural, recyclable products made
from wood grown in sustainable forests. The manufacturing processes
conform to the environmental regulations of the country of origin.

Every attempt has been made to contact the relevant copyright-holders,
but some were unobtainable. We would be grateful if the
appropriate people could contact us.

ACKNOWLEDGEMENTS

I'd like to thank Sharron for her patience and support. John Blake, Sara Cywinski for editing, Martin Roach at Independent Music Press and Tom Bromley for his editing, preliminary agent work and advice. Thanks also to Tony McCluskey for proofreading. I'd like to personally thank everyone for their belief, help and support, especially Norman Ferguson. Everyone on the tour: Eugene, James, Gordon, Naoko, Michie, Atsuko, Page, Krist, Dave and Kurt, Willie, Michael and Murray.

CONTENTS

Nevermind Tour, Winter 1991

BRISTOL BIERKELLER 4 November
LONDON ASTORIA 5 November
WOLVERHAMPTON WULFRUN HALL 6 November

(Nirvana head to mainland Europe)

BRADFORD UNIVERSITY 26 November
BIRMINGHAM HUMMINGBIRD 27 November
SHEFFIELD UNIVERSITY 28 November
EDINBURGH CALTON STUDIOS 29 November
GLASGOW QMU 30 November
NEWCASTLE MAYFAIR 2 December
NOTTINGHAM ROCK CITY 3 December
MANCHESTER ACADEMY 4 December
LONDON KILBURN NATIONAL 5 December

INTRODUCTION
ON STAGE
WITH NIRVANA

LONDON KILBURN NATIONAL, 5 December 1991

Sometimes life hands you a moment. It's encore time. You can't believe it. Is this really happening? It is. I'm here. I'm not dreaming. Concentrate. Even at this exact moment in time, in my life, on stage with Nirvana on 5 December 1991, in a heaving, jam-packed Kilburn National, drumming to 'Molly's Lips' by The Vaselines, even at this precise moment, I know it's probably the coolest thing I'm ever going to do in my life.

I also realise my biggest adversary is creeping up on me: lack of concentration. I can't let it beat me. Within seconds, despite being excited and joyous, I sense its sinister approach. I start to look around and see the crowd. Stop over-analysing. Keep the beat. For once in your life, concentrate for more than 30 seconds. Keep your head in the game. It's a strange feeling standing on stage beside Dave Grohl, in front of a pulsating Nirvana crowd.

I'm hammering and trashing the life out of Dave's drums.

3

I'm attacking the floor tom with what I think are clever triplets and flams but in reality show as much grace as a sexually frustrated builder with a hangover taking a sledgehammer to a wall. Dave is smiling at the chaos. He's sober. I'm pished. Keep your head in the game. Dedication. Application. Thought.

I'm watching Dave and then I look over at Kurt Cobain, who looks so happy. I look over at Krist, who is barefoot, locked in the groove. He's some height. From the drum riser he makes Kurt look tiny. Even with his slouch, Kurt's got to be 5'9", which makes Krist at least 6'7". Kurt has to stand up straight – it's bad for your spine to slouch like that. Bit like that myself, I never stand up straight; you make yourself more of a target. I'm good at that, guessing heights and weights. Our singer, Eugene, is doing handstands. Normally he's good at them, though not tonight, his balance has gone, he's pished too. I try to keep up with Nirvana as they rip through 'Molly's Lips'.

On stage you notice how much a full venue smells. You can smell people's breath, good and bad. You can literally feel and smell the electricity searing from the amps and the PA, the dust burning on lights, the sweat, and the excitement. It smells of energy, a life force. It smells of power. It smells of love, fear and frustration. There's a tremendous heat that hits you when you run on stage. It's similar to the feeling that cold Scottish people get when they step off a plane on holiday. You notice the lights from up here. They add to the intensity. Setting the tone. How would you start to paint this? Harsh reds, delicious greens, warm violet, some purple, some lavender, then they switch to a stark, volatile orange. The cues seem to come from Dave. When he rattles both crash cymbals the lights switch, as if he's triggering a plot change.

Bodies fly everywhere. I see beautiful girls look up with wide-eyed abandon. I see one in particular who looks right into my soul. Fucking concentrate. She can't be looking at me. I look at Dave and gesture and nod toward him. Come on, forget about her, keep the beat! She shakes her head and points to me. I start a conversation with her through nods and eye gestures. *Yes, you!* she says. She has the most beautiful smile. My eyesight's great – it's my ears that will go first. She looks like she just stepped out of *The Great Gatsby.* How would F. Scott Fitzgerald describe her? It's the Jazz Age. Bobbed, coquettish, pale and pristine; a distinct, angular beauty. Strong featured, striking, different-looking, would photograph really well. I am Trimalchio, welcome to my feast. Keep in time. Concentrate. Fucking hell, concentrate! Look at Dave, all focus and power. I watch him and struggle to find the appropriate analogy and metaphor. Grohl drums like a stuntman in a monster truck speeding toward a cliff, with an unnerving tendency to wait just too late before jumping as the cab careers off the ubiquitous cliff and explodes for dramatic effect to close the scene. Concentrate. Fuck! Just focus! Dave rockets through songs like a punk rock, animated mini John Bonham, a taut powerhouse, all hair, tattoos and elbows. He's in a shower of sweat and splinters as his sticks slay cymbals, and it's terrifying trying to keep up with his intense, ferocious playing. This is like appearing in the ring at Madison Square Garden and trying to spar with the world heavyweight champion while trying hard not to look like a fanny. Stop!!! Stop with the analogies and concentrate. My drumming has to be spot on; any lack of concentration is highlighted, especially when alongside someone as good as Grohl.

It's strange to look up and play and actually notice thousands of people. They all look so happy. How fucking cool is this? A swirling cloud of humanity, cool indie fans, post-punk fans, rock fans. All wearing their Ramones, Mudhoney, Beat Happening, Megadeth, Sonic Youth, AC/DC and Beatles T-shirts. Loads are wearing long-sleeved black Nirvana hooded sweatshirts. There are just so many different fans that don't care and just love music. There are sensitive shoegazing Smiths fans nervously clutching their *Penguin Classics* and breaking into a shy smile. There are smartly dressed Mods stage diving. Cynical Northern Soul fans and bikers, now all believers, embrace like a Klan member and a black minister on a tacky American daytime show. Everyone seems mesmerised; all disparate factions, coming together. There's something definitely happening here. All their faces share one of three expressions; enthralled, elated, ecstatic. Caught up in the power. The volume. The pop. The punk. The rock. The emotion. The energy. The sheer unadulterated joy. A visceral, pulsating, excitement.

Fucking concentrate! No, not too hard. Relax, keep in time. It's true what Charlie fucking Brown says, 'The harder I try the worse I get.' Just find the zone. Relax tension. Keep your head in the game. DAT: Dedication, Application and... ha! Look! There's the Mod. Go for it, son. Where's the girl from *The Great Gatsby* gone? Maybe not *The Great Gatsby*. Who is that painter? She looks like a punk version of the girl from the painting in the Hunterian Museum in Glasgow. Stanley Cursiter! That's the one: 'The Pewter Jug'. Why did they always have the models in paintings holding jugs? Can you do something with your hands, sweetheart? Here, pick up that pewter jug and look out of the window. Give me enigmatic, baby! Excellent! That's the one. She's gone – ships that pass in the night. It was lovely knowing you, however fleetingly. We could've been made for each other.

Crack. Fuck. Just snapped my left knuckle with my right-hand stick. Smile through, no one noticed. Is that bone chipped now? I notice my fingers have new muscles on them. Tiny little six packs. *Come on, tour! Work out a new muscle programme for those flabby fingers!* There's so much magic in the air. There's endless stage diving. I could never do that, they'd let me fall. It's about trust, they say, go for it, believe! If I did it, just like Lucy did to Charlie Brown, she'd pull the ball away as I was about to kick it. I'd go up in the air but they wouldn't catch me and I'd land on my arse. Concentrate. Someone gets on stage and sprints toward Kurt's monitor and uses it like a springboard; jumps off higher than the others, like an Olympic pole vaulter.

Oh, my knuckle hurts, that's a bruise. That's the secret – the approach. The run up, the momentum and speed to get the required height, relax into an arched shape; spin before gravity thinks you're a smart arse and drags you down. One of his Converse sneakers goes off in mid-flip and ricochets in the opposite direction. This is fucking painful. I can't concentrate. Why am I fucking bothering? Why do I have to keep noticing every detail? I notice things that are unimportant and ignore the important ones like right now. Just play drums.

I notice that Dave sings backing vocals in a punk scream and also in a tender, melodic harmony. I see two girls at the front in all the chaos who are trying to pass notes to Kurt, stoically keeping their place as the venue sways and booms. Kurt doesn't see them or, maybe from their demonic look, chooses not to.

They haven't smiled or sung and their very white make-up is still intact, there's no sweat on these two. They're made up like a Victorian version of Courtney Love, hoping to catch Kurt's eye. Then I wonder about all these older venues and their history. Is this place haunted? Are they fucking ghosts? Shite, where have they gone? Keep the beat. They've vanished. Oh thank fuck, no, they're back. Bobbing up and down like Siamese twins adrift on the ocean, they still manage to skilfully dodge the flotsam and jetsam and kicks in the head from flailing sneakers and Doc Martens.

Kurt looks round and smiles at his drummers. Is it sarcasm or delight? Are we there yet? Are we fuck! Only halfway through. The harder I try to focus, the more difficult it becomes. You're fucking so right, Charlie Brown! Oh fuck, keep him out of this. I look at Dave again, he smiles. Krist dances a disjointed punk rock pogo with a Peter-Hook-from-Joy Division classic pose. Kurt looks joyously happy, so alive and in control. This is his turf. He turns again to his drummers, smiles that smile. All is well with the world when he's in full throttle. He has refined the three-minute post-punk song. Like a modern-day John Lennon, bringing his lyrical sarcasm, wit and idiosyncratic style, making the song, not the guitar hero, the central character. He makes firing through 'Molly's Lips' appear so effortless.

I notice how bands interpret songs differently. Nirvana's version is more new wave, more heightened frenzy, part angst and melodrama, part post-punk bubblegum compared to The Vaselines' shambolic and more innocent original. For trivia fans the Molly in question is an old Scottish actress called Molly Weir, who presented a show on STV called *Housewives Tales* and played Hazel McWitch in the BBC children's show, *Rentaghost*. Eugene used to delight his family by kissing her when she came on the telly.

Just for that brief moment I think about Nirvana. The three guys I've got to know. This is happening to them every night. We are so fortunate to be part of all this. I try to analyse the reaction, the cross-section of their audience. There's five hit singles on *Nevermind* surely. Fuck me. Imagine that? They're going to be bigger than Dinosaur Jr., The Pixies and Sonic Youth, whether they like it or not. These songs sound so great on the radio but seem to take on a life of their own in their shows.

You get the feeling from speaking to them and their frustration at how commercial *Nevermind* sounds that they'll want to do more leftfield, underground punky albums too. Who fucking knows? Concentrate. I look out at the swaying, pumping, swollen river of humanity and I'm sure I recognise someone from Airdrie float across the crowd in his Mod parka. The band all seem so cool about it, relaxed, getting close to the end of the UK tour. Just a bit to go…

Here comes the cheesy rock 'n' roll ending, loads of noise and cymbals… I can do that – bum-ba-baboom, ba bum-boom boom ba, ba ba-boom. I'm still hitting the cymbals and shaking my head. How the fuck did I get here?

CHAPTER 1

'OUR NEW DRUMMER:
ANDY BOLLEN.'

It's the hot summer of 1991 in my hometown of Airdrie, 12 miles east of Glasgow. I bump into Gordon Keen, guitarist of the BMX Bandits, as we read the music papers. People in bands in small towns naturally gravitate toward one another, being kindred spirits, empathising with each other's predicament. Stories to tell. Bitching about this one or that one and wondering how this band got a deal and we're still signing on. We would bump into each other in WH Smith every Wednesday afternoon and read the music papers *NME* and *Melody Maker*. *Sounds* had gone out of business a few months before, in April.

After about an hour, we'd get a bit paranoid about spending too long in the same shop, then we'd cross over to John Menzies and continue our chat about music. After finishing reading the papers, we rarely bought them, preferring to keep our money for coffees in Sharelles. There we would spend the rest of the afternoon talking a good game; we always liked the same groups, though different football teams.

One week, Gordon was more excited than normal. He'd been helping Eugene Kelly from The Vaselines with a new project, a band called Captain America, and said they needed a drummer and asked if I would be interested in auditioning. Their temporary drummer was Brendan O'Hare of Teenage Fanclub. He was going to be busy playing gigs and promoting the singles 'Star Sign' then 'The Concept' from their album *Bandwagonesque* (which would be released to critical acclaim later that year in November), so Captain America needed a permanent replacement. At the mention of The Vaselines, I remembered going into Glasgow on Saturday afternoons to look at the girls and walk between Virgin and HMV, and always seeing Charlie Kelly, their drummer, in a full-length leather coat. I thought he was coolness personified. Funnily enough, Charlie is still something of a stylish and dapper dresser; it always seems to come naturally to some.

I was intrigued about the offer of an audition, but remained non-committal. Privately, I was considering a career as a writer, maybe trying journalism. I also had a very secret fancy for hairdressing. Surely anyone who can make a woman more beautiful would be popular? Of course, being from a housing scheme in Airdrie, I was very *secretly* considering being a writer, as such aspirations – being an actor, a hairdresser, or a writer – were viewed upon as a sure-fire sign, if one were needed, that you were gay. In this particular small Lanarkshire town, homosexuality hadn't been invented yet but if it had, the first one would've been a writer, with sideburns, a penchant for hairdressing and called Andy. I would willingly go into battle for many gay friends but times then were different. The very thought of anyone wishing to do something that didn't involve Buckfast, dope, Indian ink tattoos and stealing a car to pull a bird showed a lack of ambition. Bear in mind these were the days before Billy Elliot made it OK to have ballet dancers in every housing scheme. What a trailblazer. Grand Jeté! This was before gap years, fuck buddies, Brit Schools churning out industry cash cows and government funding to encourage lazy 16-year-old guitar heroes to get out of bed.

Captain America had played a few gigs and Gordon had mentioned they had a tape of a live show which he promised to bring next week. I realised there was a sense of urgency as he phoned that evening to suggest meeting up the following day to give me the tape. When I listened to it on the Walkman and played along I was surprised as The Vaselines' songs I knew as introverted and shambolic were now turbo-charged rousing epics. Instead of The Pastels they sounded more like The Pixies.

A few days later I got a phone call from Gordon asking if I'd be interested in coming along to see Captain America play at Glasgow's Third Eye Centre, now the CCA: Centre For Contemporary Arts, on Sauchiehall Street. He suggested I'd be perfect as they really needed a reliable drummer. In musical terms, a reliable drummer is someone who does what he's told, shows up for rehearsals and, hopefully on gig nights, sober. Everything happens for a reason. Things flow in their natural order. The red man comes on at a pedestrian crossing, we stop. If we don't, we get hit by a psycho driving the 201. The story continues. The beat goes on.

The gig at the Third Eye Centre was incredibly hot and intensely loud. My immediate impression was the energy, tension and raw power between Brendan on drums and James Seenan on bass. All good groups need a titan on bass and James fitted the bill. He was clearly a fan of Joy Division, Jah Wobble and Killing Joke. I made a mental note for the next day: *Listen to Dinosaur Jr. and Neil Young's Crazy Horse*. The hi-hats were loose and the drums loud and I knew if I wanted the gig, I'd need to hit them really hard, keeping the hi-hat very loose for that swirling sound.

I was then invited to Aberdeen to see a gig at The Lemon Tree. I was picked up at home; first everyone came in to do a piss, then into my bedroom to check my record collection. I was in, or at least in the van. Gordon was chuffed that I was being myself and getting on with everyone; apparently I was making a good impression. Brendan was in good form, trying to get a picture on a small hand-held TV, almost space age in 1991. The Fanclub were all over *NME* but I was more impressed by the van. It had seats, windows and a kindly temperament allowing it to move in a fluid manner. I was unaccustomed to this kind of luxury.

Still, I wasn't too keen. Captain America were impressive live but I had grown tired of being in bands. Yet something must have intrigued me because I practised again to the live tape of the Third Eye Centre gig. I made another mental note: *Play hard as fuck, do more Led Zep fills*. Oh, the precociousness of youth, kind of! I was 25. Not that I'm comparing myself, but at the age of 24, Paul McCartney wrote and devised the idea for *Sgt. Pepper* flying back from holiday in November 1966, so in terms of age, I was playing catch up. Why even bother to keep going at 25? It's a young man's game.

Maybe my confidence had gone. I had started looking at old

diaries, old notebooks full of song titles, of unfinished ideas with plays, badly drawn cartoons, plot ideas and sketches. I was formulating my next move. I was tentatively thinking about writing. This is just daft. I'm kidding myself on. You can't start again in a new band in your mid-twenties. Everything flows and things do happen for a reason.

On Friday, 16 August, I was watching *Tonight with Jonathan Ross* when the phone rang. Gordon nervously explained that they couldn't get a hold of Brendan and begged me to 'Get in here, we need a drummer, now!' They were supporting Mudhoney and Hole at Glasgow University's Queen Margaret Union. I was driven there by Tom, dad of Sharron, my girlfriend at the time, now my wife. I made my debut for Captain America, strangely, just for a few songs and that was it. The backstage area for QMU is four or five floors up, something I always found funny from a comedic point of view. Couldn't they raise the stage? Clearly health and safety issues with stage diving.

Mudhoney were the American kings of grunge, Sub Pop's finest, and vastly underrated, formed (after Green River split) in Seattle, Washington in 1988 by singer Mark Arm and guitarist Steve Turner. They were promoting their second Sub Pop album, *Every Good Boy Deserves Fudge*, and the single 'Let it Slide' was high up on the indie charts. Due to the volatile, unpredictable but always entertaining nature of their shows, they had a big punk and indie following. Backstage at Glasgow University's QMU, they were around and very friendly. I spoke to their drummer Dan Peters and bass player Matt Lukin. They were friendly, relaxed and very down-to-earth. I was nervous backstage, up five flights, and before going on stage sat with Hole guitarist Eric Erlandson. I was petrified. He assured me in a soft, compassionate, measured tone that it would be fine. He did this for a living though and was brilliant on stage. I liked him a lot. He was rangy and sharp featured and reminded me of a young Alice Cooper, a lovely person and a calming influence.

I am incredibly nervous of walking into any room so walking on stage is always something of nightmare. I'm OK once I'm there and I'm sitting behind the kit or have a guitar but I'm shy and self-conscious. I realised that without even a rehearsal, I would, in effect, be auditioning as drummer for Captain America in front of a Mudhoney audience. I tried hard to focus on just getting from backstage (down five flights on a lift, shall I keep this going?) to the drum kit without falling. My stomach was in a knot. There were some shouts from fans of Brendan, then that awkward moment when you hear everything before a band plugs in. I can't recall ever being more nervous in my life. I tried to psyche myself up by imagining, and I have to emphasise the word *imagining* here, that I could play like Clem Burke from Blondie and John Bonham and concentrated on getting on stage, and behind the kit without falling. Anyway, I played loud and straight, probably actually overdoing it a bit, just to get the point across.

After a couple of songs Brendan walked on stage. Was this some kind of test? See if we can get Andy in from Airdrie to stand in for Brendan? Get him on stage, see what he can do? Years later I found out that Brendan had genuinely forgotten about the gig so there was no hidden agenda from Captain America. I was actually relieved when he showed up. Eugene announced to the QM audience, 'Ladies and gentleman, our new drummer, Andy Bollen.' I remember thinking at that point, *Not sure pal, not sure if I like this much drama.* I looked over at James, who was angry I wasn't staying on. He shook his head but I smiled, happy that Brendan had showed up. James applauded loudly, as did a sizeable part of the small-to-middling audience but he sought me out straight afterwards to tell me I should've stayed on stage. I found it all a bit traumatic and I don't like doing things unless I'm prepared and have rehearsed. Fail to prepare, prepare to fail. People get annoyed with these little truisms but my head's full of them. You will have gathered by now that I have the attention span of a lobotomised gnat so I find their conciseness helpful.

After I came off, I didn't want to hang around and so I headed upstairs to the backstage area, five flights up, and first to greet me was Eric Erlandson.

'Brilliant, Andy. Told you it would all work out well.' A bit more relaxed and chatting to Eric, I was about to tell him I'd heard their name came from a line in the Euripides tragedy, *Medea.* I love the Greek stuff but then I was knocked off-kilter by Hole's lead singer, Courtney Love. Wearing her prom-queen-trash-bridesmaid look, she was carrying a half bottle of Bells whisky and an unlit, bent, Benson & Hedges cigarette wedged between two of the biggest, lipstick-smeared lips I'd ever seen. I found her simultaneously frightening, endearingly vulnerable and, to be frank, she gave me the horn.

'Hey Andy, do you have a light?' Fuck. Courtney Love knows my name. Eric had obviously been filling her in on the bedraggled but happy guy's audition. 'No, sorry, I don't smoke.' It didn't come out in my normal low register but in what sounded like a high-pitched camp castrato. She was interested in getting a light and walked off but as she left, she turned round and opened her eyes wide, smiled and winked. She petrified me but was so much nicer than the way she was being portrayed in the music press at the time. I was expecting to meet a modern-day Medusa who would turn me to stone upon sight. She was lovely and only wanted a light for her cigarette. Nab (really Stuart McNaughton, who doesn't like getting called Nab but that's what everyone calls Stuart McNaughton), my mate from Airdrie, was the only witness to the whole night. He didn't bother with Captain America – Hole were powerful, Mudhoney were incredible.

Me?

I was in the band.

CHAPTER 2
SMELLS LIKE MUDHONEY

It's Thursday, 22 August 1991 and it's a very hot summer's evening. It's the evening before Nirvana's legendary Reading Festival performance. I'm playing drums in Captain America, in my first full gig at The Venue in New Cross, London. The promoters have banned anyone in the bands from leaving the venue. None of the acts are allowed to leave because the area is so violent, apparently down to gang culture. I'm curious enough to want to get out and go for a walk to loosen up but I'm warned against it.

I've just seen Nirvana for the first time. I was expecting sicker and grumpier-looking people and a more robust three-piece – they almost look the wrong shape for a band. I didn't speak to them: they seemed amiable enough and approachable but I leave them and get on with stretching. The singer is happy, relaxed, laughing in a self-deprecating way as he talks to Sonic Youth and Mudhoney's drummer, Dan Peters. He looks over at our company; he has longish dirty-blond hair and is wearing a cool, brown, retro leather jacket. His jeans are ripped at the knee but surprisingly he has thinner trousers, like pyjamas underneath. He looks small beside the tall and thin bass player, who is wearing tight red-orange trousers that seem to go up to his chin. The drummer looks a bit shy, nods politely in the conversation and smiles a lot. He is also thin and small framed.

James is warmly greeting Nirvana's bassist Krist Novoselic. They'd met before; in 1990 The Vaselines reunited to play a show with Tad and Nirvana at Edinburgh's Calton Studios, at the request of Kurt, who was already a huge fan of their work. The Vaselines had no gear (as in equipment, not smack) and borrowed amps and guitars from Teenage Fanclub. My immediate impression, from about 20 feet away, was how a skilled cartoonist would find them easy to caricature.

My attention turns from people watching to the inflamed pain in my back and neck. I continue to stretch, trying to straighten and realign it. I was nervous having to play in front of all these cool influential people but at that moment I could hardly stand or bend. The longer than usual nine-hour drive, crushed between amps and my drum kit, had taken its toll. It was the Thursday of a Bank Holiday weekend and everyone seemed to have decided to leave work early, get in the car and drive off to somewhere more exotic only to find themselves stuck in their car, in front of us, for hours.

Delayed in traffic and with exhaust fumes that made me nauseous, tired and stiff, I needed to find a quiet corner and do some stretching. I knew I looked like a total twat but I didn't care – my neck, back and now my calves all ached. It wasn't really the thing to do in such a scene of indie cooldom, to look or do anything as sensible or athletic. As I did stretch I found myself engaging in something I'm bad at: small talk. I went over to the rider, picked up a bottle of water and right in front of me were Don Fleming, producer and frontman of Gumball, and Thurston Moore of Sonic Youth. Don wore a Russian-styled hat even though it felt like the hottest day of the year. He talked about stretching and being stuck in the back of a van. Thurston had a cool fringe, pretty much like he's always had. I'm subtly trying to stretch while I nod and chat, making weird noises – a mixture of pain and relief as my neck and back click into place.

A good tip when you meet someone cool – and believe me, Sonic Youth are cool – is to maybe stop twisting your neck like a psycho about to go into a boxing ring. Keep it short and sweet. If there was a cool Olympics they'd be first, second and third. It's best in these rarefied moments to keep it regular and polite.

'Hey!' Thurston's wife, Kim, said as she joined in. By now I'm working on groin and hip twists and feeling loose. In hindsight I probably looked more like Alan Partridge dancing in front of commissioning editor Tony Hayers for another series than an indie drummer in the first band on the bill.

'Bit stiff.'

What did I just say to Kim Gordon? I need to keep my mouth shut. Just smile.

'Tough drive, eh?'

I smiled. I couldn't believe I was no longer capable of speaking to Kim Gordon. A good tip when you meet someone famous is to say fuck all. If you have to say anything, say 'Great work'. Kim Gordon was the coolest person on the planet. There she was, standing in front of me. My stomach was churning in her presence. I was so nervous. She was just as laid-back and cool as you'd imagine her to be. Eugene had told me they were doing festivals and had flown in from Ireland.

'Were you playing festivals in Ireland?'

'No, we played some pubs.' Kim smiled, playing it down. I thought she was being New York sarcastic. They had played a pub, Sir Henry's in Cork, on 20 August and The Top Hat in Dun Laoghaire on the following night. This is really going well.

'We just played with Nirvana and tomorrow it's Reading. You guys are coming, right?' asked Thurston.

'I'm not sure. I think Eugene's going. Nice to talk.' Soon we'd find ourselves walking by Nirvana, Sonic Youth, Mudhoney and Hole through the small stage door and I was thinking *It's like a Who's Who of indie royalty* and wondering what the fuck was going on in my life. The strangest thing was how nice they all were to us and how we had the cheek to feel at home. Then we were through another door, on stage and were really well received. I remember being relaxed enough to take some photos before we started and in between songs. Playing drums in front of 800 strangers seemed much less traumatic than making a fanny out of yourself trying to talk to Sonic Youth. Peer group pressure made us play better than expected despite only a few rehearsals.

Nirvana in that crowd were modest, unassuming and low key. Later, we were offered weekend backstage passes from Nirvana and Mudhoney for the Reading Festival. I never went to Reading as, given the chance to be home in six and a half hours (best way to travel home from London, during the night, much quicker) and sleep in my own bed, I always take the bed option. So James and I went back home with the gear and I was sound asleep by 7am and got home to go out with my friends that night.

Reading's now viewed as a pivotal and defining moment in Nirvana's career. They had been blowing everyone away while supporting Sonic Youth on their European Tour, mostly festivals. The tour is documented in the film *1991: The Year Punk Broke* by Dave Markey. They had been playing all the new material from *Nevermind* live for months now and by the time they reached Reading were more than worthy of their mid-afternoon spot on the bill.

Nirvana played a blinder. Eugene joined them on stage to do 'Molly's Lips' and at the end Kurt dislocated his shoulder by diving into Dave's kit. Served him right – don't hit the drums, man. I missed a great show, but in effect, I gave up a weekend pass at Reading to get home to see Sharron and go down the pub with my mates and I'd do the same again.

From August 1991, the momentum started to grow with Captain America. After my first gig with Mudhoney and Hole at the QM then in London, even at this point, I was still unsure. I should've been honoured and flattered to be playing cool support slots with such elite indie company. Deep inside though, I still harboured notions of doing a journalism degree. I'd even picked up a shiny, glossy prospectus. The girl on the front was cute, wearing trendy media glasses and pensively pouting with a pencil provocatively placed in the corner of her seductive mouth. The buttons of her blouse were undone ever so, just enough as to submit to the promise, her notebook was spread out, ready, waiting and willing, but she was definitely not on the course. If she was, it would've been oversubscribed.

My brain was saying time to grow up, you're past it. But my heart was saying give it one last shot and enjoy yourself. They seemed like decent guys and I got on well enough with them and there was – even at this early stage, the dreaded cliché – 'a buzz' about them. Two things happened on the same day that made me go along for the ride. In Eugene's flat we heard an advance copy of Teenage Fanclub's 'Star Sign' and then Nirvana's first album, *Bleach*. My love for pop was reawakened twice that day, with TFC's delicious swirling pop harmonies and Nirvana's first album with 'About a Girl' and 'Floyd the Barber' pointing to both sweet melody and punk. Count me in.

On 11 September we played a show at Falkirk College with Brendan as my drum tech. We played well to a very punky Goth audience. Eugene goaded the Goths, who were sitting down on the floor, all attitude, irony and eye liner, by saying he didn't know he was playing a Spina Bifida gig. Miraculously, instead of becoming abusive at the insult, they responded in kind by getting up and joining in. Before the gig, we are invited to a house by generous friends of Brendan and get some dinner, refreshments and watch the first half of Scotland against Switzerland in Bern. Scotland are down 2-0 at half time but by the time we leave the score is 2-2. There's much hilarity when I point out the game is taking place in the Wankdorf Stadium.

We worked pretty hard around this period. There's one weekend, from Friday, 4 October, which stands out, and here is a truncated version for flavour and feel of events, a snapshot of how things were happening for Captain America before we went on tour with Nirvana.

On Friday we rehearse in Berkeley 2 in Glasgow, from 12 till 6. Teenage Fanclub are rehearsing next door and come in to see us. They are really supportive and excited by the sound. Gerry the bassist, in particular, is very upbeat. During breaks, Brendan comes in about four times and I play drums while he plays electric guitar. We leave rehearsals, swing by Eugene's flat to pick up some amps and guitars and head for a gig in Edinburgh. We leave about 6.30pm but don't get there till 9pm. There is a very nasty crash on the M8, which we eventually pass later. The venue has given up on us so the promoters are happy when we arrive. The support band had hours to soundcheck; we have exactly four minutes before the doors open. Stephen, my brother, and his pal Hugo are there. They have come straight from work, looking out of place dressed in suits, shirt and tie. Everyone thinks they are A&R men. Stephen later told me that Hugo remarked I played drums like John Bonham. If only I could make them sound like him. We aren't on till 1.30 in the morning, play OK, have played better but there is a great crowd response. It's loud and very hot but *NME*'s Innes Reekie says he'd seen us better and didn't put a review of our gig in.

We don't get to bed till about 5am and we're up at 7.30am to get to London for a gig at Camden Underworld. The B&B is called the Four Seasons – I'm not sure if it's still there. I shared the room with James, Eugene and Yvonne (Eugene's girlfriend at the time), all with our clothes on. We have a great breakfast and despite the few hours sleep, I feel quite good. It hasn't gone unnoticed in the irony stakes that we have a guitar/drum tech and roadie all rolled into one, Mark Hughes, from Superstar, and Murray Webster – a driver/

sound man/ tour manager. Tour manager? Can a tour consist of two dates? Both Mark and Murray were excellent at Edinburgh. We must be getting so professional – someone to set up and pack away my drums? Sean Webster was a very friendly guy, who seemed to be around at the start of the story with Brendan at Mudhoney and Hole shows, he worked with Paul Cardow more. He then probably had better things to do than lug gear around.

We get a good drive to London for once and arrive at Camden Underworld rather professionally, intact and on time. The Underworld is one of the hippest gigs in London. On a Saturday night, once the bands have stopped playing, it becomes a great Indie Club. At the venue we're treated – well, choices galore: pizza or chicken-in-a-basket for dinner, how cosmopolitan. Before the sound check, there's a shower in the dressing room so I jump in before going on stage, to loosen up. We also sign the contracts and are now officially on cool, London-based independent, Paperhouse. It's a subsidiary of Fire Records and run by the affable Dave Barker. We play a blinder of a gig and it's full of amazing talent. Everywhere you look there's cracking-looking girls. If they could just move all this up 400 miles to Glasgow I'd be a season ticket holder.

After the gig, I have another quick shower. This time, as I'm drying off, the door opens and I get a visit from a pretty faced young woman with long dirty-blonde hair. She's around 22 and is standing watching me dry. She's wearing a denim miniskirt and a cool biker's jacket, which I recognise. Fucker. She's stolen my jacket. She informs me rather poetically that she was feeling a bit blue because it was her period.

'What, like Picasso?'

'You what?'

'Forget it. Get my jacket off.'

She whipped off her T-shirt as well. She went on to explain that as it was her period I'd just be getting a tit-wank. My soul remained intact but the unnameable was keen.

'Nah, yer OK.'

'You what? What? Are you knocking me back? You must be fucking gay!'

She threw the jacket at me and made me feel cheap for trying to be faithful. After locking herself in the toilet, she left, leaving a huge shit floating in the pan. I tried to flush the fucker away but even her shit seemed to be shaking its head at me. At that point I was still dripping wet, running about looking for a bottle of water to help flush away the offending article. After drying off, I felt guilty and went to see how Mark was getting on packing up the drums and amps. What a difference it made having someone look after your gear, set it up and check while you were playing. As I watched and continued to feel guilty standing watching Mark moving all the gear, a gorgeous black girl nervously asked me back to her flat in New Cross. I reluctantly declined and eventually got back to our digs.

We were staying with Helen, a mutual friend of both Teenage Fanclub and people from Paperhouse, the record company. She shared a place with Dave Rowntree, the drummer from Blur and someone from Swervedriver. I had a great night's kip though I have to say it's with some sadness that I have to report that for me at least, Dave Rowntree's record collection was shocking. We slept late and after a cheap Sunday brunch in a greasy spoon, we left Camden at 2pm and drove to Edinburgh to park our gear at the studio where the next day we'd be recording. Then we headed back across the M8 and I was home in Airdrie for 10.45pm. Knackered. On Monday, 7 October 1991, we began recording our first EP with Jamie Watson at Chambers Studio.

We continued doing more gigs and interest in Captain America had started to increase. There was a definite rise in the profile of the band and expectations were high as Eugene Kelly's new project was much closer to The Pixies than the expected Vaselines style. This meant more press and interviews. One particular newspaper interview came a bit later, on Tuesday, 14 January 1992, with Alistair McKay of *Scotland on Sunday*. I was more interested in his method than what I had to say to him. It was brilliant to watch how he approached the piece. We were in The Griffin bar, he'd taken time to get to know us, spent the day listening to us and he skilfully distilled the whole piece, had a theme, a narrative. We then went for a photo shoot and on to listen to the DAT [Digital Audio Tape] of the second EP. I made notes about how he structured the whole article; how he captured every aspect of the band at the time – the vibe and the dry humour of the group.

This was in stark contrast to an *NME* piece we did with Steve Lamacq. He hung out with us for a few beers, and we had a conversation bordering on a debate, about music. He said we were just another Teenage Fanclub 'being from the same Glasgow patch as TFC and signing to Paperhouse Records, first British home of Norman's conquerors.' The article opened with a line about Bobby Davro and mimics, with a small headline saying 'I'm Your Fan! More heroes from the Glasgow Guitar Club'. I did learn that no matter how convincing an argument Gordon Keen and I put up about our favourite bands, we failed to realise one of the most important rules: the journalist always has the last word. Lamacq knew his stuff but I felt I knew as much about pop music as he did. The *NME* was past the halcyon days of the late 1970s when writers like Nick Kent, Tony Parsons, Julie Burchill and Paul Morley attracted circulation figures of up to 250,000 readers. Whatever the figures were in late 1991, Lamacq certainly had more influence over what passed as being hot and what was not, than I had.

I also learned that there was a gulf between the shape, style and tone of a weekly Sunday broadsheet and a pop newspaper. So I was watching and learning and deconstructing what writers and journalists were saying about us; how they shaped, structured and topped and tailed their work. I thought it was incredible how they were dissecting every little nuance but you just didn't know how it was going to turn out until you read it in print.

We were invited on *NB*, a Scottish Television arts show and recorded a video for 'Wow', in the Tramway Theatre. The director wanted us to stand around a burning supermarket trolley, looking cold and moody. Out of boredom I kicked it over. Oh, how the director loved it, seeing my inner demons released. My friend, John Sheridan, who will now be known as Sherry, his dad taped it and anytime I visited the first thing he did was put it on to slag me off. One of the many perils of being a drummer is losing the drum stool. To expand a bit, the drum stool is split into two: the crown (the seat) and the stool. Like odd socks across the nation, most drummers have at one point either lost or inherited the stool or the throne. So at some point I lost the seat part and while filming at the Tramway searched for something to sit on. The presenter, a charming, affable chap called Alan Campbell, helped and I found a prop: a small log.

'Oh look, that'll be the Captain's log then?' Oh, how we laughed. One of the things I remember most about that show, apart from making a fanny of myself on national TV, was that they recorded it on Betamax. Even in 1991 that was outdated. The girl filming said it was because if the tapes went missing they would be difficult to replicate. One of the most noticeable advances since 1991 has been in technology – there were no laptops, or phones, or digital cameras. The photos that I have from the tour were taken on a small Kodak Instamatic 92, which was state of the art in 1976. I'm sure Eugene and I were the only ones who even thought about taking a camera.

After recording the show and heading home in the dead of winter, I saw the Thrashbush bus and ran for it. I met a mate – Andy Marshall – as I struggled onto the bus with my cymbal case and bags. He was genuinely excited by what he'd heard about Captain America and I told him we were just filming a video for *NB* and it was all going a bit nuts. It was the first time I'd spoken to anyone outside the band for a few weeks and someone whom I trusted, who wasn't full of bullshit, and for the first time I felt it was starting to become quite serious.

However well we thought we were doing, nothing could come close to how Nirvana's trajectory was set to trash and burn the music world. Leading up to the milestone 1991 Reading performance they were playing a blistering set incorporating the best of their older stuff and loads of new songs from their next album, which apparently sounded more like The Smithereens and The Pixies. The live reviews were fantastic as the band propelled toward September and the release of a new single called 'Smells Like Teen Spirit'. A few weeks later *Nevermind* knocked the music world for six. Word had also filtered back from Seattle that there was chaos at an in-store gig at a hip record shop called The Beehive. When Nirvana had shown up to play on 16 September, there were queues for hours and there were 300 inside a shop which legally could hold no more than 120. The crowd was full of Seattle's musical hierarchy – The Screaming Trees, Tad, The Fastbacks, The Posies and Soundgarden – but also the most important barometer; it contained real music fans who were going crazy.

There was a reason why we were watching on excitedly. Apart from an offer of backstage passes for Reading, Nirvana had asked us to open for them on their European tour in November and December.

CHAPTER 3

WHERE DID YOU SLEEP LAST NIGHT?

BRISTOL BIERKELLER, 4 November 1991

It's 7.30am on a very wet but surprisingly mild November Monday morning. Two guys look out of place amongst the thousands of depressed commuters going to offices and banks. They wear inappropriate attire for office work and appear full of the joys. They are happy, wide awake and getting inquisitive looks from bank managers and insurance brokers who used to speak to them at school but pretend they don't know them anymore. Both need a haircut, carry small bags over their shoulders, enough for three days' worth of essentials. They both have a similar look, wear leather jackets, faded jeans, long-sleeved T-shirts and sturdy footwear. They're both full of optimism, fear and nervousness, but they should be pleased with themselves. While the others on the train face another day of stress and pressure from a boss they fear and loathe with equal disdain, these two guys are going to Bristol. First, they're heading to Glasgow to meet the rest of the band and crew then drive to the Bierkeller to open up for an American band most people on the train won't have heard of.

They've heard a tape of a tape of a tape of an album called *Nevermind* by a band called Nirvana and it's so good it's changed their opinion of music. They are listening to a tape of a tape of a tape of an album called *Nevermind* as getting the album is just about impossible. On the day of release there were 40,000 copies available in the UK. A few fans had a copy but actually having the record in your hand was like finding the Holy Grail. The album would create a sub-genre, redefine a generation, spearhead a musical movement unparalleled since punk or even Beatlemania, yet it sold out as soon it hit the shelves, and so finding *Nevermind* was almost impossible.

The first time I heard the album was on a TDK90 cassette. I had this tape lying about my bedroom for years and used it to record from another tape Eugene had received from a friend. The music industry slogan at the time was *'Home taping is killing music and it's illegal'* – bet they didn't see the Internet coming – but we'd have been lucky if we knew one person who had a copy of the record. Once we finally did get to see the album, we realised this wasn't your average rock 'n' roll band. The sleeve of *Nevermind* was challenging and reflected the band's attitude to what they perceived as selling out. We are used to the album cover now but at the time there was quite a controversy about the content. An innocent newborn baby swims underwater, trying to grab a dollar bill from a hook just out of reach. Innocence versus corruption; the corporate monster and capitalism trying to hook us in from the moment we're born. Maybe too much is being made of it but it's certainly a memorable first impression.

So we're off to tour with Nirvana, the exciting US post-punk band. There's loads of talk about them in the music press because of their Reading performance in August and the festival tour dates they did with their label mates Sonic Youth. They were on Sub Pop but the current trend in the music industry is for independent record labels to have licensing deals with majors. If *Bleach* was influenced by Tad, Mudhoney and The Melvins, *Nevermind* is more polished, still heavy but has a dynamic closer to The Pixies, Killing Joke and The Smithereens but there are also elements of R.E.M. and The Police — in other words a wide ranging mainstream rock record. The songs, particularly the first five, are full of great pop and rock hooks embellished with delicious bubblegum grunge. It's uncomplicated, no bullshit and just a really great sounding album.

They're from Seattle, the Pacific North West. In music, geography is everything. Where else could the Beatles have been from and how important is their musical DNA to Liverpool with its 'Strawberry Fields' and 'Penny Lane'? The Kinks, quintessentially English and as part of London with its 'Waterloo Sunset' as Motown with Marvin Gaye, The Temptations, The Four Tops and The Supremes is to Detroit, Michigan. The Northwest is 'Louie Louie' country; The Kingsmen, who made the Richard Berry song their own, are from Portland, Oregon. It's Jimi Hendrix, it's The Regents, The Sonics, it's *Nuggets* and *Pebbles* compilations, 1960s garage punk and 1970s metal; it's Sub Pop, Olympia's K, it's Beat Happening, Mudhoney and now Nirvana.

The guitars are raw, the drumming and bass playing incredible and the songs themselves are stunning. There are no filler tracks. It's hard to describe the sound. You can't stop listening once you start; you don't stop and rewind, you need to listen to the album in its entirety. Everyone's shocked and taken aback. It's a hard thing to do but try and listen to *Nevermind* again with a fresh ear; listen to it and try as hard as you can to imagine you've never heard it before. We were expecting a natural progression from the first album but this is a quantum leap. We all have copies, with no sleeve notes or song credits; there's a strange sense of dislocation. We're listening to it and thinking, *This isn't what we're expecting*. At one point I think it might be a secret supergroup. That was the feeling on listening to a tape of a tape of a tape of an album called *Nevermind* on cassette with no information or photos. Sheer disbelief.

Buoyed with excitement and anticipation, the two guys on the train arrive at Charing Cross Station in Glasgow, just around the corner from singer Eugene's flat, above the Canton Express on Sauchiehall Street. It's 8.15am and already the van's being loaded by the roadies, Willie McGhie and Michael Ewing. James the bass player is in ebullient mood. They eventually set off but within minutes, perhaps a portent for the rest of the day, a car pulls out in front of them and they just avoid a serious crash. The van screeches to a dramatic halt and unsecured guitar flight cases ferociously hit Eugene. It could've been much worse. As their day progresses, the frustrating remnants of each passing minute highlight either terrible preparation and planning, or appalling bad luck. Think of a Kafkaesque version of *Spinal Tap* but with a macabre, nightmarish subplot full of aircraft disasters, projectile vomit and characters straight out of *The League of Gentlemen.*

Captain America never made it to Bristol. I've still never been there.

A cheap option at the van hire company meant we missed this first gig; a terrible start to the Nirvana tour but great for comedy. We broke down 20 miles from Carlisle. We then had to wait for two hours in the van and we were 'relayed' via different vans and eventually taken to an AA depot − how exciting − in Beattock. We had something to eat in a place marked 'Café' but it was actually closer to an evil acid trip, a descent into hell; the café should've been called *Dante's Inferno.* We emerged after being wrong-changed by two women with more facial hair than ZZ Top. As the rain lashed down, the thought of the one bite I had at a tuna sandwich which was still frozen in the middle came back to haunt me. I emitted a rancid projectile that NASA couldn't replicate. The tour van company were really uncooperative but eventually a van was sent. We had to unload the gear and load up the new van.

The rain was still pouring down. It was now 5.45pm and Bristol was definitely off. We were annoyed, frustrated and angry but didn't have any other option but to accept our fate. I hoped our bad luck was out of the way but I was proved wrong. We headed straight for London for the Astoria gig the next day, but as we were expected in Bristol, we hadn't organised anywhere to stay in London and by the time we got there it was after midnight. Eventually we got a hold of Stevie Gray, a mate of Eugene's brother Charlie, who thankfully, as someone previously involved in bands, empathised with our predicament. At last, we'd have a place to crash. Or, again, so we thought. We began like Spinal Tap, now it became more like Laurel and Hardy. Just as we were envisaging a bit of toast and a sleep on his floor, poor Stevie managed to lock himself out. We got so close – we could see through his letterbox. He then took us round to his girlfriend's, Deborah Wall, who kindly put us all up.

Apart from breaking down and being dumped in the wonderfully soulless place that is Beattock, Dumfriesshire, on a very wet Monday afternoon, the surreal highlight has nothing to do with rock 'n' roll. Well, I suppose pop culture, and indeed musical culture, country, jazz and soul, have all had their share of major losses to aircraft disasters so maybe it isn't so far removed. Not many AA drivers would have a call out to a bombed aircraft. As we approached Lockerbie, the AA driver – a nice silver-haired and bespectacled older gent, who clearly loved his job and was proud of his uniform – took over the scene. Each wrinkle on his face was a testament to the books he'd read, mostly manuals, probably about fan belts and carburettors. I don't drive but I do know about fan belts and carburettors as they sound like funny words.

It was only natural that we would bring up the inevitable subject of the plane crash. The driver almost seemed to look forward to this part as if, entering stage right, he'd come to perform his by now well-trimmed and tight script about the fateful night in December 1988. He hung dramatically, I'd say too stiffly, on some of the lines, deliberately using his best spanners to torque up the tension. His twists and turns added pace and gravitas but in repeating the same story without interruption and no spontaneity, verbatim, every day for the last three years, twice a day on a Saturday, I felt he was in need of a jump start. We were all too politely brought up to burst his bubble.

He continued, like a professional, describing in full his role in that evening's proceedings. He said that the AA were officially the police that night, stopping people in cars and ambulance chasers driving by to see what was going on. The thing most strongly etched in his memory from the evening was the windows in the cockpit being intact. My mind wandered as it regularly does, to thinking about how the call for the AA van closest to the disaster went.

'Eh Jimmy, there's a wee problem in Lockerbie.'

'Fan belt or carburettor?'

'Eh…'

He was a nice old guy and I felt guilty for those killed and was enjoying being safe from Libyan bombers in the AA van – a van that felt for the first time as if it wasn't about to break down. To think the day which started so perfectly at Airdrie train station at 7.30am would end in a fold-down bed in the flat of a generous, beautiful, complete stranger, in London at 2.00am. I suppose it's my fault, I did want an adventure.

CHAPTER 4
FINDING NIRVANA

LONDON ASTORIA, 5 November 1991

JESUS DOESN'T WANT ME FOR A SUNBEAM
ANEURYSM
DRAIN YOU
SCHOOL
FLOYD THE BARBER
SMELLS LIKE TEEN SPIRIT
ABOUT A GIRL
POLLY
BREED
SLIVER
LITHIUM
LOVE BUZZ
COME AS YOU ARE
BEEN A SON
NEGATIVE CREEP

ON A PLAIN
BLEW
DUMB
PENNYROYAL TEA
ENDLESS NAMELESS

woke up at Deborah's feeling like I'd been falling in and out of consciousness on an operating table. Fitful, anxious, broken, jagged stabs of short nightmares full of aching pain and confusion, all in a series – not a UK series but an American one with 22 shows in chronological order, all self-contained, all chaotic. We were grateful for the fold-down bed in Deborah's place but Willie the roadie's snoring sounded like a pneumatic drill. After breakfast in a nearby café we then headed up to Maury Road in Hackney, spending the rest of the morning at Fire Records. We had signed with Dave Barker's subsidiary label, Paperhouse, and went in to meet everyone. I got CDs and vinyl by the Spacemen 3, Teenage Fanclub, Blue Aeroplanes, The Pastels, Gumball, Harbour Kings, Gun Club, Close Lobsters, Chuck Prophet, HP Zinker and Pulp.

It's interesting that I got all these CDs yet at the time had no CD player. I have one now but I still prefer the warm, natural sound of vinyl. One of the few perks of signing a record contract – you didn't do it for the money – was the chance to get some albums for free. You were given the chance to plunder the record company's archive. That sounds like a Radio 4 show. '*Plunder!* Guests pick their favourite radio clips'. That's a winner. Either that or a Victorian sexual euphemism – 'I'd like to plunder your archive, Lady Arbuthnot'. Either way it was an enjoyable few hours, having a coffee and helping yourself to records, with Mr Barker on top form.

We were back at the venue four hours early in case we missed the second night. With time to kill, we found a pub directly across the road. Eugene, Willie and I sat in the warmth and calm of the pub in the heart of London's West End for a few hours, watching as Charing Cross Road heaved with late lunchtime workers, excited tourists and irritated locals. We discussed our dramatic start and lack of organisation, the way things were being handled and how embarrassing it was to miss the Bristol gig. Last night Midway Still stood in and by all accounts, unlike Nirvana, played really well.

Looking over I see our name in lights for the first time. I'm thrilled as I look above the door of the Astoria. '*Nirvana! The Television Personalities! Captain America!*' Excitement is overtaken by a hollow reality. There's something sad and a certain tacky shallowness to neon in the daytime. Maybe I'm just tired and melancholic. Afternoon beers don't help and we're so comfortable and warm the last thing we want to do is head for the venue. So here we are, Day Two of the initial three dates with Nirvana and we've broke down twice, slept on floors and been locked out of the guy's flat who we weren't even supposed to be staying with.

The first time I met Nirvana was in the Astoria. As ever I got lost. I always get lost – I'm a day-dreamer, I don't read the signs. It's because I don't drive. I've never driven, I leave that to others; I like to walk or use public transport. I lie that it's about saving the environment – I'm just selfish and it allows my strange mind time to think about funny things. I know Cobb

Greengrass wrote 'Tainted Love' for Gloria Jones yet I still have to check my national insurance number or phone number. I can never remember which way to turn when I'm given directions because I don't listen. I should've listened more: I know Tegucigalpa is the capital of Honduras but I can never remember my pin number.

Anyway, I walked into the wrong room and Eugene introduced me to Kurt and Dave. They seemed charming enough, pleasant, self-effacing and happy in a quiet way. They were both tired, seemed very jaded but Kurt spoke kindly – a slow, measured drawl, but articulate and sharp. Though slightly cautious and wary, I was also excited to meet up. I was still getting my head around the concept of why I was there. Pop fan first, wannabe writer second and drummer in the support band third. The room had beer, water, juice, strawberry milk, sandwiches... all the trappings of a tired, clichéd and jaded rider except for one bizarre item: Kraft Macaroni and Cheese in a box.

I felt out of my depth and unsure as I sat with Nirvana. Maybe sensing a slight look of panic, Dave handed Eugene and I two beers from the rider and smiled, then went back to playing his unplugged electric guitar. There was a sense of mischief in their eyes. Almost a look that said if they could organise an escape from all of this, they would. We chatted about the previous night's gig in Bristol. They said we didn't miss much, they hadn't played too well and they seemed interested in our previous day's drama trying to get to Bristol. What were they thinking of me? Biker's jacket, black T-shirt and denims and Doc Martens, hair in between three styles, Echo and the Bunnymen with bad Charlie-Nicholas-meets-

Oscar-Wilde short bob? Someone who wanted to be a skinny art-school guy behind the drums but being from mining stock looked like a brickie, boxer or a bouncer.

I would later realise they weren't the type to care about what I was wearing, how I looked or how I was made. Dave continued to play an unplugged, turquoise electric guitar. Complex solos, lead parts. If he can do that on guitar, what's he going be like on drums? He'd been playing guitar since he was ten or 11. He was small framed, sinewy with long hair, wore an oversized yellow cagoule and had a really warm smile. OK, I'm obsessed with teeth and hair. Dave was watching everything: always observing, tentative, taking it all in.

As the UK tour would go on, Dave would bring humour and stability. He was the most fun. He was filled with a great sense of how ridiculous everything was becoming, a bit like all the footage of Ringo during Beatlemania, refusing to get too carried away and brilliant at dealing with the extraordinary things that were happening to them every day with a great sense of normality and a concise, quick-witted retort. They were both relaxed and when they did speak, they did so in a calm, measured tone. Krist has said on countless occasions that when Dave joined the band, Nirvana really started to happen. I think that's as much to do with his personality as his musical ability.

The first thing you notice about Kurt is his piercing blue eyes. He has peroxide hair in between two styles and two colours, blond with darker roots. It looks like he's growing it in with signs of a shorter, more sensible crop from about six months before. He looks undernourished, slightly sick, as if needing or just recovering from surgery. At the time I didn't know about his prescribed medication. As a supposedly hyperactive four-year-old, he was prescribed Ritalin for a period of three months, and later in life unrelated painful stomach problems would require on-going medical monitoring. He wore gloves with the ends cut off, an Oxfam raincoat and a cardigan with holes in it. He preferred roll-ups rather than filtered cigarettes. I watched as he expertly created a perfectly formed homemade cigarette. His denims had a small chain, like an old-fashioned watch chain, from his back pocket. I was expecting at least a few signs of debauchery and hedonism and was met with calm erudition.

As we played more shows, Kurt was, as you can imagine, a touch more complex. He slept a lot and had a persona that made people wary of him. When meeting the real fans, though, he was generous, responsive and always aware of their nervousness and made them feel at ease. He never forgot that he was, despite the band's success, just like them: a fan of independent, underground music. When forced into situations with people he didn't trust he was uncomfortable and was at his most relaxed in the company of fellow musicians and bands. He had a healthy dismay for industry people and hated when they'd bullshit or cosy up and be over-familiar.

My lasting memory of Kurt is seeing him concentrate as he wrote, either in his journal or one of his many letters, to people like Calvin Johnson at K Records. He'd sit in the freezing dressing rooms of the UK, in the familiar second-hand overcoat on top of layers, always looking cold but writing right-handed. When I asked why he played left-handed and wrote right-handed, he told me he was left-handed naturally and taught himself to write with his right hand when he was a kid. I called him a smart arse and he adroitly used his left hand to give me the middle finger.

He seemed to look at the world like a cartoonist, sideways. That's maybe the best way to describe his whole idiosyncratic and creative point of reference. There's a natural line that runs through his lyrics, songs and artwork. He was at his most natural and relaxed when Dave and Krist appeared and had an infectious smile, kept mostly for his band mates. It seems strange to be talking about him in the past tense like a hollow echo, when he was so alive and happy. Now I treasure the memory of those times, seeing him laugh and at his happiest when using a great put-down, a regular occurrence that would have everyone in the room laughing.

I didn't meet Krist Novoselic till later. When I knew Krist he was called Chris and that's how I spelt his name in my diary but as he now uses the Croatian spelling and the name of his father, Krist, that's what I've called him. Gregarious, extrovert, cordial and hospitable, he was always politically informed and ready for debate. He was always ready to engage in conversation and seemed particularly protective toward the other two, off and especially on stage. At times I'd look at the long tall shape of Novoselic and worry about him hitting his head in theatres built at the time when the men building the theatres were 5'7" and they were the big guys.

My first impression of Nirvana as they trudged off to soundcheck was a remarkably strange one. I found myself wanting to protect them to the ends of the earth, a feeling that would soon be shared by millions of fans across the globe. Meeting them for the first time was similar to the same charming dismay and surprise when you hear archetypal rock 'n' roll animals Iggy Pop and Alice Cooper are mad golfers. I was so glad to be with them for this short tour and within seconds of seeing them open up on stage at the Astoria playing 'Jesus Doesn't Want Me for a Sunbeam' I was hooked. Already I was succumbing to the spell.

Memorable moments from our first night on the tour? We are on at 7.30. We are nervous but focused and desperate to just get through without any major hiccups. The sound is good and very loud. Willie the roadie has been kept busy with my kit sliding along the stage floor – I think I hit the bass drum too hard but our resourceful crew find a rug from somewhere and that does the trick. The crowd are coming in as we're halfway through and by the end there's a definite rise in the volume as we complete the set to rapturous applause. I feel sorry for the next band, the Television Personalities. The indie fans in the crowd get the TVPs but the response from the rock and punk element is just like a football crowd. They don't get the band's quaintness. Maybe it's the wrong place on the bill for whimsy but hats off to Kurt in particular for wanting to educate his new audience on his love for the fey and the true indie scene.

In one way I'm excited but equally scared. The testosterone-fuelled element of the new Nirvana audience doesn't seem the type for indie sensibility. I'm not brave enough to say to anyone in Nirvana's crew, but I want Kurt to explain to the crowd how much the band mean to him and perhaps introduce them. It's as if the Television Personalities have become unwilling participants of Kurt's guilt at Nirvana's new, polished, radio-friendly inevitable mainstream success. This is how wrong it can go if you dream too big. So many of the fans at the Astoria just aren't interested in the twee eccentricities of Dan Treacy, and that might be their loss. There's only so long before the more loutish hall, full of *Kerrang!* fans, want blood, or maybe just want Nirvana. Independent acts who find mainstream success always seem to love artists like Dan Treacy and Calvin Johnson of Beat Happening, who are almost deified for not selling out.

I feel like slapping the ones who are being abusive. This is the Television Personalities. If you don't get it, go to the bar. They at least deserve some fucking respect. Know your musical history and shut the fuck up. One of the Beavis and Butt-Head crew was pished and mouthy, and as the hall was quickly filling up it would be easy to 'accidentally' elbow him in the nose or the ribs and say, 'Oh, sorry mate'. Then you think, *No, that would be me resorting to type.* In between songs while chatting with the crowd, someone to my right clearly tells Dan Treacy to fuck off but he holds his own and reminds the heckler.

'Now, now, manners. It's fuck off, *please.*'

I whistle, whoop and laugh loudly, a much more fitting response than a slap on the face. Since November 1991, Dan Treacy hasn't had his troubles to seek but in the last few years, people like Alan McGee have been championing his cause and keeping his name alive, particularly in his *Guardian* 'Music Blog' from 4 May 2010. Treacy has become something of a cult figure, and indie fans were delighted when he released *A Memory Is Better Than Nothing* in 2010. Bringing things full circle, on 19 April that year, I reviewed this album for a music review site I freelance for, giving it a decent review. I remember the work was great but it was even better just to have him around.

In October 2011, Dan Treacy was in a critical condition

facing another long battle following an operation to remove a blood clot from his brain. No matter what happens and we all pray for a positive outcome, Dan is assured his rightful place in pop history. True independent artists like Dan are still lauded and laughed at in equal measure, like all the talented outcasts. The earlier heckler represents the mainstream. He's afraid of Dan because his unstinting creative philosophy and truthfulness makes the heckler feel culpable.

There are many similarities between Dan and Kurt, the biggest being how uncomfortable both were in dealing with their respective levels of critical success. I often wonder if Kurt could've learnt to enjoy his success, he wouldn't have been in the situation he found himself by April of 1994. This inability to accept and enjoy his mainstream success is probably at the very core of the band's, and definitely Kurt's demise. His spirit and true musical heart lay in the underground scene. To really appreciate what it was like for him, you have to understand what it would be like to go from being a high-school dropout to an international star. To go from learning chords on your own and trying to copy the same chords of Beatles songs. Then you pluck up the courage to find like-minded people who share your love of music. You mess about in numerous bands. Then you're thrown out of your house, sleep on friends' floors, sleep in hospital waiting rooms and write a song about living under a bridge where a tap had sprung a leak (even though, according to Krist, that never actually happened but why let the facts get in the way of a good narrative?). You find a focus, a friend in Krist, a drive that brings a worldwide hit three years later.

It's clear on meeting Nirvana for the very first time at the

Astoria, with the distinct lack of rock 'n' roll groupies and clichéd excess, that they view themselves as an indie band with a punk rock ethos. Everything's relaxed and low-key and there's fanzines strewn across the table. Kurt has letters out; he's reading them and responding to some. There's no major label over-indulgence. If anyone wants to truly understand Nirvana's music, then it lies somewhere between Kurt's love of punk and the music of The Beatles. He loved bands like Bad Brains, The Slits, Minor Threat, Butthole Surfers and Black Flag. If you merge the direct, punk rock approach with the sheer pop commerciality of The Beatles, you might get close to explaining Nirvana's breakthrough and how they made alternative music accessible to the mainstream.

The history of rock 'n' roll from Elvis to Kurt is full of people making it in spectacular fashion. Sometimes making it big isn't as difficult as how you actually handle it when it comes your way. He wasn't alone. Grab a ticket, take a seat: Dee Dee Ramone, Jimi, Janis or Jim? Sid Vicious? Joe Meek? Johnny Thunders? Amy Winehouse?

At the Astoria, Nirvana are welcomed on stage with a warmth and rapture I've never experienced before. Maybe it's the shape of the old venue but it's affectionate, welcoming and very loud. Kurt looks revived from earlier, wearing a white, long-sleeved Leadbelly sweatshirt. They smile bashfully and nervously wave, looking genuinely taken aback by the welcome. Krist wears no shoes and pogos nervously before the songs even start. They begin gently with 'Jesus Doesn't Want Me for a Sunbeam'. What's this, a C86 night? They then kick into turbo boost for 'Aneurysm' before melting the place with a blistering version of 'Drain You'. Everyone just goes mental.

It's mayhem and it's surreal. Like watching a film and the director shouts action and the fans go ape-shit. They play the poppier stuff and again take it to a new level. They are in control, they are loved and all I keep thinking as I look on is, *How the fuck are the same tired guys I met earlier able to do this?* As they move toward inevitable mainstream success, you wonder if their slender shoulders can take it. The Astoria show has hundreds of cynical earlier fans upset at them for 'selling out' and playing venues bigger than the local pub; the ones 'who were into them first'. There's nothing wrong with this, we've all had bands we were a bit precious about. To see your prized little band who you've cherished and could write a letter to and they'd respond, lost forever, to the normal uncool people of the mainstream.

At all Nirvana concerts, there are pockets of disconsolate early fans that were into the band before everyone else. The fans that were into *Bleach* and saw them play the students' union at SOAS in London in 1989. But Nirvana have changed; there's more power, volume and confidence. Kurt may have loved bands like Beat Happening and The Vaselines but they were always closer to a heavy punk garage band, just add in some pop bubblegum and watch her blow. The initial fans remain unsure; they know they don't want to lose them but love is like that. You grow up, you move on.

As if understanding their angst, Kurt brings a smile to their faces. Four songs into the show the opening riff of 'School' is quickly cheered by the early Sub Pop fans. Maybe a few hundred know what it is. The newer fans stand back, listen to the Black Sabbath-styled intro and immediately respond. As Dave kicks in, the place erupts, the fans sway and bounce and dance and squeal. The same thing happens later in the set when the band plays 'Negative Creep'. Both songs are from a similar place, the 1960s garage sound of the North West. It's classic garage punk. Exploding from sweet lemonade kisses, laced with speed, angst and confusion.

For me the best song is 'Breed' – it's just so commanding and potent and powerful. I'm caught between watching the band play and watching the audience go crazy. They all know the song already and are singing every word. The band look so relaxed and yet the crowd are going ballistic. You can't imagine the venue being able to take any more of it. The same director of the movie who earlier shouted 'Action!' to send the kids delirious seems to have ingested half a tonne of pure coke and wants it more intense. That clichéd but ubiquitous car crash again, this time there's just that gap, maybe five seconds while you wait for the inevitable shout of 'Run, she's going to blow!!!' It's primitive, it's vicious, the guitar starts, a 1960s garage distorted riff like 'I Wanna Be Your Dog' by The Stooges, a touch of The Sonics on 'Psycho A Go Go' or of The Eyes' 'You're Too Much'. Dave comes in with a machine gun snare then Krist joins in, driving the song forward to the explosive almost ray-gun sounding solo: a fantastic song, brilliantly executed by musicians on top of their game. You can almost smell the gasoline and the turbo-charged chaos. Fucking brilliant! I'm here for free as well. What the fuck's happening here? Something is definitely happening here.

The gig was reviewed on 16 November 1991 by Sharon O'Connell for *Melody Maker*. She was blown away by Nirvana, though not by us. The same by now familiar Teenage Fanclub comparisons: basically, that they have been doing it for a while and doing it far better than Captain America. We are a weaker strain, a second-hand version brought in by the label Paperhouse, supposedly annoyed at losing Teenage Fanclub. There's also something cheery about withering and dying naturally. At one point she compliments me at least, by calling us Ramones-esque and saying we had the poppy smugness of Marc Bolan's finer moments. I actually quite enjoy her writing style; at least she seems to be genuinely into music. Most music journalists I've met so far don't see themselves as journalists who specialise in music but are failed musicians who didn't have the ability to make it. It didn't work out, so the closest they could get would be to write about music instead.

She also used a word I hadn't heard of and I like learning new words. 'Plangency': *Resoundingly loud, especially with a plaintive resonance, as a bell.'* Apart from obvious bad jokes and cartoon pictures of a plangent bell-end, before Captain America shows, when no one was looking, I used to always make sure the ride cymbal had a mic and that it was as tight to the bell of the cymbal as physically possible. This gave a garage feel if it was struck halfway down the cymbal and a clear, resonant chime on the bell part which helped cut through Gordon and Eugene's fuzzy guitar sounds. No one seems too bothered about the review; I'm the one looking at every word and over-analysing. I liked how she set the main piece up about Nirvana, with a theme about fireworks, it being 5 November, and she clearly loved the headline act. I tell myself it's an improvement, a *Melody Maker* review of a London gig with Nirvana compared to a review in the *Airdrie and Coatbridge Advertiser* from the Club de France.

Sharon O'Connell made an interesting return to my diary

with an article in the *Melody Maker* dated 4 September 1993, this time with a brilliant review of Nirvana's third album, *In Utero*. I've highlighted her review as one of the most well-informed pieces of music journalism, up there with Lester Bangs and Nick Kent. It's informative, funny and clever, compares Kurt's vocal performance to John Lennon circa 'Cold Turkey' and even has an interesting take on Baudrillard, the postmodern French philosopher and cultural commentator. The review's worth a read for two reasons: it is an accurate and skilled piece, and it also perfectly captures the relief felt by millions of nervous Nirvana fans, as by September 1993 the chaos and turmoil surrounding the band was such that we were expecting news of an imminent implosion, never mind the release of an album. As for Baudrillard, his theories on the simulacrum are worth checking out, if only to give you a migraine.

We were supposed to be staying again with Teenage Fanclub's friend, Helen (so maybe the reviewer was right, we can't even find original friends) after the Astoria gig. Another nightmare, we ended up driving all over London to find her but couldn't. In the end, we managed to get a kip on the floor of Gordon's Japanese girlfriend, Yuka (who he later married). Her place was a bit out of the way – it was like Del Boy's high-rise in Peckham – but we were grateful.

I can't get to sleep on the floor. I'm lying there, thinking, *How can Nirvana perform so explosively and detonate like this every night?* Most have dozed off. I go into my small notebook and write down the news we'd heard earlier about Robert Maxwell's death; he was reported to have fallen overboard from his boat near Tenerife. I write some gags about it, for that show

I'm too scared to send stuff to, *Weekending*, on Radio 4. I try to sleep again, but I can't. I go into my bag, pick up *Time's Arrow* by Martin Amis, which I found discarded in the van. It's weird and unsettling; about a doctor in a concentration camp and time is passing in reverse. I can't read it when I'm sober as it makes no sense. However, when I'm pished and reading it with one eye closed with that feeling of impending doom as the room spins in that uncomfortable altered state of mind, it seems to make more sense. I'm dreading anyone asking how it is as I don't know. I'd probably say, 'Yeah, it's the usual postmodern stuff, exaggerated, caricatured, grotesque and the usual Bellow, Nabokov, Joycean envelope,' but the truth is, I don't really know what's going on.

I put Amis down and try to work out why the time feels so right for Nirvana. When The Sex Pistols happened it was against the background of a depressed 1977. What's happening in 1991? The year began with the UN attacking Iraq. The deadline for Saddam Hussein to pull his troops out of Kuwait had passed. Late night TV schedules were dropped for wall-to-wall coverage, almost like sport analysis with military experts dissecting and discussing every nuance of Operation Desert Storm. It was simultaneously riveting and sickening. In March, Rodney King was beaten by cops in LA. A bystander filmed the incident and footage caused outrage round the world. (Four LAPD officers were later charged, but in 1992 were controversially acquitted, sparking the LA Riots.) Meanwhile, Indian Prime Minister Rajiv Gandhi was shot by the Tamil Tigers and Helen Sharman became the first Briton in space. Tim Berners-Lee established the first website at Cerne in Switzerland, effectively inventing the World Wide Web. There were riots in Leeds, Birmingham, Cardiff and Oxford and Terry Waite was released from Lebanon. Yeltsin was elected Russian President – and Slovenia and Croatia declared independence from Yugoslavia.

I was aware of the fact that Krist Novoselic is of Croat descent and when I met him that November, I regret not having the courage or probably not knowing enough about the topic to engage in a conversation about it. I wanted to ask him his opinion but the time never seemed right to broach such a heavy subject. I should have. Krist is always engaging and well-informed and I wasn't surprised to hear that he eventually became actively involved in politics. Until September 2010 he also wrote a great blog in *The Seattle Weekly* online section *Reverb*, where he delivered a clever, incisive, thought-provoking style with a warmth and tone that connected. When I read it, I heard Krist's voice. He quit to do a degree and left the blog, promising to contribute on politics at the FairVote site.

Elsewhere, back in 1991, in terms of TV, the top sitcoms were *Cheers, Roseanne* and *Murphy Brown*. The top movies were *Terminator 2: Judgment Day, Robin Hood: Prince of Thieves* and *The Silence of the Lambs*. Musically the news was worse. The five best-selling singles were Bryan Adams' '(Everything I Do) I Do It For You', Michael Jackson's 'Black or White', Roxette's 'Joyride,' Scorpion's 'Wind of Change', and finally adding some much needed kudos, R.E.M.'s 'Losing My Religion'.

It's a strange time in terms of news, culture and the economy but one in which Nirvana have made a creative impression. I keep trying to work out what has brought us here – to be here, at this moment, at the Astoria, with this incredible band. What has brought them here? Well, I know they've a great album of songs with catchy hooks and distorted guitars that touch upon every emotion from elation to despair and everything in between. I know the singer's a big fan of The Vaselines. But apart from that, it feels like something's happening. Call it fate, maybe the stars are aligning, the moment definitely seems set.

By the time we're on tour with Nirvana in November of 1991, a look at the *NME* gives you a flavour of the bands that were gigging. Hole, Silverfish, Spirea X and Spiritualized are playing. The Pogues with Joe Strummer are playing Brixton Academy (it was Joe who went first – in 2002 – and Shane is still around, somewhere, who would've thought that?). The Ramones are also packing them in at the same venue, playing with The Damned. James Brown is cashing it in at Wembley Arena. Bands like The Senseless Things, Mega City Four, The Frank and Walters, Dodgy, The Cure, Curve and Revolver are also gigging.

At the same time, the music scene is full of corporate, major record company acts: Michael Jackson, Genesis, Enya, Lisa Stansfield, Pet Shop Boys, Simply Red, Tina Turner, INXS, Bryan Adams and Queen. The record industry is flabby and corpulent. The post-Live Aid stadium rock cycle has reached its nadir. The time is just right for something, anything. The moment. Now. Here.

In August, Primal Scream threatened world domination with *Screamadelica*. Everywhere you went in Glasgow you heard this really different sounding album wafting from student flats in the West End to pubs and clubs in town. At one point it even reached Coatbridge. It's dance, it's rock, it's almost perfection. What connects Kurt to all the bands like The Vaselines, Teenage Fanclub, The BMX Bandits, The Pastels and Primal Scream is their record collections. They all have a vast knowledge of the producers, engineers, studios and musicians on all the great albums and better still, on all the unknown classics.

I then try to think of bands like The Smiths, then The Stone Roses, who captured the zeitgeist and changed the music scene. Maybe this will be Nirvana's place in the future, the band that shook up the lacklustre record industry at the time. What makes them go from darlings of Tuesday Indie Disco Nite at the students' union to heavy rotation on MTV? Maybe someone at the record company or in their management was a chess player. Someone decided it was time to make a move and that move was straight through the middle. Always controlling the game from the centre, it was no longer about fanzines, coloured 7-inch singles and fan letters from 'Kurdt' (sic). It was now about strategy, attack and approach.

After more tossing and turning and thinking too much instead of letting my brain switch off, I finally manage to get a few hours kip. I woke up on one occasion dreaming I was having my balls eaten by three big black rooks and it was so real it started to hurt. I woke up in pain because it was so cold my balls were freezing. I should've started to rub them, see if I could see my future. What I really needed to do was imagine sinking into a hot bath to bring them back to life.

We got up, got a bite to eat then headed for Wolverhampton. That was the plan at least. The way things were going we might be involved in a 70-car pile-up or the first ever earthquake to hit the Midlands. It's around 110 miles from London to Wolverhampton. It took us over four hours to get there.

CHAPTER 5
NIRVANA GEAR

WOLVERHAMPTON WULFRUN HALL,
6 November 1991

JESUS DOESN'T WANT ME FOR A SUNBEAM
ANEURYSM
SCHOOL
DRAIN YOU
ABOUT A GIRL
FLOYD THE BARBER
SMELLS LIKE TEEN SPIRIT
POLLY
BREED
SLIVER
LOVE BUZZ
LITHIUM
ALL APOLOGIES
BEEN A SON

NEGATIVE CREEP
ON A PLAIN
SOMETHING IN THE WAY
BLEW
DUMB
SPANK THRU
RAPE ME
LOUNGE ACT
TERRITORIAL PISSINGS

We're stuck in the traffic jam from hell. I'm looking around at concerned faces and wondering what did we do in a previous life? I listen to *Nevermind* again, knowing that it'll have an added dimension now I've seen the band perform the songs live for the first time. Just like that feeling of being 16 and your favourite band were playing in town and as soon as you got home and all the next day, you would be listening to their new LP with a different perspective, I was now a fan and couldn't wait to get to Wolverhampton to see them again. I'd heard *Nevermind* loads of times but seeing them live seemed to reaffirm how great the songs were. Now there is a tangible connection.

The journey to Wolverhampton is tense and traffic problems only add to the misery. We agree that everything has to be sorted for the remainder of the tour. After tonight's show, Nirvana are off to mainland Europe and we join up again in Bradford on 26 November. As all around argue, I decide to focus on getting a good feel for the music and turn up *Nevermind* on my Walkman. I love music for that – blocking out the shite. I think of the guys who are playing on the album who I met yesterday and make mental notes to place in the diary later. I'm blown away with the power and strength they show on stage and find it hard to believe this can come from the three unassuming guys I met offstage.

I spend the next few hours dreaming of being able to even come close to writing songs as good as the first five on *Nevermind*. At this point, I realise how far away from making it as a musician I am. My heart isn't in it anymore. I'm faking it here. This isn't what I want to do with my life. I keep formulating ideas and angles and looking at things like a writer not a drummer. I hate the arguing and the negativity. I lock myself away amid the mounting anger and chaos in the van, wishing I had the balls to take out the diary and start scribbling down everything in my head. I have so many ideas, then more ideas coming from those ideas.

It occurs to me that if Nirvana keep performing, keep on writing and playing like this live, they will be massive and this could be in the Top 20 albums ever made. I'm too embarrassed to go on about how great a record it is. I know pop music, I used to work in a record shop, I love music. You'd need to be stupid, deaf or insane not to like this record and recognise its massive commercial crossover appeal. Since we're on the bill with them, we are naturally playing it down and want to stay a bit cool about the situation but I'm so excited by how good this album is and how powerful Nirvana are live. I just wish we would channel our energy into not letting them down. Right now what is actually happening is everyone's fighting and arguing, wanting some decent equipment, a safe reliable van, decent B&Bs to sleep in and some food. All art school coolness and indie sensibility has gone out of the window as it gets heated and candid about the practicalities of being a touring band.

Nirvana are fans of Eugene and James's old band and seem to respect us an awful lot. I feel a bit guilty to be there, it should be Charlie Kelly from The Vaselines who is drumming. I keep wanting to shout, 'Do we really know how lucky we are to be on this tour?' Take away all the bad luck and breakdowns and the missed first gig. We need to put that behind us, we can't change that. There's no point in wasting any energy even thinking about it. Let's just really appreciate it and when we get to meet up later for the remainder of the UK tour, let's be fucking brilliant.

On the tedious journey, I keep comparing *Nevermind*'s first five songs with those on other classic albums. The first five songs on *Sgt. Pepper* by The Beatles: 1. 'Sgt. Pepper's Lonely Hearts Club Band' 2. 'With a Little Help from My Friends' 3. 'Lucy in the Sky with Diamonds' 4. 'Getting Better'. 5 'Fixing a Hole'. All brilliant – but the best five openers? I know it's about opinion but the songs on *Sgt. Pepper* aren't even as good as the songs on other Beatles records. It's the colour and the concept and the excitement of the sound and the advanced recording techniques that make it a groundbreaking record as opposed to the best ever. For me the songs on *Revolver* are better: 1. 'Taxman' 2. 'Eleanor Rigby' 3. 'I'm Only Sleeping' 4. 'Love You To' 5. 'Here, There and Everywhere'. But are they as resounding as: 1. 'Smells Like Teen Spirit' 2. 'In Bloom' 3. 'Come As You Are' 4. 'Breed' 5. 'Lithium'?

I know it's about the positioning of songs and I'm not saying Kurt Cobain's a better songwriter than Lennon and McCartney. I'm also aware that in the 1960s, LPs always had great opening tracks on each side. The Beach Boys *Pet Sounds* is a great example of this, starting side two with 'God Only Knows'. It opens with: 1. 'Wouldn't It Be Nice' 2. 'You Still Believe In Me' 3 'That's Not Me' 4. 'Don't Talk (Put Your Head on my Shoulder)' 5. 'I'm Waiting for the Day'. All great but nowhere near the first five on *Nevermind*.

Also, *Pet Sounds, Revolver* and *Sgt. Pepper* were well on in the respective careers of The Beach Boys and The Beatles. *Pet Sounds* was The Beach Boys' eleventh studio album. Does this mean 'Smells Like Teen Spirit' is as good a song as 'Good Vibrations' or 'A Day in the Life'? I'm talking about the quality of the first five songs, the impact of the band and the fact this is only Nirvana's second album. This is coming from someone who thinks the guitar, bass and drum sound as well as the vocal performance by Lennon and McCartney on the opening of *Sgt. Pepper* is one of the finest moments in the history of pop.

Again, *Sgt. Pepper* and *Pet Sounds* seem to suffer because we almost know them too well and both albums are so familiar to us, so my assertions could be a trifle over the top. Maybe *Nevermind* should be looked upon like those albums which come along and change the music scene. Albums such as *The Velvet Underground and Nico* from 1967. An influential record as the first real art rock album, without it we'd have no Roxy Music, David Bowie, Jesus and Mary Chain or Primal Scream. Or an album like The Byrds' *Sweetheart of the Rodeo*, which changed the rule book and gave us a new genre, country rock. Like NWA's *Straight Outta Compton* or Public Enemy with *Fear of a Black Planet*, all critically acclaimed and important albums within their genre. Or like Marvin Gaye's *What's Going On*, which became the first (and only?) civil rights concept album.

Maybe it was the way *Nevermind* stood out from the crowd, like Patti Smith's *Horses* or The Stooges' *Raw Power* or The Clash's *London Calling* or Television's *Marquee Moon*.

It's funny how we get so worked up and worried over saying the right things and upsetting everyone but that's what I think. My favourite Beatles and Stones albums can vary from *Let It Bleed* to *Revolver* but equally at times I love *Their Satanic Majesties Request* and *Yellow Submarine*.

While the critics and fans talked up *Nevermind*, Nirvana always played it down in a self-deprecating way, preferring to criticise the over-polished sound than accept plaudits for the success of the album. I know from talking to them that they knew 'Smells Like Teen Spirit' was an OK song but even their management and record company used it as an introduction to the band. 'Come As You Are' was seen as the sure-fire hit that would propel them into the mainstream. *Nevermind* was then and is now a cracking album and whether Kurt was alive or not I still think it would be topping classic album lists. I get self-deprecation but Nirvana took it to a whole new level.

I love nothing more than bursting the bubble of pomposity. I learned some time ago that it's a good trick in life and especially in comedy. It comes in useful when you end up in a conversation at a party or in the pub about, for example, the greats of celluloid history. When bores drool at the mouth over the clichéd soundbites you've heard a million times before about the cinematography and the deep focus of *Citizen Kane* or the Odessa Steps sequence in Sergei Eisenstein's *Battleship Potemkin*, it's great to just say, 'No, for me it's *Naked Gun* or maybe *Rocky V*.' When the literary classics are reeled off and the work of Nabokov is God and Joyce the only choice, get out ahead of the curve, throw a cultural grenade into the debate and say, 'No, for me no one gets close to Dan Brown or Ben Elton.'

Nirvana really worked hard at their craft and their reward was a groundbreaking album that, in effect, created a sub-genre. People are so dismissive about what it takes to be successful in any form of creativity. The effort required to just be ordinary, never mind have a major breakthrough on Nirvana's scale, is beyond the understanding of most people. They say to be a good writer you have to be a good reader. To be in a band you have to listen to all kinds of music – the blues, jazz, rock 'n' roll. To be a painter, understand and study the techniques of the greats. It would amaze you how many people don't get it and don't even think along those lines creatively. All three members of the group understood the template, the natural order. Whether that meant listening to The Minutemen or Black Sabbath, they were listening with a musician's ear. The same way a young Lennon and McCartney would work out Eddie Cochrane's 'Twenty Flight Rock', the chords and shapes of Chuck Berry, mimic the vocal technique of Little Richard and the songwriting structure of Buddy Holly. The way George Harrison would learn difficult Carl Perkins and Scotty Moore solos. Once The Beatles were established, they embraced Motown with covers of Barrett Strong's 'Money' and The Marvelettes' 'Please Mr Postman'.

Kurt was convinced that he'd unlocked the code to writing Beatles songs after assimilating himself in their early albums and analysing their structure. The result was 'About a Girl'. It's about the lengths you go to, the effort required to understand and improve your art. Those who work harder at their craft find it easier to get what's in their head on to canvas, vinyl or in print. They'd probably be embarrassed to hear this but here's my theory about Nirvana's place in the natural running order: Robert Johnson gave us the blues, then came Elvis Presley and Chuck Berry, Little Richard, The Beatles and The Stones, Led Zeppelin, The Sex Pistols and Nirvana. They are on that first branch of music's family tree. Then closely connected are millions of artists like The Kinks, The Beach Boys, The Byrds, The Small Faces, The Ramones, Sonic Youth, The Stooges, Dylan and Hendrix. It's not only the music but the impact and the sea change in the musical landscape.

Before the gig in Wolverhampton I phone Mum in Airdrie to check in and have a chat and to tell her we're recording a video for a TV show on the Friday. Everywhere she goes she hears Nirvana on the radio and they're never out of the papers; she tells me to watch myself. I tell her not to worry, they are all lovely guys and the way they're being portrayed isn't what they're like. They're really kind and funny and generous, and if she met them she'd like them.

I reassure her that there's nothing to be worried about and just before I hang up, I ask her to watch *The Word* on Channel 4 on Friday and record it for me. I was going to be away recording a video for 'Wow' on STV's *NB*, and there was a whisper that Kurt was going to wear a Captain America T-shirt. By now the world knows this is where Kurt says, 'I'd like all of you people in this room to know, that Courtney Love, the lead singer of the sensational pop group Hole, is the best fuck in the world.' Thanks for that, Kurt – my mum nearly killed me.

After their soundcheck at Wulfrun Hall, Dave was doing a TV interview. While in the middle of it he saw us setting up my kit and shouted, 'Andy, shove your drums on the riser so we can see you. In fact if you want, just use my kit?'

· 'Really? Are you sure?'

'Fuck yeah, it's cool.'

I've known bands who wouldn't let you borrow a plectrum. Some are really precious about sharing their amps, drums or equipment. Nirvana were one of the most generous bands I've ever worked with. Happy to help and support, always laid-back and selfless when sharing the stage with all the bands they worked with. We were given full access to all their equipment.

Only once have I come across a similar attitude from a band happily letting you share their gear. A few years later, in a band I formed called Boomerang, we played a gig at Bellshill Academy with my pal DD's band Boyfriend. The gig itself was a surreal event, MC'd by none other than legendary Mr Superbad, AKA Freddie Mack. Sadly he died in January 2009 but only after an incredible life worthy of a book itself. From cotton plantations in South Carolina to being a childhood friend of Floyd Paterson, he reached third place in the world light-heavyweight rankings. He turned to acting and appeared in *Cleopatra*, as a slave, carrying Elizabeth Taylor into Rome, and in The Sex Pistols' *The Great Rock 'n' Roll Swindle*. Anyway, back to the point: Boyfriend's guitarist, Stephen Jollie, let me use his beautiful Vox AC30 amp and at the soundcheck I blew a valve in it. He shrugged his shoulders, went home and brought another amp over. I blew that one too. Not a word was said, just a rueful 'Shit happens' shrug. Good guys. They're still doing their thing as The Epicureans and DD with his project The Dead Agenda.

With *Nevermind*, Nirvana were now, whether they liked it or not, in the same league and rubbing shoulders with major acts in the mainstream. They refused support slots with Metallica, U2 and Guns N' Roses, but instead decided to use their fame and influence to help bands they were fans of, like Half Japanese, Daniel Johnson, Shonen Knife and Captain America. Even their beer was handed over to us every night. Can't imagine many rock stars being so generous with the rider or amps but strangely I can imagine Keith Richards would be like that – 'Take it, baby, it's yours.'

We are warmly received in Wolverhampton with clear shouts for an encore. Uncharacteristically, we do the right thing and get off stage. It's Nirvana's show, not ours. They meet us as we come off.

'Great show, Andy.'

'Thanks, Dave. Great kit. It's the best kit I've ever played.'

'Yeah, right.'

'No, seriously, it sounds amazing and I don't need to pack it away, so it's the best kit I've ever played.'

We did play well, perhaps because we were using Nirvana's gear but it was the best we've played since I joined Captain America. We were solid, powerful and confident. I'm glad we left them wanting more. Maybe it was the steam being let off from the drive up to the Black Country. I felt more concentrated during the show, feeling I had to play at my best. I'm more relaxed than normal with a bit more focus. I think it's because I've been listening to *Nevermind* all the way up from London and for some reason feel obliged not to let Nirvana down for asking us on the tour.

Nirvana's performance at Wulfrun Hall was brilliant and long. Three songs stand out tonight: 'Lithium', 'Floyd the

Barber' and 'Love Buzz'. 'Lithium' takes on a life of its own. Rousing, dynamic, great drumming and the crowd sing along; it's bedlam. Krist, as ever, controls and cajoles, Kurt twirls and thrashes his guitar; it splinters to the thunderous drumming, mirroring Dave on the down beat. The lyrics are strange, hinting at Kurt briefly finding God after living for a short while with his friend Jesse Reed's family. They were devout born-again Christians and Kurt for once found some temporary solace, even attending services but later decided it wasn't for him. The quiet dynamic of the verse, when Dave and Krist play, is straight and simple, a good foundation for Kurt's vocals. I look around, and everyone knows every word. Everyone is singing and by the time we reach the first chorus the crowd can't hold back any longer and just lose it. They bounce up and down, then sway and pull as Nirvana completely control and orchestrate them. Kurt has them in his grip; it's really noticeable how relaxed he appears while the band continue unleashing such devastating power.

A word rarely used to describe Kurt was laconic. He was also far more courageous than he's ever given credit for but we'll talk about that later. He could be terse and stunningly brief, especially when frustrated and a quick escape from an unwanted conversation was required, and indeed could be curt by nature. However, he could also be warm, kind and sensitive. If he was fond of you, he would show patience, relax and just chat.

He was similar as a songwriter, economical, succinct and this style is perfectly shown in 'Floyd the Barber', living up to American short story writer Raymond Carver's maxim of 'get in, get out, don't linger' (if ever there was a great hypothetical

Nirvana album title, that was one). Tonight in Wolverhampton, the Nirvana fans old and new love the live favourite. The song is magnificent, with an extra zeal and maybe seems tighter and punchier than the actual record, with its opening riff engulfed in feedback, distortion and fuzzy hardcore punk, so the song sounds bigger than it does on *Bleach*. Filled with irony, humour and tonight fortified with punk rock cough syrup stolen from the medicine cabinet of The Ramones. There's a huge slice of Black Sabbath and again that 1960s garage punk, making 'Floyd the Barber' sound like a modern garage classic.

If 'Floyd the Barber' seems like the natural connecting point between *Bleach* and *Nevermind*, then 'Love Buzz' is the song, even though it's a cover, which would point toward grunge pop – a loud distorted sound but a central theme of 1960s punk bubblegum. Krist's bass is pounding, sharp, full bodied, yet with a high end treble sound that drives through the whole set and is perfectly highlighted on 'Love Buzz'. I liked this song a lot but noticed that they didn't play it again after the Astoria and Wolverhampton shows.

'Love Buzz' is now regarded as the song that gave Nirvana their first break. From the tentative phone call to Jack Endino to book some time in Reciprocal Studios in January 1988 to record a song called 'If You Must' with Dale Crover of The Melvins on drums, to knocking Michael Jackson's *Dangerous* off the Number 1 spot with *Nevermind* on the US *Billboard* charts in January 1992, it's an incredible journey. The demo of 'If You Must' isn't amazing but what strikes you immediately is Kurt's voice. The power of his rock scream is indisputable, and it led Jack Endino to inform Sub Pop's Jonathan Poneman of the skinny little guy's potential.

The label subsequently offered them a chance to put out a single. Surprisingly, they looked toward The Netherlands and chose a band from The Hague called Shocking Blue. They had numerous hit singles in the late 1960s but in 1970 had a massive worldwide hit with 'Venus', which topped the US *Billboard* charts for three weeks. 'Love Buzz' was another of their songs. Krist found it on a 1960s compilation album in a charity shop, and it was a song the band had made a live favourite in their set.

Tonight in Wolverhampton, 'Love Buzz' is sensational. Nirvana demonstrate why they're fast becoming the hottest band in the world with an incredible show. They seem relaxed and the sound is powerful, feeling gigantic yet intimate at the same time. Maybe it's as much to do with the venue as the mix from soundman Craig Montgomery. Standing in Wulfrun Hall in the centre of the gig, the feeling is like an assault in the midriff. You can physically feel the impact of the bass drum and snare hit you in the solar plexus. The only other band I've experienced that with is Killing Joke. After a while it's so powerful you start to feel nauseous; then you get used to it and want more.

I thought the higher profile gig at The Astoria in London was maybe pushing Nirvana to perform a bit above their game. But I'm wrong. It seems they might be relentless every time they play. It sounds very obvious but it's fascinating to see how good they really are. Way out of our league. If I can learn anything from this, then it's to try and stay focused and in the game. As I've mentioned countless times before, my biggest weakness is lack of concentration. Tonight I wasn't as bad as I normally am (there were still moments, though) but when I concentrate, we definitely seem to play better. I'm always thinking about that day's entry in the tour diary, which ironically I'll be doing from home tomorrow. This is becoming surreal.

In 1968 a band from Detroit, Michigan, called The Amboy Dukes had a classic garage hit called 'Journey to the Centre of the Mind'; here's a journey into mine while I'm supposed to be drumming. The onstage thought process generally goes something like this. I'm playing in front of 12 people in Wulfrun Hall, opening for Nirvana. I'm really sharp, aware, playing hard and loud to our set opener, 'God Bless Les Paul'. As we begin, the crowd becomes maybe 50 or 60. Sometimes I can even do a more accurate head count while playing as I can see them from my view, high up on Dave's drum riser. I look around to see if I recognise anyone. I then look around to check out the talent and see if any cool girls are in.

By now there's maybe a few hundred people coming from the bar to see what the noise is. Then my mind tells me to refocus. I play well again. I'm on the ball. Then after ten seconds I'm drifting again, thinking about my bed tonight, about the day off tomorrow. I'm looking out at the crowd, gathering slowly and checking faces and expressions to see people's reactions. Now there's maybe about 200 slowly congregating. Some are moving their heads to the beat but most are staring and checking us out. Those ones are probably in bands. I'm looking at the lights and thinking how it's nice that we get some. The lights are done by Susan Sasic, who has worked for Sonic Youth and is now in charge of bringing light, colour and drama to the *Nevermind* Tour. I'm thinking she may be the coolest woman we've ever met. She's just so hip.

I'm wondering if Nirvana are here for the long haul. Will anyone care about these three guys, these generous self-effacing musicians? Then, before I go to play a fill and move to the ride cymbal in the chorus, as I seem to do constantly, I click my knuckle off the snare as if someone is telling me to concentrate. Then I sit up and for the next few songs, I'm sharp, clear and doing my job. Then I tell myself, while playing, that if we continue to play collectively as well as we did on those last two songs, people might be surprised at how good we are becoming. However, as we're quite loud and whether good or bad, hard to ignore, as the set progresses more and more, people get curious. By the end of our set there's maybe 450 genuinely into us.

As I'm looking at the architecture of Wulfrun Hall, a very grand venue with a long illustrious history, I rattle a stick off the snare mic instead of the snare and scare myself into focus again. I noticed posters when I came in to the venue advertising Nirvana's gig, incongruously placed between future gigs for Roy Chubby Brown, Vic Reeves Big Night Out and Chuck Berry. Then we've finished, there are calls for more but we come off stage and my job's over for the day.

Nirvana's characteristic live sound, evoking the garage punk of the 1960s, sounds that way tonight because of the muddy, fuzzy, distorted sound from Kurt's amp. It's a reference to the *Nuggets* and *Pebbles* series of compilation albums. When I first actually heard Nirvana, I was amazed to hear how much they were influenced by the compilations of psychedelic garage punk bands that made the Pacific Northwest area famous in the 1960s. By 1972, Jac Holzman of Elektra Records had released *Nuggets*, a double album compilation of garage rock singles from the mid-to-late 1960s. The liner notes were done by Lenny Kaye, who went on to become guitarist in the Patti Smith Group, and in his fanzine-style notes, Kaye sets the scene perfectly, even using the phrase 'punk rock' for one of the first times in print.

Actually, here's one for the fanoraks. According to Jim DeRogatis in *Let it Blurt: The Life and Times of Lester Bangs* the word 'punk' as a musical term was first used in an essay for *Fusion* magazine by Nick Tosches in July 1970. The phrase 'punk rock' was first used by Dave Marsh in his 'Looney Tunes' column of *Creem* magazine in May 1971 describing a live set by Question Mark and the Mysterians. Interestingly, for those of us in our shiny new anoraks, the term 'heavy metal' was also used for the first time in the same issue.

In the mid-to-late 1980s Rhino continued the tradition and released a series of 15 albums called *Pebbles*. Not everything is great but even the bad stuff has charm. Both the *Nuggets* compilations and those of AIP Records' *Pebbles* are an incredible canon of work and should be essential listening to any discerning music fan.

The influence of the *Nuggets* and *Pebbles* compilations on Nirvana is clear from their debut 'Love Buzz' through to *Bleach* and especially on 1990's 'Sliver'. Equally, it could be that Nirvana were influenced by their local heroes from Seattle, The Melvins and Mudhoney, who were also heavily influenced by their musical predecessors from the 1960s. Underneath the distortion and the dirty guitar sound and pounding beat, with *Nuggets* or *Pebbles* bands there's usually a diamond of a song to be unearthed. I would spend hours over those compilations dissecting every nuance and chord change and drum beat and hook and lyric and hope to find songs to rip off or cover. The sound and feel of those records excited me. The music fan in me loved reading the small biogs of the bands featured on the series. It was great to hear that even in the 1960s young bands in the States were taking Romilar cough syrup, forming a band, making a record and getting girls. This is why the series is so important and often ignored. If it wasn't for these garage bands there would be no Stooges, New York Dolls, Sex Pistols, Ramones or Nirvana. These groups invented punk. They invented the underground indie scene. There's also a definite lineage from the groups right through to many of the acts on Sub Pop.

We head up the motorway for Scotland straight after the Wolverhampton show, and tensions, which were festering earlier, now explode. By the time we reach Southwaite Services in Cumbria, Paul our manager and our guitarist Gordon are having a blazing row. Again I stay out of it. I talk to James, our bass player, most of the way up and we see the funny side of it. He starts just about every sentence like a stand-up comedian with a funny tendency to say 'You know it's bad when...'

'You know it's bad when those two are up for a fight. I'm starting to enjoy this. Fucking hold me back.' James continues to laugh and shake his head. We give out what's left of the lager from the rider and I doze off. Things of course are going too well on the mechanical side. I wake up suddenly, thinking I'm on an airplane that's plummeting and drastically changing gear in a rain storm. We are in Carlisle. I curse the angry gods as we're driving through sheets of unforgiving rain.

I fall asleep until we're outside Calderpark Zoo (gone now, flats or houses) east of Glasgow, about five miles from home.

My nightmares stop due to a strange lack of movement. The van has stopped working, it's just dead. We ran out of petrol and had to get out and push it up a hill and then toward the nearest petrol station, the Gulf on London Road. Don't think I'm a lunatic but at that point I'm thinking of using the Gulf garage's name as a sign of a gulf in the band, that kind of shite, or the Gulf War, warring factions, the gulf in class between us and Nirvana.

Eventually, I get home, go straight to bed at 5.30am and don't wake up till 1.30pm. Best of all, it's a day away from everyone, and a chance to get everything processed, sorted and scribbled down before meeting up tomorrow to record for Scottish TV's arts show *NB*.

As previously mentioned and what is apparent from the diary is the truncated nature of the tour. Originally, as Gordon excitedly called the Bollen hotline every five minutes with updates, we were to be touring all of Europe with Nirvana, wait for this, visiting Berlin, Hamburg, Vienna, Amsterdam and Barcelona. Initially, Nirvana wanted us to play the whole European, Irish and UK tour but we couldn't afford it. They even offered to help with travel and hotel costs by letting us travel and stay with them but we couldn't make it work. Initially, though I'm sure that arrangement would've changed after their breakthrough – they would be off for five days during the tour and on those days we would have to pay for our own hotels, food and travel.

In the end we were all desperately disappointed not to go to Europe with Nirvana. Instead, we'd resume the UK tour with them at Bradford University on 26 November. On the current evidence it's difficult to imagine us skilfully navigating the autoroutes and autobahns of mainland Europe when we couldn't get vans out of Glasgow without breaking down. It's incredible looking back how unprofessional and amateurish it all was. But I was having a great time, remaining optimistic, always hoping things would improve. I was more relaxed as at least somewhere in the back of my mind, I knew I didn't want to be a drummer but a writer. This was going out on a high. It was all too tense to last any longer than a year. I would try and remain focused, absorb everything and see if there was anything worth writing down. In retrospect, with the mechanical and emotional breakdowns, and the banter and the drink, we did, for the most part, have a great laugh and we should all be at least grateful for that.

CHAPTER 6
INFLUENCES, POP MUSIC, COMEDY AND THE MONKEES

As Nirvana go on to attack mainland Europe for the next 20 days without us, there's a natural break in the story. Perhaps a good time to map back from November 1991 and see if we can find a few moments when I connected with music and it all made sense. A time to ask what brought us here? It's important for things to connect and make sense. Like the day you started to understand cryptic crosswords or when algebra made sense, thanks to a decent maths teacher using real-life tangible examples to explain it. When suddenly, things became clear, that moment when you truly fall in love with music.

I'd have been about two or three and at Airdrie Fair Day. In the centre of the town, just along from Airdrie Cross, there used to be a stage and a natural slope which would become like The Hollywood Bowl, not the ubiquitous bowling alley franchise but the natural amphitheatre. I was still in a pushchair which I remember but I'm told I heard a band, with a PA, a real group and held my arms up, and my mum picked me up and later said I was mesmerised. The song was a cover of 'Red River Rock' by Johnny and The Hurricanes. Each time I hear that song I'm taken back to that hot summer afternoon and Airdrie Fair Day. I can still smell fried onions, hot dogs, feel the excitement and squeals from the older kids at a fairground, see a man like Oliver Hardy selling ice cream and candy floss from his golden coloured van.

My life would change forever when I was six. That's when I became a true pop fan. Not that I was shyly forming opinions and writing bad poems for girls I fancied, that would come later. My mum's sister, Ellen, gave the family her old record player, as she was getting a new one. It was a Scottish version of the Stack-O-Matic. You could play six singles at a time. From then on I was in love with music. Ellen even gave us a small blue overnight suitcase full of old vinyl, which intrigued more. Amid the dust jackets and sleeves, there were singles with two songs: an A-side, the better song, and the B-side, which was supposed to be not as good but on many occasions was just as good, if not better. I dusted and cleaned them all and placed them into the correct sleeves. Labels like Decca, Parlophone, Pye, EMI, Epic, Motown, Atlantic, Bell and Rocket.

Each song had a narrative, usually about love. It didn't matter if it was the confusion of the man in the Manfred Mann song who longed to marry a pretty flamingo and make her his own. About Marie being the name of Elvis's latest flame. The B-side to that was 'Little Sister', equally as good. The Archies and a funny song called 'Sugar Sugar'. There was Cliff, happy to remain a life-long bachelor, which kind of became prophetic. Gary Puckett and the Union Gap had a strange song about a girl he was too old for but he had a funny surname as it sounded like 'bucket' and rhymed with 'fuck it'. Amongst the singles from Aunt Ellen was 'Ticket to Ride' by The Beatles. It was scratched at the start and jumped but when it kicked in, it made me so sad. The Beatles were good and The Stones were devil incarnate. They even had a song called 'Sympathy for the Devil' but I loved their tunes too. Even then lines were being drawn.

The stories in the songs gave me goosebumps. I understood it was a new way of communicating, these people were writing songs, short stories, putting music to them and having them played on the radio with records. There was a connection; suddenly I understood that the music played on the radio was being played with records, by a person called a DJ. The music on the radio was chart music and if the radio played it, people bought it and the more it was bought, the higher up the charts it went – if it was really good, it got to be Number 1.

I was spellbound by the music on the record but equally by the artwork and information on the vinyl itself. The label – Stax, CBS, Warners, Island. The colours – the distinctive reds, oranges, greens and blues – the serial numbers, the smell. The information was endless. When I got older I'd have to read everything on the sleeve before I even played a new album. Which studio was it recorded in? Who was the producer? Who engineered it? The titles and hopefully the lyrics. The artwork of every record sleeve, the colour of the vinyl.

The artists at this time always seemed to be up against each other. There were my sister's *Jackie* magazines and posters of David Cassidy and David Essex; her friends preferred Donny Osmond. There was something visceral and totemic, there was a scene. There was rivalry and excitement. There were Saturday mornings watching The Jackson Five and The Osmonds cartoons and listening to the bubblegum music in *The Banana Splits*. I didn't know it was bubblegum then, just that it was pop music and it made me feel good. It took me away from the violent, aggressive world I was in. Strange how colourful in the mind they are, even though we were watching in black and white. There were the charts we'd record from a transistor radio every Sunday on to a portable tape recorder. Sometimes the ice cream van would pass just as Number 1 was being announced and its jingle would ruin your recording. There was Bowie on *Top of the Pops*. The Sweet were good bubblegum and the Bay City Rollers were over-commercial and too formulaic, bad bubblegum, but we still loved them (Kurt liked the Rollers incidentally, that's a fact and a sublimely humorous one).

The 1970s were a harsh time economically and emotionally, not least for my family. I remember at seven or eight thinking I had to get out of this. I didn't know how it would happen but there had to be somewhere better than this. There was so much frustration and pent up aggression but I noticed when *Tom and Jerry* cartoons came on, the violence in the real world would stop and the laughter would begin. Maybe if I can make them laugh?

Along with the small suitcase of records, it was The Monkees on TV who helped me escape from all this. I've said on countless occasions that The Monkees shaped my life and it's not an exaggeration. They gave me hope, some light in the dark. Something happened. They detonated my imagination. This band lived together, had amazing adventures and drove around in a cool car. For 20 minutes, once a week, I'd be transported to this wonderful world of fun and incredible pop they inhabited and was left heartbroken when they sang their final song as this meant the credits would be next and that was it for another week; the dream was over. Reality time again. Of course at that age, you don't know that can be a job, or a career. You do understand it would be noble to aspire to, mainly as it seemed to irritate sane grown-ups.

Along with *Bilko* and The Beatles, The Monkees and *The Banana Splits* probably shaped me more than anything. They both had fantastic bubblegum pop music interspersed with mad chaotic slapstick comedy and sketches. At the time I didn't think anything of it but looking back, this could be where the love of comedy and music started. How you see the world, forming opinions, how things flow, looking at the world differently.

On the radio, the BBC always had *I'm Sorry I Haven't A Clue*, and the repeats of *Hancock's Half Hour* and *The Goons*. I remember telling my dad that Kenneth Williams's voice was the same man who was in the *Carry On* films when I heard him on *Hancock* when I was six and he looked mildly surprised at me as if I was a strange child. I also loved *Steptoe and Son* on TV and from an early age Galton and Simpson were as important to me as Dalglish and Jordan and *The Broons* and *Oor Wullie*. I remember being allowed to stay up on Christmas Eve, when the magic of Christmas was still around in the house. I was all shiny and clean, after a bath with fresh pyjamas on, cuddling into my mum (who hated *Steptoe*) and watching the 1973 Christmas Special when Harold books a holiday in Spain to get away from his dad. *Steptoe* had a grip on me – I felt like a millionaire watching them in their abject poverty and even then knew Harold would never be able to get away. My mum explained I was born in a lift at 9.26pm on the way to theatre at Bellshill Maternity hospital and that my dad missed it because *Steptoe and Son* was starting.

When I was in my mid-teens, I bought a big box of old cassettes for a pound at a jumble sale. I had a quick rummage around and got some weird looks but underneath the debris and dust and James Last Orchestra cassettes were about a dozen BBC audio tapes of comedy shows. I almost felt guilty, as if it was wrong to waste time doing something like this instead of studying for exams and trying to get a decent job. That's what you were supposed to do. I'd listen to them constantly, really got into them. I understood the beat. I could hear the same pattern working its way in. I knew when the joke was coming before the audience did. I'd write down the actual dialogue longhand and underline the lines that people laughed at. I would sit and stare at the words as if they were a cryptic crossword puzzle. Sometimes it would be obvious. Other times it just wasn't that funny but then I'd learned they were saying it in a funny way. I was off in a private world. I kept it all hidden, along with my diary, I was more embarrassed than precious about. In between collecting second-hand football programmes and cataloguing them, I'd be looking for books on comedy or comedy artists. At the time it was just something I really enjoyed, I didn't know then it was something you could have a career in.

When I was around 13, at a Christmas fair in St Columba's Church in Airdrie, I found an old *Scotsport* annual with Arthur Montford on the front (*Scotsport* was a very popular Scottish football TV show) and a hardly touched, new book, an assortment of S.J. Perelman and his short stories. I couldn't believe the haul I'd just plundered. The *Scotsport* annual intrigued me because it had behind-the-scenes photographs of the show and how it was put together. As for the Perelman book, it may sound naïve but till then, I thought comedy really only existed on radio and TV sitcoms like *Hancock, Bilko, M*A*S*H* and *Steptoe and Son* or in sketch format with shows like *Monty Python*. On the back cover of the book, it said he had written for the Marx Brothers and the quick glance through made me physically laugh out loud. It explained he was a columnist and writer for the *New Yorker*. What a job that must be, just making up funny stuff for people to laugh at and get paid for it! I got the comedy straight away. I heard his voice. All these people were writing in a humorous way on very unimportant things and expanding the minutiae. I got it. Music and comedy, is there a degree course? Can I sign up?

In the three weeks until we met up again with Nirvana, Captain America have a few days off – no gigs, just meeting up for rehearsals. We do a session for Radio Forth in Edinburgh, recording 'Bed In', 'Butter Milk', 'Flame On' and 'Indian Summer'. We are all definitely quiet and somewhat flat. At the back of our minds we are thinking how incredible it would've been to be opening up in The Loft in Berlin along with Nirvana on 10 November, then taking in Hamburg, Frankfurt, Munich, then Vienna, through Italy and a show in Ghent, Belgium with Hole, when things would go particularly crazy. The rumours were that Kurt wasn't showing up for soundchecks and his behaviour was becoming erratic. James was convinced Kurt was on heroin but I didn't want to know. I'd met him and I liked him. Though you know deep down when someone like Kurt is in Berlin and Amsterdam, he isn't visiting the art galleries.

Two big pieces of news would cheer us up between Wolverhampton and meeting up again with Nirvana in Bradford on 26 November. The first was all over *NME*, or at least the front page. On the front cover Kurt was wearing a Captain America T-shirt. Not only wearing it, but opening his coat to advertise us. I found this a bit surreal. It was incredible to think this guy was wearing our T-shirt but as a broke musician I was thinking, *He's doing this to give us some profile, knowing kids will want to wear the same T-shirts as him.* It was a brilliantly executed piece of marketing by Kurt. What had happened was they did all their publicity, interviews and photo shoots on the one day for all publications. This meant he had worn it on TV doing *The Word* and now all over loads of music newspapers and magazines. That week we were on Kurt's chest on the front cover, we were also on the inside with an article by Steve Lamacq, a single review, we were on the *Turn Ons* feature which highlighted what the *NME* staff were listening to that week and appeared in two adverts – one for our EP, and a much cooler one: a mention as support band on the Nirvana *Nevermind* Tour.

I remember reading the article at the time and being amazed at how it perfectly captured the way Nirvana were to outsiders and journalists. I had only been with them for a few dates but saw another warmer side. When I went back to read the article again when writing this book it took me back to the sight, sounds and smell of the time I spent with them, and if you can track the paper down or read on the *NME* online, it's well worth the effort.

'You'll probably barely recognise the name,' said the *NME*'s Mary Anne Hobbs. That's right, with Nirvana on the front cover of the *NME* dated 23 November, even up till this point, they were still something of a precious indie band, a well-kept secret from the Pacific Northwest. The last days of their ambitions to sell a few hundred thousand copies and dream of being as successful as Sonic Youth and having that artistic freedom were being played out. But soon they would become, as Mary Anne informed us, massive. The article went on: 'By the time this page is ink on your fingertips, Nirvana will have sold 1,000,000 copies of their new LP.'

The *NME* piece is excellently written and immediately captures the spirit and dynamic of the band. It's almost a portent of what was to come. Kurt's moodiness is highlighted, as is his medicine bottle for his stomach ailments and his habit of trying to rest or sleep, hunched in the foetal position. The piece also focuses on Nirvana's music and they are placed alongside their contemporaries. The *NME* already recognise, unlike many who didn't see it, that *Nevermind* is as important and iconoclastic as Primal Scream's *Screamadelica*, Teenage Fanclub's *Bandwagonesque* and Ice-T's *OG: Original Gangster*. I have heard the first two of those LPs a million times (forgive the slight or more likely monumental exaggeration), but I'm somewhat ashamed to say I've never heard Ice-T's. By this point, as Mary Anne reminds us, *Nevermind* had reached the *Billboard* US Top Ten in under six weeks. There was also reluctance throughout the article to accept their current predicament. Depending on whether your side of the fence was indie or mainstream, Nirvana were either on the verge of unimaginable success based on the quality of the songs on their second album, or on the edge of a precipice gazing into a dark abyss that Kurt would never be able to accept.

What is also captured in the article is the relentlessness of their schedule and the palpable pressure they were under. The band, Mary Anne explained, were 'suddenly found diving on the media trapeze between a thousand grinning interviewers, whose common opening gambit is: "Hi! So, why did you decide to call the band Nirvana?"' It must be emphasised the piece was written just before it went chaotic, just before 'Smells Like Teen Spirit' changed the band's life forever.

The second piece of news, revealed the same day, was even harder to believe. Eugene found out that Nirvana were going to cover his songs, 'Molly's Lips' and 'Son of a Gun', for the B-side of their upcoming single, 'In Bloom'.

CHAPTER 7

SHONEN KNIFE, LAMINATES AND GOTHS

BRADFORD UNIVERSITY, 26 November 1991

DRAIN YOU
ANEURYSM
SCHOOL
FLOYD THE BARBER
SMELLS LIKE TEEN SPIRIT
ABOUT A GIRL
POLLY
LITHIUM
SLIVER
BREED
TALK TO ME
D-7
BEEN A SON
NEGATIVE CREEP
ON A PLAIN

BLEW
SOMETHING IN THE WAY
JESUS DOESN'T WANT ME FOR A SUNBEAM
TERRITORIAL PISSINGS

Set off today for Bradford and a gig at the city's University Union, to hook up again with Nirvana and meet Shonen Knife. We all loved Shonen Knife, a three-piece all-girl group from Osaka, and wanted to take them home with us. They were wonderfully warm, gentle and kind. Naoko Yamano sang and played guitar, her sister Atsuko Yamano played drums and Michie Nakatani played bass. When I knew them, Atsuko played drums but before leaving the band some years later, she also played bass and designed the band's cool outfits. Atsuko was so talented and my favourite. We all looked forward to meeting them at the soundcheck each day and seeing them play each night on tour. Beneath the cute pop songs about animals, sweets, riding bikes, collecting insects, banana chips, cookies and sushi, there was a skilled underground garage band.

As well as having a cult worldwide following, they had huge fans in influential bands like Redd Kross, Sonic Youth and Nirvana. I have a signed single, with kisses and love hearts of 'Space Christmas' and 'Bear Up Bison' on the Seminal Twang label, which I treasure. Seminal Twang was an extremely cool off-shoot of Paperhouse, run by Dave Barker. It's similar to the Sub Pop Singles Club and contains bands and artists like The Springfields, Half Japanese, Velvet Crush, Redd Kross, Jad Fair and Daniel Johnston. Shonen Knife later released a live mini-album called *We Are Very Happy You Came*, which I used to own but lost somewhere. It's worth buying if you come across it, as it captures the band's set at the time. On the sleeve notes I get a thank you and my name is beside a guy called Cobain in the credits, more for alphabetical reasons than in order of importance.

With songs like 'I Eat Choco Bars', 'Lazybone' and rocking covers of 'Suzie is a Headbanger' by the Ramones and 'Goose Step Mama' by The Rutles, they won over loads of new fans in 1991 on the *Nevermind* Tour as the 'super-eccentric-pop-punk-cult-band-Shonen-Knife!' I loved hanging out with them and we'd spend hours talking about nothing really. Nice and relaxed. One conversation I remember was about the complexities of how the Japanese language was written and the importance of the shape of the word, as it's about the sound each letter makes. They then wrote my name out in Japanese. I'm amazed at how neat and detailed their handwritten letters and notes are. The band's underground garage sound and quirky Buzzcocks/Ramones pop is still going with Naoko Yamano at the helm, but it's the line-up of Naoko, Atsuko and Michie that I knew and liked the best.

Bradford is the first day of the tour proper as we meet again after Nirvana's European dates. We are more organised this time, learning from the mistakes of the previous three dates: Bristol (not made, broke down), London (no accommodation organised), Wolverhampton (ran out of petrol five miles from home and had to push van to a petrol station). I decided to drive down with Michael and Willie (hereby known as the crew) in the van with the gear as there's a decent seat at the front and more of a laugh. Michael and Willie are nuts and have a great attitude. The others are on the tour bus, which is more like a large minibus with windows and some decent leg room.

We are all full of the joys as we set sail for the good tour Nirvana, optimistic as always, until the van breaks down near Custom House Quay by the Clyde in Glasgow city centre. We phone the AA, again, who come out and recharge the battery.

Now the pressure is on. When we get going again, it's 3pm and we are two hours behind schedule. We arrive at Bradford at 7.15pm and I'm on stage 20 minutes later. Despite the panic to get there, the gig was fine. I still feel traumatised after the white knuckle ride to the gig and after an uncomplicated set, I head for the bar. While having a beer, I get chatted up by a woman wearing a Nirvana T-shirt. I couldn't take my eyes off her, not because she's gorgeous but because she looks like Iggy Pop with long hair. In fact, kind of what Iggy looks like now in those insurance ads he does. She was nice enough but a bit abrasive and very uninteresting. The only thing remotely interesting that made anything stand to attention were my ears, when she said we sounded like The Pixies.

I'm bought a lager by two girls who are far more interesting. One looks like Siouxsie Sioux and the other like a punk version of Liz Hurley. They're from London, posh and talk all the way through Shonen Knife. I always hide my laminate but tonight I realise my pass is out and shining and luring all kinds of weird and wonderful creatures toward me. There definitely is a look you get when people are talking to you but their eyes are staring at your pass. It's not you they want to be near; it's the band you're working with. If you've ever been in a band, your first vicarious thrill after a blowjob off two drunken students at a party in Gartlea is the day you're handed a sticker with your band's name and the words 'Access All Areas' on it and it's placed over your head like an Olympic gold medal.

It doesn't matter if it's King Tuts in Glasgow or The Vogue in Seattle, getting your first pass for a gig in a decent venue is like a rite of passage. Now imagine you're given one when you're touring with Nirvana? You would be as shag-worthy as someone who works at a model agency with a card in his pocket at a party going up to prospective models with the promise of a shot at stardom and a one-way ticket to fuckyouville. That's what happens when you're wearing an Access All Areas laminate. Suddenly you become someone worth approaching and talking to, someone witty and erudite, a modern-day Noël Coward or Oscar Wilde. 'Oh look, is that F. Scott Fitzgerald at the bar? Oh he's so full of put-downs, attractive and appealing and so worthy of attention.' That's why I always tried to hide my laminate. I didn't like the falseness of the situation or being the centre of attention and hating the deceitfulness of strangers I'm talking to, thinking they know me really well and assuming I can sneak them in to meet the band, no sweat. Even if I could, which I might do at a push, there's millions of people who deserve that before any of the strangers in front of me.

There are a few good reasons why you have to wear a laminated pass around your neck. So you don't lose it and so you can be quickly recognised as part of the touring party by the security at each venue. I'm on the periphery of one of those empty, facile conversations with about seven or eight people; our guitarist Gordon and our bass player James are holding court, Eugene and I on the edges of it. Nearby some people are talking about themselves and I'm faking interest, pretending to listen and looking really attentive but I'm brilliant at that. I'm not listening. It's like a Tom Stoppard play, all witty statement, pun, cleverness and innuendo with everyone thinking they're being philosophical and truth-seeking and idealistic though really they're just using you to get close to people who aren't even your pals but you were thrown together in a situation. I was just as bad as them, standing there as if I'm best mates with Nirvana.

As my enigmatic laminate flapped around, many people crossed my mind who I wished were there. People who supported me when I was starting in bands, when I was 15 and 16 and wanted to be in this situation so much, to have records out, to play drums every night to appreciative, if not huge crowds, just to share a piece of this and meet the band. Like my big sister Maureen, who had a yellow Ford Fiesta that I managed to squeeze a five-piece drum kit and cymbals into and be driven to Glasgow many a time for a gig in the Rock Garden. Sharon Galway (my then hairdresser and still now, poor woman). The old girlfriends like Patricia, who I spurned in order to practise and rehearse. Friends like Mark Leslie, who gave me a tape with *Rubber Soul* and *Revolver* on each side and got me into The Stooges before anyone had heard of them. Like Tom Roche who would generously lend you huge swathes of his cool record collection for years to enhance your taste, and who also gave us his cherished Rickenbacker every Sunday to rehearse in Pet Sounds studios in Maryhill when we didn't have a guitar, without ever complaining about it. People who cared and were supportive. To guys like my old record shop manager at Our Price, Matthew Cassan, who paid for early demos and considered managing Ben Mullen and me in a folk-rock project. He would've been a brilliant manager.

And the one person at that moment in time who I wanted there was a girl I truly fell in love with. After years of writing, rehearsing and hopeless gigs, she deserved to be part of this. That moment when you look at someone and your eyes meet and you've connected. Someone so beautiful and cool that you can't believe she knows you exist, never mind smiles and chats to. By then I was going through my Morrissey naïve romantic and poetic stage but wished I was going through my Iggy stage. Her name was Liz Shanks and she was older than me, a couple of years older; this seemed important at the time. She'd drive me to gigs and be so cool, and we'd sit in her yellow Mini and chat. She always smelt so clean and beautiful. Her job took her off for a year's work placement in the States and she'd send me postcards from Washington, Boston and wherever her travels took her. Eventually her postcards inspired me to get up and get over to America for my own trip. She was the daughter of a farmer and we'd go walking through the fields and one day she squealed at me to stop. Her experienced eye saw a rusty hunting trap big enough to catch a deer. It was all set and primed and if she hadn't squealed at me to stop, my leg would've been gone. I was too busy being a romantic dreamer. Elizabeth Shanks should've been the one, but she was just too cool for me.

Now I wanted her and any of the people who had been there for me to be around, especially when I started out playing gigs. I knew it wouldn't get any better and felt that this tour was as good as it was going to get and I wanted them all there to share in the excitement. The Liz Hurley lookalike and her friend are actually quite cool and didn't know I was in the support band till the woman who looks like Iggy comes into the conversation and informs them. Liz and the Banshee are surprisingly warm to her in return. Like all women when they get together, it sounds like they've changed the language so men don't understand. The two friends are following the band to Birmingham and Sheffield then the last night of the tour at Kilburn. They're staying with a friend who attends the university and lives just two minutes away. If I fancy it, as he – their friend – is away, they offer a place on the floor. I buy all three a beer and the Iggy clone, in a less erudite fashion jokingly roars, 'Bring condoms!' A woman who looks like Iggy Pop. Just hold that thought in your mind, OK.

I head backstage for some of the lager Dave has delivered to our dressing room and make my way to the side of his kit sitting adjacent to his drums as Nirvana deliver a breathtaking show to an enthralled Bradford. I didn't think they could improve any, but they have. There's a clear, no-nonsense atmosphere at the soundcheck and around the venue before the doors open, there's a degree of tension. At first we think it's because of the growing pressure of being under the media spotlight, and the impetus and momentum over the last three weeks of 'Smells Like Teen Spirit'. However, I'm told by the crew that the band's seriousness is down to a rather chaotic night in Amsterdam. There's a significant change in the way they kick off their set from the first three dates. Instead of lumbering up with an atmospheric cover of 'Jesus Doesn't Want Me for a Sunbeam' by The Vaselines, they blow the place away with 'Drain You' and 'Aneurysm'.

I'm gob-smacked. I'm happy. I'm confused. I have goosebumps. 'Aneurysm' starts like a zombie waking up and having Prozac for breakfast, building up tensely before exploding into a 1960s psychedelic hardcore anthem. It sounds like a different Nirvana song; it's not the usual structure or shape. Dave is all elbows, attacking high and floor toms so hard, building up the tension, locked in the groove. Krist and Kurt both watch Dave and smile. Kurt then kicks in, taking the masses to post-punk pop oblivion. The crowd sway and move like a sequence of waves, bouncing off the back wall from back to front then ebbing with an incredible mathematical looseness from side to side. All as one, hypnotised. The song is cleverly truncated with a riff that reminds me of the start of 'Teenage Kicks' by The Undertones. It then keeps kicking back into Dave's clever, dominant and robust drum parts. It builds up to a great post-punk crescendo with the rhythm section playing against Kurt's guitar, as he is pleading his aggressor to kick the shit out of him. The song ends with the zombie running amok, going out of control, as the band get quicker and faster yet keep it under control.

During 'Lithium' I see the Iggy clone stage diving. I look over at the bar and can actually see Liz Hurley and her friend and they look even more beautiful in that twilight area of most gigs between the atmospheric lights of the stage and the garish, fluorescent, unnatural lights of the bar.

We all know this is a moment. But of course we play it down. We have to, it would be so wrong to show your true excitement. Now is the time to stay like Nirvana, keep level-headed and underplay it. Eugene and I shake our heads and shrug in disbelief as we hear Nirvana's management nonchalantly inform the band that there will be a *Top of the Pops* appearance for 'Smells Like Teen Spirit', which has entered the charts at Number 9. Out of all of Nirvana, Krist is the most animated.

'Cool, *Top of the Pops*, man.'

There's a feeling on the tour of suspended disbelief. Everyone senses the excitement of a sea change, the feeling something is starting to happen for the band. Their days seem more hectic since we met at the shows in London and Wolverhampton. During their three-week absence, as they toured mainland Europe, they seem to have gained more confidence, but at the same time seem tired and frustrated. There are more interviews, TV, press and photo shoots. They look exhausted. When we sit down together for a beer or at dinner, no one speaks about it. It's almost a bit too uncool to talk about something as unfashionable as having a smash hit. There's a surreal nature to it all. Maybe it's just the band's modest nature. No one speaks about it. Don't mention the elephant in the room. (I hate that irritating idiom for an obvious truth but feel its use is worthy of inclusion.) Perhaps it's the realisation that the momentum is really starting to move, but the band's early punk ethos is making them keep it all low-key. Kurt, despite the laid-back image, was ambitious to make it. Now it was really starting to happen for him but we all wished the band could enjoy it more.

I'm so knackered and drained from attempts to make Bradford on time that I renege on the small party and even though I'm very tempted by the presence of Liz Hurley and her pal, the Iggy lookalike unsettled me a bit. Instead, my conscience guides me back to a hot bath and an early night in the calm and tranquillity of the small family-run bed and breakfast.

I ended up lying in bed, two single beds, chatting to Gordon about a decent single review (not brilliant but not shite) in *Melody Maker*, for our first release on Paperhouse, the eponymously titled *Captain America* EP. The rest of the night was rounded off by making up surreal psychedelic lyrics for the same guitar riff for an imaginary *Nuggets* band we were going to form. As you do. It was funnier than it sounds now, you'd have to have been there. As ever, I couldn't sleep so I put the TV on; in the news was a story about condoms being handed out to thousands of New York High School students. It was as though even the news was mocking me for my early night.

CHAPTER 8

NICE T-SHIRT, KURT

BIRMINGHAM HUMMINGBIRD, 27 November 1991

DRAIN YOU
ANEURYSM
FLOYD THE BARBER
SMELLS LIKE TEEN SPIRIT
ABOUT A GIRL
POLLY
LITHIUM
SLIVER
BEEN A SON
ON A PLAIN
NEGATIVE CREEP
ENDLESS, NAMELESS

The overriding feeling as we approached Birmingham wasn't a good one. It just didn't feel right. Something wasn't flowing. The Sword of Damocles, or more appropriately, the

Converse sneaker of the Indie Kid, was hanging precariously over the city, the venue and the gig. It was tense, frightening and scary. This was evident in Nirvana's performance as they went on stage crankier than normal, irritable and tired. They played a truncated, abridged set, the shortest on the tour by far. It was the first time I'd seen anything in Nirvana's locker that pointed to being difficult. I saw them arguing with their own management and the local promoter. Everyone was fucked, and at the end of their tether, but however short their set was, Nirvana did perform for their fans.

We've already established that Nirvana were a band that used their profile to amazing effect. Both Captain America and Shonen Knife were given full use of their equipment, drums and amps. Thanks to Kurt's deliberate piece of marketing, in wearing a Captain America T-shirt on the one day Nirvana did all their press and photo shoots, this primitive yet effective strategy meant loads of Nirvana fans would check us out and thankfully would buy the T-shirt he was advertising too.

We made it to Birmingham in good time but once we got there, found it difficult to get around, or at least I did. I was with Michael in the van with the gear and we couldn't find the Hummingbird. Eventually we got there, then had to dash off to the B&B to check-in. Birmingham was a nightmare to get around but even more difficult to get out of. We drove around so much we ran out of petrol and had to push the van again to the nearest petrol station. But as was the case with Michael or Willie, no matter how bad things got, a great laugh was never far away.

At one point, amid all this chaos, we stop to go into a newsagent. I tell Michael I need a huge fart and that I'm going to let rip really loudly. I look around and see a target, an annoying precocious brat bullying a few others, and tell Michael we're blaming him. After I unleash a rocket, we chastise the lad for his bad manners, leave him speechless and with an incredulous look on his face. While we create a distraction in the queue, Michael ingeniously slips a copy of *Big Jugs* into his shopping pile. An array of old *Carry On*-style jokes duly followed about being antiques fans of ye old pewter jugs. Oh, it's all very immature and sexist, I know, but it was funny.

Eventually we made it out of Birmingham city centre and got to our B&B but were late and had to get back to the venue to eat and soundcheck. James and I grabbed about 15 T-shirts from the box but Gordon, Eugene and our soundman Murray thought this was a bad idea as we were running low and felt we should try and ration them a bit. We headed back in again to the Hummingbird. Murray had asked me to remember how to get there. So futile, as I've said many a time I'm crap with directions as I don't drive. There's actually a good reason for that: a recurring nightmare. I have a dream that's gone beyond recurring; it's now just like an irritating continually looped rerun of *Friends* in my subconscious. I'm part of a daring bank heist, which involves robbing millions from safety deposit boxes and I'm the getaway driver. But I can't drive and I flood the engine and panic and stall the car.

As a non-driver, I was pleased with myself for identifying a landmark on the way back to the venue. That's what the intrepid adventurers always did. I remembered that we had turned left at that McDonald's. Great. There we were, heading back to the venue, all going splendidly. The place did look different as the late afternoon lumbered into the early winter evening. Now it was dark. We were a bit out of the city centre, beside Edgbaston and near the (since closed down) BBC Pebble Mill studios. How was I to know there were more than one McDonald's in Birmingham? You'd think it was a franchise. So we turned left, and were heading the wrong way toward what might've been Greenland. Murray eventually made it by using the more conventional method of following road signs.

We reached the venue a few hours later and despite Murray going mental at us, managed to eventually make the stage and play well. When we walked off stage we were told we'd ran out of T-shirts. Eugene and I volunteered to jump into a taxi. Having just played, we were choking for a drink so we grabbed four cans of beer from the rider to help us on our expedition. The taxi driver wouldn't let us drink the beer and as he knew where he was going, we quickly got to the van and grabbed the remainder of the tour currency, the T-shirts, and headed back to the venue. I noticed when leaving the venue that security was particularly tight. There seemed an aggressive aspect to it. We looked at each other and both knew it was going to be a nightmare. Having watched the reaction to the band at previous gigs we sensed a really bad vibe in the building and, worse still, outside.

All the shows on the tour were robust, with loads of stage diving and people enjoying themselves, but I never saw one bit of trouble or a fight. In fact the only fight I saw was a food fight in Newcastle between us and Nirvana. Things were at worst boisterous. But in Birmingham, the atmosphere seemed strained. As we approached, about 30 feet from the front door, the mood deteriorated. The bouncers outside had what was left of the queue of Nirvana fans all in line. I sensed it was going to be difficult. A woman on security wasn't pleased with us for showing up with a box of T-shirts. She called in the rest of them. This one huge security guy was well over 6'4" and around 22 stone, all muscle. 'Where the fuck are you two going?'

'Into the venue,' I said sounding hard as I tried to look up and eyeball him.

'Nah nah, no you don't! Put the box down.'

'We're the support band, we ran out of T-shirts. We've passes.' Eugene was trying to appease.

'I don't give a fuck if you're with the band. You're out here now,' he growled.

'Get Alex MacLeod, Nirvana's tour manager out, he'll vouch for us,' I said, trying hard not to back down.

This was clearly his patch and he intended to keep it that way. He bent down to look at the box, making the mistake of giving me a clear punch at his temple. I could see the vein pumping away: one sharp elbow on that and he's out cold, big fucker or not. The Nirvana fans queuing up started to notice what was going on. It could turn into a riot if I created a distraction. I was three seconds away from a clear knockout; I was in that zone. I didn't like the guy and knew I had the clear hit. All I had to do was scan the area for the best way of escaping to safety. I looked around, and knew some of our people would be at the front door if we could get to it. Most of the bouncers were over at the queue searching Nirvana fans and only a couple were at the door. I was scanning the place, looking at the big picture. I couldn't work out what was going on, I became confused and for a brief second as it got more surreal, thought I might be having a bad dream. I could hear American accents in the crowd. The security guard rummaged through the box. I didn't like the atmosphere here at all. Things seemed to go into slow motion. I was convinced I could hear New Jersey and Brooklyn accents. It was all just weird shit. At that point, just as I decided to calm down, the security guy found our cans of lager.

'What the fuck's this?' He held up four green cans of Carlsberg.

To him, though, it was contraband. We were smuggling beer into his venue and not paying for it inside. He looked around at the pandemonium, was nervous and distracted.

'We took it from inside,' I said, still trying to stare him in the eye, though inside I feared the worst. He stood up again. I honestly thought I had to be dreaming at this point – all the aggro and the American accents. He looked at us both, then for some reason, probably boredom, nodded for us to go in. We met our manager, Paul Cardow, and threw the box at him.

A few minutes later I met Dave and Nirvana's tour manager, Alex MacLeod. They were concerned when I told them about the incident. In the dressing room I got my thoughts down quickly while I chatted to Krist. Kurt was sleeping. The big sleep.

Alex MacLeod was quite a ferocious character who didn't take shit from anyone and kept things running as smoothly as possible. He was gruff, had curly hair usually tied back in a pony-tail, and was a tough, no-nonsense and uncompromising guy. His job was to take care of Nirvana and he was brilliant at it. If he liked you, you knew it.

Dave's snare is fucked at The Hummingbird show and I see Alex struggle with it between songs. I run out from backstage and bring mine from the van and give it to Dave while Alex tries to fix Dave's broken one. Earlier he'd ask if he could use my cymbals, one of which was an incongruous black Paiste Chinese symbol, bought in '83 at the height of my art school Steve-Jansen-from-Japan 'Art of Parties' and Simple Minds 'I Travel' phase. The other was a Zildjian 18-inch crash cymbal which Dave liked the sound of – either that or he hated it, he hit it so much it split. I wasn't going to say anything. I'd been rattling his kit every night on tour and never a word was said to cast up anything. In a perverse way I thought it was cool that Dave, who was such a small, skinny guy, could actually break a cymbal. Mark Elliot finally destroyed the cymbal, as drummer in Boomerang and still has it somewhere as a weird sculpture and doorstop.

The official line on why Nirvana's Birmingham show was much shorter than normal was that they were late and tired having just recorded *Top of the Pops* at Elstree studios in north London. This might have explained the reason for the spare snare and what I noticed was a different hired kit. Maybe the spare stuff was in another van. Maybe it was tiredness. Their playing was perfunctory and powerful as always but for once there was definitely a different, angrier side to the group that night: frustration and tension.

I don't know what's happening; maybe it's the way certain people in the support band are being treated. I walked by the promoter earlier and saw their tour manager and the band deep in discussion. After the drama at the front door of the Hummingbird, I make it to the side of Dave's kit as the band take the stage. I have two cans of beer, a glass filled with ice and I pick up a litre bottle of water sitting beside me: you've got to stay hydrated. Kurt looks around for a drink before starting the set and I realise I've picked up his bottle. I hand him his Evian by awkwardly stretching through the cymbal stands. He nonchalantly takes a drink without thanking me. There's me thinking I'm saving the day by returning what was actually his.

Kurt looks over to Krist waiting on him, then plays an A chord. He plays a short, sharp punky chord a few times then turns around and for once, almost tentatively starts the opener, 'Drain You'. Kurt kicks a distortion pedal with his left foot and the drums and bass join in. Bang on cue, the Hummingbird fans go crazy. Just at that point the bass seems to go. I look over and Krist's bass strap has loosened off, but he quickly sorts it and we're back on course. I sit crossed leg, taking it all in. Two things stick out: the clarity of Kurt's vocals through Dave's monitors and how loud Krist's bass is for the drummer. I laugh at the lyrics. I can hear Kurt's lyrics and I've never noticed exactly what he's singing till now. Dave is concentrating and watching Krist pogo like he does, out of time and disjointed but his playing is always exact. I'm knackered just watching the drumming, powerful and accurate, exactly like the record. He sits very low in the stool and with the lower centre of gravity is almost pushing all his weight into the pedal. Most drummers have their heel flat but he doesn't, he has the ball of his foot kicking ferociously as though using a foot pump, transferring an incredible amount of power despite his small frame, which steers the band along. He is only halfway through the first song and already you see his importance to the dynamic of the group.

In most bands, drummers are there to simply keep the beat but Dave's style of playing is much more powerful and clever than that, taking the songs down with intricate work between the bass drum and the ride cymbal, then coming back in with a powerful machine-gun-like drum roll with a clever bass drum triplet and we're away again. The phrasing and technique would make you think he was the songwriter. I've already started copying him on tour by hitting both crash cymbals at once and incorporating, whether the others like it or not, some triplets into the songs. Something I didn't do before.

Now 'Drain You' is in the middle-eight and Dave counts the build up by hitting the ride cymbal on the bell, builds up then unleashes it, bringing it home with a superbly tight single-stroke roll and Bonham-esque fill before driving on to the next verse. It's as though each specific part is crucial to the song. When the aforementioned snare problem emerges later in the set, I immediately fetch mine to help out and Alex MacLeod, the tour manager, is grateful. He tries to fix Dave's snare as he uses mine. Dave winks and smiles his appreciation at the work done to get his snare sorted, then he shrugs his shoulders at the kit and laughs. I ask Alex what he's laughing at and he says it's a hired Yamaha kit.

The momentum and the pressure are building and you can feel it in Nirvana's performance. Everywhere we go there are film crews, journalists and radio stations recording interviews or journalists from the music press around the band. At every turn the band are taking the piss out of how polished the production is on *Nevermind*. I feel like shouting, 'It's a hit, why be bashful?' I suppose if you have a vision and you don't get to see that in the finished product then as an artist that's your opinion but it's hardly Huey Lewis and the News. I think they're just embarrassed by how successful it looks like it's going to become. It doesn't sit with their punk rock values; they think they're selling out because they're popular. The Sex

Pistols were popular. It feels like it's starting to really happen for them. Earlier we saw them nervously head off as if attending a court hearing. They were going to record *Top of the Pops*. Fuck me, how cool is that? *Top of the Pops*! It's Nirvanamania, which is kind of like Beatlemania only without the hysteria, the mania, or the Beatle part. After this, for them nothing really would ever be the same again.

At the encore, Krist confirmed the *Top of the Pops* story. He came on buttoning his sweating brown shirt and engaged with the fans.

'We just recorded *Top of the Pops*. It was really stupid. You gotta watch it tomorrow night on TV, if they show it. Kurt did a mighty fine Morrissey impersonation.'

Then began as vicious a version of 'Endless Nameless' as I've ever heard. Maybe it was the long day. I was behind Kurt's amp and to the side of Dave and was inches from him as he brutalised his guitar off the poor defenceless machine.

On the way to Sheffield the next day, as the others sleep, daydream, or chat about the Birmingham gig, I find a bit of courage and take out my small pocket notebook, mainly for prompts and ideas. I give myself an impossible task. I attempt to see if I could describe, distil and dissect Nirvana's music and their career path in as few words as possible. I managed with great difficulty to get it down to three words and write down 'fragmented with fluency'. Then I started to get frustrated and felt it would be remiss and flippant to over-simplify how good they were on the dates we had just seen them play. Even on bad nights, like last night, they may have been angry but the show was really power-charged, if short.

I then decide to expand on this idea, and use the journey to see if I can nail why so many fans were buying *Nevermind*. What makes them so special? What sets them apart from bands like Big Black, the Butthole Surfers or The Melvins? Pare it down to basics. What do Nirvana have? At the very heart of their work, from the earliest songs like 'Blew', 'Floyd the Barber', 'About a Girl', 'School' and 'Negative Creep' on *Bleach* to the release of 'Sliver', two minutes of post-punk perfection, were the quality of the songs and the fact they sounded different.

It all points to one thing. Yes, there's heavy punk rock from the 1960s garage scene like Blue Cheer, whose album, *Vincebus Eruption*, was a definite template for the Seattle grunge scene. The album from the San Francisco trio still sounds incredible in its explosive intensity, especially when you consider the backdrop at the time of the hippy movement. There's the Black Sabbath riffs and the chaotic rifferamma of Mudhoney and the independent art school vibe of Sonic Youth. Yet what sets Nirvana apart is that, meshed in amongst all the anger and loud guitars, there are glorious pop songs of tremendous quality.

The sign of a great song is that no matter the genre or style, whether it's performed by an orchestra or acoustically, if it's well written it will come across. Equally the sign of a great band is how generous they are in their interpretation of other people's songs. This could explain why 1993's *MTV's Unplugged in New York* proved so successful for the band. If you include the many different types of music fan who loved the record, then you have a commercial breakthrough and smash hit record. Indie fans love them, metal fans love them and the mainstream pop fans are getting it. I head to Sheffield genuinely happy, excited and buoyed for this incredible story to continue.

CHAPTER 9

GETTING THE TAPE, TOUTS AND TOTPS

SHEFFIELD UNIVERSITY OCTAGON CENTRE,
28 November 1991

DRAIN YOU
ANEURYSM
SCHOOL
FLOYD THE BARBER
SMELLS LIKE TEEN SPIRIT
ABOUT A GIRL
POLLY
LITHIUM
SLIVER
BREED
BEEN A SON
NEGATIVE CREEP
ON A PLAIN

BLEW
ENDLESS, NAMELESS

Kurt is sullen, more so than normal. The darkness descends. Those around him every day recognise it but journalists and TV people don't. The talk backstage is that they're wary of opening up or trusting journalists as earlier in the year they naïvely welcomed a journalist into the inner sanctum on the tour bus, letting them witness them at their most vulnerable. The same journalist later portrayed them as delinquent TV-trashing cretins. All trust is gone and their guard is always up. Any interview is generally interspersed with Kurt criticising the polished sound of *Nevermind*. It's easy to gauge how truculent it's going to be for those on the receiving end by measuring the angle of Kurt's stoop. He alters his posture to varying degrees of happiness or discontent. When people in other bands or fans approach, he is upright and smiling and relaxed but when he is unhappy he starts to stoop, becoming more fractious and bad-tempered.

During interviews Krist is the star. Dave is happy to laugh, will engage with a few good lines if he's in the mood but also looks wary and on edge. Kurt nods in agreement with most of what Krist is saying. Krist is the same – funny, sharp, ready to bob and weave and debate, great with a line, personable and approachable. Dave and particularly Kurt are more defensive as soon as a TV crew show up or a journalist brings out their tape recorder or notebook. They are in demand. Everybody wants a piece of their hot little grunge ass and they just don't want to speak again about 'Smells Like Teen Spirit' or *Nevermind*. They even discuss the ubiquitous snooker coverage every time they come to the UK rather than talk about the success of their second studio album.

Nirvana always had strong pockets of support in the UK from the start. It's strange thinking of the very first time I heard the actual name Nirvana. I thought it was a terrible name; the name and feel of the word. I like my bands to have descriptive names, like The Chocolate Watch Band, The Strawberry Alarm Clock or The Lemon Pipers. Nirvana just seemed a bit boring in terms of a name and I always felt the font – Bodoni, extra bold condensed, for those interested – was a bit heavy metal, like Slayer or Metallica. There's actually a font called Nirvana now. How cool is that? Not only did they create a sub-genre, they also have a font.

I honestly felt the branding was a bit mixed and confused. It didn't seem to represent the band's sound. I thought it was a clichéd, normal, everyday, overused term. If it's going to be a one-word name, make it sound interesting. Oasis is a crap name and boring, whereas Television, Japan, Wire or Magazine are imaginative single-word names that sound interesting. It's actually really difficult at times to come up with a decent name. Kurt came up with it and is on record as saying it's the attainment of perfection but I always thought it was a crap name, so it shows you what I know. I felt it sounded like they had to quickly come up with a name to have something to spray on their gear before someone else stole it.

Nirvana were always loved and embraced by the indie fans in the UK but the press weren't always so sure. Around the release of *Bleach* they were hardly unanimous in their praise. Some respected scribes slaughtered them, didn't get it and were dismissive. Others with a more discerning ear could hear something. The most commonly held view was that Nirvana were Sub Pop's heir apparent to Mudhoney's crown.

Despite his strong indie ethos, Kurt was an ambitious and driven individual. One who clearly wanted to make it and to make it big, despite his diffidence when it arrived; when things escalated, it would be enough for Nirvana to be as successful as The Pixies. By *Nevermind*'s release and the 1991 tour, the band could've played every venue three times over and still left some disappointed. Even by the final UK tour for *In Utero,* scheduled for spring 1994 which never happened, the UK dates for major arenas sold out in a day. Given all this, looking back it's astonishing to see how unprepared people were for what was about to happen.

As I got to know the band, they openly discussed their dismay at *Nevermind*'s production. In one particular conversation I suggested that it was an amazing record and they should be proud as fuck of making such a brilliant album. I understood their reticence, modesty and indie spirit; we all shared in their success and kindness even if it was three crates of beer, or using their gear every night. I argued there was nothing wrong with being commercially successful but maintaining artistic credibility and cited R.E.M. as a band who managed to sell by the truckload but still, at least in 1991, had kept quite cool.

Even so, Nirvana were so fed up and frustrated, maybe even fearful, that their hardcore fans would hate them for 'selling out' that it almost became their default position to criticise the album. Krist Novoselic told me 'Smells Like Teen Spirit' was 'Louie Louie'-meets-'More than a Feeling'. The former song is the benchmark to which all rock 'n' roll bands should aspire to, the other is a Boston song. So, we had a band who'd released an album that fans were finding hard to track down and the group who made it didn't like how it sounded. That's right, folks, a great and auspicious start to the record that would redefine a generation.

I would sit close by as TV companies from France, Japan, Belgium and America interviewed Kurt, Krist and Dave and they would be berating *Nevermind* and 'Smells Like Teen Spirit'. For the UK show *Rapido*, I sat beside Dave's kit as they recorded incredible versions of 'Aneurysm' and 'Lithium'. The reaction every time they played the songs was always very positive. I tried to analyse the record many times in the pages of my diary. It struck me that if they came from LA or New York, they'd be more hip but probably not as successful. Being outsiders, they were looked down upon, even by the Seattle bands – they didn't have that snobbery or desire for coolness and pretension. They liked what they liked and didn't give a fuck what you thought about them. They loved The Vaselines, The Stooges, The Pixies, The Melvins, Black Flag and Black Sabbath but they also loved Aerosmith, R.E.M., The Beatles and Bowie. In other words, they were just probably listening to all kinds of music, from punk, new wave to folk and not giving a fuck about 'scenes'. Who were the last band to namecheck Leadbelly? The band, and especially Kurt, would take in all these groups and quite rightly be influenced by anything around him, then add that distinctive clever, acerbic, ironic, dark melodramatic writing. I just didn't like the fact they were slagging off their own record, though why was I bothering and being so precious about it? It was their album, if they wanted to be dismissive about it then let them.

I've had many surreal things happen to me in my – at times – bizarre life. Two memorable little things happened one day at Sheffield University. I enjoyed Sheffield; the people were warm and friendly. Around the university area there were market stalls. They sold mostly second-hand records, books, old leather jackets and cool old boots. This really was nirvana. It was good to get away from the rest of the crowd, just lose yourself checking out CDs and vinyl. Hidden amongst the usual crap people throw away, there is the ubiquitous shite you see in every charity shop: *No Parlez* by Paul Young, *Push* by Bros, *Face Value* by Phil Collins, and the inevitable *Kids From Fame* album. There were some decent 60s compilations, in great condition and underpriced, but my eyes kept going back to a stall with cool biker boots. I was trying a pair on, 15 quid (this was '91, remember). I had 15 quid saved from my fiver PDs (*per diems*; your daily allowance on tour), mainly for juice, chewing gum, a magazine or a newspaper. Meals, accommodation and transport were laid on, as was drink from our own, Shonen Knife's and Nirvana's rider. I quite liked the regime of touring but it was hardly a world tour, just a small British tour.

'Just get them, Andy,' suggested the smiling American, 'How much do you need? Here, take it.' I was embarrassed, but being shallow also chuffed at the same time because the two guys on the stall couldn't believe Kurt knew me.

'No, you're alright. They're a bit tight and I've my eye on a *Pebbles* album over there. But thanks. What are you doing out here? You not supposed to be soundchecking?'

'I sneaked out. They're fixing some shit.' 'Fixing some shit' on tour could mean anything from changing a battery in an effects pedal to a major rewiring job with the PA. One could take 30 seconds, the other hours. Either way, for Kurt it meant a taste of freedom and a chance to sneak off.

'Let me buy you a coffee then, since you nearly bought the boots.'

'Cool.'

As we wandered off, shuffling past stalls, Ian Beveridge, Nirvana's road manager, came out from nowhere and grabbed him. From the fire exit door at the arena I could hear 'Drain You' without guitar or vocals. Kurt laughed as he was caught trying to escape. Ian shook his head at me as he huckled him back to the soundcheck.

As I walked back to the venue the stallholders who had offered me the boots for 15 quid were suddenly very friendly. Then I counted the seconds before the inevitable question came.

'12 quid and two free passes.'

'So, let's just think this through...' Their eyes were working out figures. Nothing against them, they were traders, living on their wits but they didn't look or seem like Nirvana fans.

'OK, we can go to ten for the boots.'

'Ten? I don't want your fucking boots! Before you saw me talking to Kurt Cobain, you were charging 15 quid!'

'That's business. Come on mate, that's a great deal. You must be able to get some passes?'

The younger, slightly cooler one pointed to my Access All Areas pass: the pass without which you could do nothing, even if you were in Nirvana. I made the mistake, because the stalls were so close to the venue, of wandering out without hiding it. I honestly wasn't being flash.

'Kids have been going mental all week, asking if we had any tickets. It's a sell-out. Tickets are like bloody gold dust.'

'You know what, tell me three Nirvana songs. You tell me three songs by the band you want a free pass for and I'll sort it. But you can't 'cos you're not fans, all you want to do is scalp real fans. All you care about is money. Just like earlier, with your fucking 15-quid boots you're now selling for a tenner.'

'Who the fuck are you to talk to us like that?'

'Me? I'm just a fucking nobody, but I've got a fucking laminate pass, ya scalp bastards!'

I've always hated anyone who rips off music fans. I walked away as they started calling me a 'fucking stupid *Scotch* bastard,' which always annoys me. I'm a stupid fucking *Scottish* bastard, *Scotch* is a drink. I know even writing this it sounds absurd to say how much that irritates me and probably most Scottish people too. It's the same thing when Cockneys call Scottish people 'Jock'. In Stewart Lee's wonderful book, *How I Escaped My Certain Fate: The Life and Deaths of a Stand-Up Comedian*, he dissects his comedy routine and explains the inner mechanisms of his thinking and how he knows the Scots hate being called 'Scotch' and he explains in great detail why he does it. He had recently found out that he was 'half-Scotch'. It's all about context. He's clever though, these two were just dumb. *Oh, we'll fucking see who has the last laugh*, I thought.

On the way back into the University I noticed a cool indie couple who I later found out had hitched overnight from Carlisle. They were sitting on the bench adjacent to the market, eating a shared late lunch. When I was with Kurt I noticed them looking over all starry-eyed, nudging each other and pointing. I knew it wasn't for me. As I walked back they smiled and I started to chat. I asked if they were looking forward to the show. It was then they explained how they had journeyed down to see the band and couldn't get a ticket anywhere. They hoped to buy tickets but couldn't afford them at the prices touts were charging; they also said the guys from the stall were doing a roaring trade touting.

'Do me a favour, don't give them a penny.' I took a receipt from my pocket. 'Write your names down and I'll get you on the guest list. I'm not sure whose list you'll be under – Captain America's, Shonen Knife's or Nirvana's – but you'll get in, no problem. My name's Andy Bollen, I'm the drummer in Captain America. If there are any problems, which there won't be, ask for me at the door and I'll come and sort it out. Just don't buy tickets from them.'

It was true I was being nice out of badness and the couple were elated. I hope they enjoyed the gig, they deserved to – they were genuine fans. They had nice Tupperware; I liked that. Very neat. Ever noticed how you never buy Tupperware, you just inherit it? No one ever buys it. You just lose it then inherit it again and don't return it.

I'd already noticed how people's reaction to me when I was in Nirvana's company was changing. It was interesting to see their eyes when Kurt was speaking to me, as if he was a Beatle or something. I know I'm writing this and trying to work it through in my head decades after I met him, but it's something clearly evident from the diary and he'd hate me for saying it but he did have a star quality. He had a certain something about him; people couldn't stop looking at him. This was three years before the post-suicide iconic shit started and even here, at a small market stall, with about 20 people milling around – just hours before his appearance on *Top of the Pops* would be broadcast – you could see and feel people looking at him in a different way. The more he tried to be normal, the worse it seemed to get for him. I remember thinking that day at the market stalls that he seemed ill at ease. You could see people nudge each other and point and nod and talk about him. He was laid-back but there was an edge and nervousness, maybe just a bit of wariness, as he sensed the reaction around him. As we checked out the vinyl in a box, he nudged me.

'Andy, what about the Bay City Rollers?'

'Bad bubblegum.'

'I used to love them, a lot.'

'"Shang-a-Lang"'s great for a party but I'd keep that quiet.'

If you thought Kurt wanting to buy you boots was cool, later that same evening we congregated in Sheffield University's anaemic common room to watch *Top of the Pops*. We were excited; Nirvana's crew said the band had refused to mime to 'Smells Like Teen Spirit'. They were asked to lip-sync over a pre-recorded version of the song but wouldn't do it. A compromise, with some comedic value was reached, when they agreed that Kurt would sing live, like a Gothic-sounding Morrissey over the pre-recorded music.

It should've been a momentous setting, like being centre stage in the chariot race from *Ben Hur*, but sometimes these momentous events have a backdrop of profound normality. Everyone always says they remember what they were doing when John F. Kennedy was assassinated. Most housewives in the UK in 1963 were said to have been ironing when news broke of his death. Looking around at this common room, the setting for Nirvana's *Top of the Pops* appearance was like any generic common room, with orange chairs and worn, dark-brown carpeting, all adding a pathos and sadness of their own. The heating was low, despite it being late November. There was a camaraderie but also a nervousness in the air. Like watching a football match, we all had our beer and settled into the high-backed cheap waiting-room chairs around the TV.

Don't ask me why but I was really nervous for Kurt, Dave and Krist. This was fucking *Top of the Pops*! I couldn't believe it. After all those years growing up watching it at home, now I was watching Nirvana, watching themselves on the show. 'Where were you when Nirvana played *Top of the Pops*?' Oh, I was sitting with them. No one would believe it. I watched Kurt slowly slide down his chair in sheer and total embarrassment. I nudged Dave as he mimed drumming like Keith Moon. He looked at me, nervously chewing gum and shaking his head as if to say, *What the fuck?*

Kurt coming on in sunglasses, playing the fool. Dave kicking in, parodying the many drummers who rightly don't like having to mime. Krist immediately picking up on Dave's piss-take and yielding his bass like a horny giant in need of a shag. Kurt deliberately playing guitar like a lunatic who has never played guitar before. The humour again, ridiculing the song that everyone was tuning in to *Top of the Pops* to witness. Kurt is a hammed-up Ian Curtis in the verse and Morrissey on Mogadon during the chorus. Krist wielding his bass again, Dave playing *à la* Keith Moon.

Of course the band were sick of having to play the same song every night but every record company knows *Top of the Pops* is watched by millions and for them it's a chance to do things record companies love to do – really interesting stuff, like finding new demographics, maximising exposure, breaking new territories. They usually work whole campaigns around

TOTP appearances, so you can understand their frustration, having to witness Nirvana's madcap, comedic performance as they throw a spanner into the normally well-oiled PR machine. There is so much effort behind the scenes, from radio pluggers to distributors, so you could see why the record company might be pissed off.

Nirvana weren't corporate though, they were from the indie punk scene. This was their way of making a point about how futile a hit record is. Their way of saying, 'This isn't what we're about – we want to be like Sonic Youth.' Now they stood on the precipice of a mainstream breakthrough. They almost seemed embarrassed about the success of 'Smells Like Teen Spirit' and in my mind were saying, 'Don't get into the group if you think we take this seriously. We aren't that kind of band.' Either that or they were just supremely confident in the fact that they would make it anyway, with or without the help of an institution like *Top of the Pops*. How cool were they, and how punk rock to sabotage the performance? They still had that punk bit in them, that attitude that said 'Fuck off!'

It takes balls to go against the record company and management and do a performance like that. Perhaps Nirvana hoped it would separate the wheat from the chaff, lose the mainstream fans and keep the punk rock indie fans, who already knew about Nirvana. Millions of bands would kill to be in that situation. At the time *Top of the Pops* was a big, big thing.

Back in the common room, both Kurt and Dave are now cringing and sliding down their chairs so much that they are almost on the floor. Krist is also on the floor but because he's so tall, we can still see his head. With hindsight, this was a watershed moment. On the show they seem supremely confident amid their buffoonery and clowning around. In the common room, for a brief moment, the look on all their faces is one of vulnerability, shock and embarrassment. As soon as the performance is over, we all clap and howl and whistle.

It was probably my favourite memory of the tour. What an incredible moment to be part of.

Nirvana had started out as an underground post-punk band and ended up popularising a sub-genre by bringing alternative music to the mainstream. It's quite a thing to create or be a leading light in a sub-genre. Take Elvis Presley, for instance. He went from being a truck driver to making records that eventually shook the world. He took rockabilly, an up-tempo mix of country and R&B, added a backbeat and became one of the leading lights in rock 'n' roll by embracing African-American sources, principally gospel and the blues. His performances made him popular but controversial and he eventually died prematurely through a mixture of bad diet, ill health and a penchant for prescription medication.

Fast forward to the early 1990s and Nirvana were rock's new heroes. They had a singer, writer and artist who looked at the world in an idiosyncratic way. They had a bass player who encouraged and pushed the singer's creative momentum, and both would find an even better drummer who fitted perfectly, get a major deal and make a well-produced, polished, crossover album. The album in turn, because of the quality of the songs, became a scene-shifting moment and because of this, the band found themselves in territory no one could have imagined, in the same league as Madonna, Michael Jackson, Guns N' Roses and Metallica. Nirvana were the coolest band in uncool waters.

This was what Kurt had striven for, only to realise once it

had been attained that it was shallow, corporate and soulless. 'Smells Like Teen Spirit' kicked in the door, but by the time the mainstream were singing along to the lyrics of 'In Bloom', few realised Kurt was having a clear shot at the abusive macho men and the rednecks who had bullied and been abusive to him, the same ones now singing along to his radio-friendly hits. It's indie kudos versus corporate rock.

Lyrically, 'In Bloom' seems to encapsulate the contradiction. The beautifully poetic and the dark sense of humour merge seamlessly. Kurt derides nature then goes on to use the most wonderful and perfectly nuanced poetry. It's as good as Samuel Taylor Coleridge or William Blake. One of my favourite poets is the American Robert Frost and I often wonder if Kurt liked him.

Kurt was a complex, strange and at times, weird guy. This was a guy who as an artist would sometimes wank into his paintings and now his art was in the same box in the back of a van with bad Phil Collins, Enya and Simply Red albums. For any independent artist to be accused of selling out was the ultimate insult. Kurt was polemic, deliberately demeaning 'corporate rock' and intentionally taking a controversial stand in print and on TV while at the same time benefiting from major label backing in recording and promotion. It always seemed to be Kurt's Achilles heel. Always wrestling with his indie punk rock ethos while engulfing the mainstream. R.E.M. and The Pixies were always cited as alternative bands with an indie spirit who had commercial crossover appeal. Of course Nirvana's best way of showing their indefatigable indie spirit was to say no to stadium support slots with corporate acts and continue to promote artists by inviting them on tour, wearing their T-shirts and giving unprecedented free promotion and exposure to their favourite artists to millions in interviews or photo shoots. Maybe that's why, right now, at the tail end of 1991, when they should all be so happy at the incredible success of 'Smells Like Teen Spirit' and *Nevermind*, they seem so unhappy. You could be forgiven for wondering why within months it felt like Nirvana were standing on the edge of an abyss.

The gig at the Octagon in Sheffield, in the heart of the university's modern campus, is loud. It's so thunderous at our soundcheck without people in the hall and quite easily has to be the loudest sound I've ever made in a band in my life. It's brash and piercing because the sound is bouncing back so quickly off the walls. It improves when people come in and become musical shock absorbers. Shonen Knife are loud, we are extremely loud, and Nirvana just sound like a fighter plane taking off. The crowd that night were really cool too. As ever, we are on shortly after the doors opened at 7.30pm and things are now taking on a familiar shape; we start and by the end of the set, more and more have grown to appreciate what we're doing and by the end the reaction is warm and enthusiastic.

It's weird but the gig passed by and it seemed so effortless and workmanlike. Maybe we're finding our major tour support slot feet. As we're using Nirvana's equipment every night, it's starting to become familiar and it feels, at least for me, like a security blanket and I'm more relaxed. I'm still having trouble focusing, though; during one song we do, called 'Bed In', I found myself thinking about how our B&B is really nice, probably the best yet and how I'm impressed with Sheffield, or as much as I've seen of it, around the university area and how the students are very attractive, hip and cool, and I think I will come back here one day when I'm not touring. Then you get a cold chill and realise for the last three minutes you've been daydreaming when you should've been concentrating.

Something which becomes really apparent when you watch Nirvana from the side of the stage is the way the band propel this powerful sound and how intricate it all is. I was intrigued by how only three guys could create such power as a unit. Knowing I'm asking as someone who is a music fan and part of the touring party, Kurt explains in a warm and forthright manner, 'We just all had to learn our parts. Everyone just learns their little bit as well as possible, then we rehearse for hours concentrating on our parts. When we started out, we'd rehearse all day… Period.'

'And drink a lot too!' Krist knew Kurt was starting to sound too uncool.

'Before we went in to record *Nevermind* we locked ourselves away and rehearsed till we could do the parts in our sleep. Just relentless shit, man, working our parts.'

That brief chat sums up what anyone starting out in a band needs to know. Go read it again if you're starting up a band. If you're not, let's continue; if you have read it again, welcome back.

I'm not a mathematician but at its simplest, with Chaos Theory there's always an underlying order in the chaotic randomness. All the systems obey rules but are so sensitive that small changes can cause unexpected final results, thus giving an impression of randomness. Like the day Kurt bought a distortion pedal. Small action, massive consequence, that's not the chaos theory bit just yet – that's something else, happenstance or coincidence. The band themselves are on stage obeying the rules, staying in control but all around things are happening and nobody has a clue what's going to happen next. The live experience is one of a whirling chasm of confusion, disarray and anarchy, yet there's also something ordered and in control at the centre of the storm and in the uplifting truthfulness of the music. Completely different in size and shape, Nirvana work magnificently as a group. Dave looks over in between songs and laughs. He should be laughing at me. It's halfway through the set and one minute I'm there, the next I'm not. I keep jumping in and out to the front of house to hear the band. I've walked from the mixing desk to the centre of the crowd. Now I'm back and I'm writing my thoughts. I'm thinking of words, I'm listening to Nirvana. I'm lying on the floor as if I'm doing my homework while watching TV.

But I'm not sitting watching TV, I'm the happiest and luckiest guy in the world. Right now, I'm watching one of the best bands in years, at close hand and while they're playing I'm trying to think of words that can justify, convey and express the startling power and dynamic of Nirvana. Tonight 'Smells Like Teen Spirit' is warmly received but the fans at Sheffield go crazy for 'Sliver', 'Floyd the Barber' and, once again, the devastating opener 'Drain You'. I get it. It's music in its purest form. Punk, pop, rock… like The Stooges doing Beatles covers. The way it should be, just loud, glorious, energetic and one second away from bedlam.

Everyone is just falling in love with this band. This is so unbelievable. The crowd are looking at one another and asking is this band for real? How good are they? I'd go as far as to say, if based purely on Nirvana's impact on tonight's crowd, this band will be as big as The Beatles. Call me crazy, everyone does.

(It's important to qualify and emphasise at this time, 'Smells Like Teen Spirit' was their only hit to date. I considered taking this part out of the book. It looks like I'm saying this with the benefit of hindsight and despite the excitement and furore; it might've been their only hit. Of course Nirvana didn't come close to being as big as The Beatles but I've kept it in to capture the feeling of the time and well, because I did actually say it in the diary. There's also an absolute absurdity in the tone and the use of 'will', as if it's beyond doubt, it's certain, which makes me look even more of a twat and that's the job of the clown in society, to make you laugh at my inadequacies as a cultural commentator and indeed as a drummer.)

In late 1991, music journalist Dave Cavanagh did the single reviews in *Select* magazine. His review of 'Smells Like Teen Spirit' is understandably an upbeat one and signs off focusing on the lack of clarity on the mystery of the lyrics: 'Kobain is not singing "Win a Lada Mrs Davies" but with the lights out, it's less dangerous. Dang. Still marvellous.' Kurt at the time was spelling his name Kurdt Kobain. Elsewhere in the magazine there's a live review of the Astoria show by Andrew Perry; he calls the singer Kurt Kobain. Maybe it was the writer in me seeking clarity. It's not an editorial oversight, but at this time was part of the contrary and mischievous nature of Kurt. Eugene had received a letter from Kurt where he had signed off as Kurdt.

To give an idea of the bands around at the time, others on the singles page are Guns N' Roses, Sinead O'Connor, KLF and the Happy Mondays. The very last one was a review of the *Captain America* EP. Here it is in full:

Eugene Kelly and James Seenan of Captain America used to be in The Vaselines, noisy Glaswegian guitar types who influenced Nirvana across the ocean to such an extent that they're still covering their songs live today. Nirvana in turn inspire Teenage Fanclub. This EP calls to mind the first Fannies LP, *A Catholic Education*. Somewhere in that mess though lies the acceptable face of hero worship: there's a track called 'God Bless Les Paul' and drummer Andy Bollen sounds like he could easily understudy Ralph Molina of Crazy Horse in an emergency.

It's interesting to note that when we recorded this song, at the outro instead of percussive handclaps I slapped my arse cheeks, as that's the sort of thing us crazy wacky drummers do, right? Dave Cavanagh went on to write a highly regarded tome about Creation Records called *My Magpie Eyes are Hungry for the Prize*. The detail for the night Oasis were signed is accurate and well-informed. I was there, along with very few others.

So that was Sheffield, and sitting with Nirvana, watching them watching themselves on *Top of the Pops*, will live long in the memory. Kurt offering to buy me boots was cool too. The next morning, on leaving to head for Edinburgh, there is excitement as we get to read the *Select* review. I'm not too bothered or fussed by it but Eugene and especially Gordon think this is absolutely amazing. All I think about when I read the review is my diary entry after seeing Captain America for the first time, to keep hi-hats loose and listen to my brother's Neil Young records. Practise with a loose swishy hi-hat, hit the crash cymbals along with the lead guitar and get a rocking swaying feel. Keep it loose. I'm glad they like it but I play it down by deliberately confusing Ralph Molina with the actor Alfred Molina, who is married to former *Gentle Touch* actress Jill Gascoine. It gets a laugh.

CHAPTER 10
KURT'S THROAT

EDINBURGH CALTON STUDIOS,
29 November 1991

I'm back home in Scotland and looking forward to a few nights of decent sleep in my own bed. Maybe as I'm sober, I start to notice how we seem to be together all the time. I have this claustrophobic feeling as I realise that I spend most of my day and night with the others. Maybe it's the confinement of the dressing room in Edinburgh's Calton Studios. I start to think about what's actually happening every day. We travel together in the van between gigs. Once we arrive, we check-in together at the B&B or cheap hotel. Then we leave together to drive to the venue. Sometimes we arrive at the venue first, usually when we're running late, caught in traffic, getting lost, van breaking down, running out of petrol: always together. Once we're in the venue we'll eat together then soundcheck together, then we'll play our set together, come off stage together, watch Shonen Knife together. Then, once Nirvana come on, I might start in the centre of the venue but usually come back to watching the show beside Dave Grohl. Another thing that is strange but freaking me out is the amount of doors I seem to go through: every day, about a hundred doors. I seem to go in one door then out another one, never the same one.

In Nirvana's dressing room if you sit too close to Kurt you can smell his stomach: sick, hungry, acidic, gaseous and in pain. Not pain as in heartache but the smell of something you know just hurts like rotten burning flesh. This isn't the smell of fear, ambition or hunger, it's the smell of a sick stomach. I think about all the adjectives used to describe Nirvana since they came on the scene. It's all *visceral* and *seminal, embryonic, explosive, volatile, primitive* and *eruptive*. All sound like adjectives used to describe a painful symptom. All excruciating, like a ruptured appendix. All from the solar plexus. All splits, cracks, fissures, tears and perforations. Maybe all music comes from there? Is that why you vent your spleen? Kurt seems in continual torment. It all comes from the underbelly. The singer should sing from the stomach, not the throat.

The only night of the UK tour I didn't sit beside Dave's kit and watch Nirvana was the Edinburgh show at Calton Studios as Kurt was sick. There wasn't enough room on stage to swing a cat, never mind settle down to watch Dave drum again. Kurt's voice was gone. What seemed to make it worse was the almost Dickensian state of the tiny, damp, cold backstage area at the venue. Kurt's throat was raw, inflamed and he couldn't speak, let alone sing. The room was full of tension. It looked like the tour might have to be cancelled or at least some shows rescheduled. We were sitting in the tiny backstage area with

Above: Me (right) with Ben Mullen, circa '88 country folk Gram Parsons period. Matthew Cassan, my manager at Our Price, managed us and funded demos.

Below left: Drumming with Captain America at King Tuts, Scotland, in October 1991. Picture taken by Gregor Dick.

Below right: I love this grainy picture of Kurt, probably because it was my view of him for most of the tour.

Left: Opening for Mudhoney and Hole, New Cross Venue, London, August 1991. I was relaxed enough to take this photo of Eugene from behind drums, even though it was my first full Captain America gig and we had just walked passed Sonic Youth, Mudhoney, Hole and Nirvana!

Below: As Nirvana rarely stuck to their set list, I'd copy Dave's set list into my small notepad and amend the changes as the band played. These are from Birmingham Hummingbird and London Astoria. I always tried to keep an original set list for the diary but Nirvana fans would ask for them.

Birmingham Hummingbird NOV 27TH 91

Drain You
Aneurysm
Floyd
Teenspirit
About a Girl
Polly
Lithium
Sliver
Been A Son
On A Plain
Neg Creep
Endless, Nameless

* Shortest gig of tour :recorded TOP OF THE
POPS → very tired?

*Unhappy?

Astoria: NOV 5TH 91

Jesus/Sunbeam
Aneurysm (?)
Drain You
School
Floyd
Teenspirit
About a Girl
Polly
Breed
Sliver
Lithium
Love Buzz
Come as you Are
Been a Son
Neg Creep
On A Plain
Blew
Dumb
Penny Royal Tea
Endless Nameless,

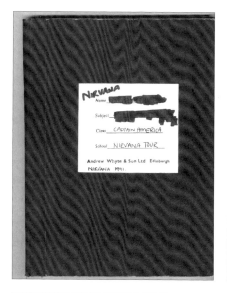

Above left: Glad I kept this: my sturdy old hardback science notebook I used to keep diary entries.

Above right: The only one I kept. I found this set list before it was thrown in the bin. It's written by Krist, but normally written more neatly by Dave.

Below: A smiling Kurt: one of my favourite pictures. A second after this picture was taken, Kurt began to set a Scottish note on fire!

Above: Kurt, me and Gordon Keen. Kilburn National, London, December 1991.

Below: Kurt and Gordon unaware of a huge bucket of water being thrown by Nirvana's tour manager, Alex McLeod. Turns out there wasn't any water in it and the result was this unflattering photo!

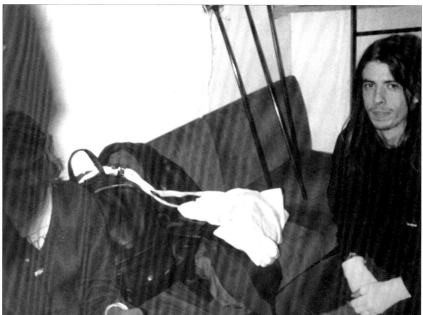

Above: Kurt asked our roadies, Michael Ewing and Willie McGhie (pictured) to dress as mad professors and walk on stage with the feather duster to clean the mics. A nice picture of a happy Kurt.

Below: A young Dave.

Fun backstage.

Above: Michael Ewing, Krist, Kurt, Gordon, Willie, Shonen Knife, Craig Montgomery (Nirvana's sound man) and Alex McLeod. Kilburn National, London, December 1991.

Below: James Seenan, Gordon Keen, Dave Barker from Paperhouse and friend (above), and me and Shonen Knife (below).

Above: Me and Gordon backstage with Shonen Knife.

Inset: Photo sent from my pals. Love those shoes! This was from a chaotic Rough Trade Shop in-store gig, December 1991. It was mobbed, and we ended up signing inside and outside.

Below: Redd Kross, backstage at a Teenage Fanclub show. BMX Bandits also on the bill. Town and Country Club, London, February 1992.

Kurt deliberately wore our T-shirt on a day full of photo shoots and promotion.

Dave and Krist, plus their agent and tour manager. Dave had a magic 8 ball toy and was trying to lighten the mood by asking it some hilarious questions, beginning with one about their record company's executive.

'Does David Geffen have our best interests at heart?'

'ASK AGAIN LATER.'

'Shall we stay with Danny Goldberg at Gold Mountain Management?'

'IT IS CERTAIN?'

'Well, that can't be right. Are we sure?'

'DECIDEDLY SO.'

That summed up Dave in a nutshell. When it was getting tense he would do something to break the ice. He was always playing it down. Two nights before, at Birmingham Hummingbird, he told me when it was getting particularly scary that he didn't know or understand what all the fuss was about. Krist was concerned earlier as he watched Kurt self-medicate with different throat infection concoctions. Kurt was now huddled up on his chair and looked sick, weak and really fragile. It was a nervy time. Kurt was seriously ill; we're talking cadaverous, yellow. It was clear to me at this point that James was right: Kurt looked like a heroin addict. I looked at James and nodded. I didn't have to say anything. James told me later he could read my mind. He patted me on the head and gave out Nirvana's beer to everyone.

There's no glory or honour in something that can do this to you. I'm reminded of a beautifully written and extremely candid line in Nick Kent's fantastic memoir of the 1970s, *Apathy For The Devil*, which sums up the harsh reality of heroin addiction. Kent, referring to Sid Vicious and Nancy Spungen, accurately demystifies that clichéd glamour often associated with the drug: 'Only twenty years old and already they have the smell of death in their young pores. That's not something that deserves to be romanticised throughout the ages'. In less than two-and-a-half years, Kurt would be dead.

In Edinburgh, Kurt was definitely ill, rundown and had a serious throat problem. He had a jaundiced look, unusually lifeless eyes and the poor guy's stomach, it really did smell terribly, right there in front of us. This is it, the tour's over, I was thinking. Just as we were getting really good on stage and Nirvana were our new mates. But like the previous generations of rock 'n' roll and old jazz and blues casualties, the physical cost of touring was part of the deal: the show must go on. Ruthless and brutal as it may be, the kids want a show. In my opinion, the show in Edinburgh, and the next one in Glasgow on the Saturday, should've been rescheduled but Kurt wouldn't let the fans down. There was to be a rest day on the Sunday and the few hours' travel to Newcastle Mayfair for Monday gave him a possible chance to recuperate. When he tried to speak, his voice was gone and his throat actually sounded inflamed and swollen. It must've been torture.

It was now late November and they had been playing shows all year. To coincide with the release of *Nevermind* they embarked on a US and Canadian tour. Added to that, Kurt's famed vocal style and well-documented rock 'n' roll scream, a black hole of angst and rage, didn't help. When a doctor was called, a dour faced, bald, no-nonsense GP arrived. He looked out of place in the small, dank and damp Calton Studios backstage area but had an air about him that garnered respect. He was guided straight to Kurt and asked him to stand then gently felt his neck at the glands. The doctor opened his mouth wide and Kurt copied. He looked down Kurt's throat. 'No, show's over,' he said. 'You need rest. I'd suggest complete rest, at least a week. You also have to learn how to sing to save what's left of your voice box.'

'Can't I play tonight?' Kurt croaked.

'If you do the chances are you may lose your voice for good. I'm saying complete rest, no talking and no work.'

He wrote out a prescription for more antibiotics and pain killers. There was nothing remotely funny about this as it sounded like we would all be going home, but for some reason myself and James were amused by the idea of Kurt Cobain of seminal Seattle rockers Nirvana getting a sick line from a Scottish doctor excusing him from work.

'That means Kurt's on the sick,' I whispered to James.

'I know, it's fucking mental. In Scotland two minutes and he's phoning in sick. That's him officially Scottish now.'

Kurt gave James that insurance line or another prescription slip and he still has it. I think he's been offered serious cash for it too but refuses to part with it. I noticed that, out of everyone assembled backstage, even though we were concerned, Krist looked the most worried about his friend's health.

We played to some familiar faces at Edinburgh; I saw Boogie and Lesley from Airdrie and loads of new regulars we'd previously won over. But the sound on stage was poor. I looked at James, who despite being the most punk rock, was really annoyed at the monitors on stage and kept gesturing to the mixing desk that he couldn't hear anything. Eugene and Gordon were also both suffering with the sound on stage. Throughout the tour we had become used to decent on stage monitor mixes. At Calton Studios, though, the sound was so bad all we could hear was what the crowd were hearing as it bounced back, swirled and rattled around the venue. Shonen Knife had offered to go on before us for the Edinburgh, Glasgow and Newcastle shows, so there were also changes in sound and tweaks in equipment after they had finished. We were getting tighter and more efficient as a band, which came in handy for the show at Calton Studios as, not being able to hear anything properly, we just battered on through. After the gig I said to Alex MacLeod that the sound on stage was shit.

'It's because the stage is so fucking low, it's a cunt, cheers.' Alex responded in characteristic fashion, as he sprinted by me to check it. Murray, who was doing our sound, said that since our gear was already packed in the van, he was going through to Glasgow in 20 minutes if I wanted a lift. He could drop me off in Airdrie. We'd both agreed we didn't want to see Kurt play a show. That suited me fine; I could meet up with my friends. I was dropped off in Chapelhall as my girlfriend Sharron worked in a pub there at the weekend.

I came in the door of the pub with a bag full of dirty laundry, my Access All Areas pass, notebook and a smile. Sharron was chuffed to see me but the others in the pub were less accommodating. Maybe it was the culture shock of coming off a tour with a cool band and straight into a small village pub but either way I sensed I had to leave. I put my stuff into Sharron's car, got a taxi to Dellettes, the old man's pub my friends drank in as it was cheaper, before going to the dancing at the Double A. It was brilliant being among your own again, though someone who never spoke a word to me in my life came up to me and said, 'I thought you were fucking touring with Nirvana! You lying cunt, what the fuck are you doing here then?'

It was my first aggressive brush with very minor fame.

'I'm at the circus watching the world's first talking fanny.'

Life in a small town, summed up in a short vignette. Oh, the banter.

By all accounts Kurt made it on stage that night, showing a courage and conviction that I keep highlighting for anyone interested in the real Nirvana story. According to observers, those in the crew were amazed that he could even stand, never mind deliver a powerful performance. With medication and dedication it was indeed a miraculous recovery, but I couldn't listen to that scream knowing the pain he was in. In some ways, I'm glad to report, especially after seeing how sick he really was, that I'll never know what songs from the Edinburgh gig went down well since I wasn't there.

CHAPTER 11
'I' VE GOT BLISTERS ON MY FINGERS.'

**GLASGOW UNIVERSITY QUEEN
MARGARET UNION, 30 November 1991**

L'AMOUR EST UN OISEAU REBELLE (Bizet's *Carmen*)
DRAIN YOU
ANEURYSM
LITHIUM
SCHOOL
FLOYD THE BARBER
SMELLS LIKE TEEN SPIRIT
ABOUT A GIRL
POLLY
SLIVER
BREED
COME AS YOU ARE
BEEN A SON
ALL APOLOGIES

ON A PLAIN
UNKNOWN (punky, Black Flag cover? Was in toilet.
Too much detail?)
RAPE ME
TERRITORIAL PISSINGS

As you'd expect, on the Saturday evening after 'Smells Like Teen Spirit' charted, the Glasgow show was chaotic. The phone never stopped ringing, with everybody wanting guest list places. We were only allowed two per band member, but Nirvana and Shonen Knife gave us theirs so we had four or five each. Paul Cardow, who as well as managing us was also promoting the gig, said I owed him a fortune, claiming there must've been about 60 people from Airdrie who got in saying they knew me and they were on the list. Pandemonium.

Gordon phoned and suggested we go in early to get away from the calls and I agreed. We had come out of the madness of the tour for some stability at home but now it was so mental at home we just headed back to the normality and safety of the Nirvana tour. So we were back at the QM for about 4pm. My brother, Stephen, showed up asking me and Gordon to sign an EP. Strange. My eldest brother, Gerard, a history teacher who didn't know who Nirvana were (but loads of his former pupils and their friends did), kindly promised them all that his brother would get them on the guest list. Gerard seemed to enjoy himself; while playing I remember seeing him swagger and sway in a corner, pished as a fart. On one of my many trips up and downstairs, avoiding Cardow in case he saw my guest list numbers, I bumped into Nirvana as they arrived at the venue.

'Hey Andy.'

'Hiya Kurt. How was last night's show?'

'Weren't you there? I thought I saw you.'

'I took a chance of a lift home. I didn't want to see you sing after what the doctor said last night. You sound a bit raw.'

'I'm OK. Nervous, I guess.'

I found it hard to believe he could possibly be nervous but he was. I also found it hard to believe he was standing but he was.

During last night's Edinburgh set, I dropped a drumstick or maybe I threw one into the crowd. I love doing that with other drummers' sticks. I went to pull one out without missing a beat, as is the way with drummers who throw sticks at the crowd, and managed to pull the stick out the wrong way round. I could see the splinters embed into my thumb, loads of them, bang! Blood everywhere. After the song I quickly poured some water on it and towelled it down without anyone noticing. By the end of the set the white towels were red rags. By the time Saturday came I had two huge blisters and one looked poisoned.

It was Dave who noticed them.

'Hold on, Andy. We got to get that shit out.'

He went off and returned with what looked like a puncture repair kit for blistered drummers' thumbs. After placing some white spirit on the thumb to clean it, he then cut the blisters open and carefully removed the skelfs (splinters) with tweezers, then strapped it up. Nice work, Dr Grohl. I was grateful but I'd be more grateful in future if he placed his drumsticks into the stick holder on the floor tom the right way up, so that when I'm throwing his sticks away to fans on his behalf I don't get lacerated. But I just said thanks.

I really liked Dave a lot; everyone who meets him does. At

the soundcheck in Sheffield I remember watching him mess around quietly on the kit as Earnie, his guitar tech, sorted out Kurt's effects. It was unusual for Dave, who was always professional and economical about drumming, aware that he may be putting the others off as they worked out a problem or tried to get a level right or locate a dodgy lead. I watched him as he effortlessly got locked in this quiet freeform jazz groove. The backbeat was intricate and clever, metronomic on the ride cymbal, a confident bell sound swayed, and the hi-hat on the second beat was certain and locked. He efficiently added dynamic and pace, bringing light and shade with astonishing clarity, even though he was still playing quietly, then skims lightly over the high and floor toms and effortlessly flourishes the jam with snare and bass drum triplets. He was doing a muso pattern which the world's super drummers can do, like Ian Paice of Deep Purple, Neil Peart of Rush or Ginger Baker from Cream, the kind that seem outrageously difficult to mere mortals. Accompanying no one, he was in a zone, grooving out with Charlie Mingus and Thelonius Monk, and free-forming with John Coltrane.

Dave is a musician who understands his role in the dynamic of the band and adds incredible harmonies as well as complex drumming. He is relaxed, takes everything in his stride and what you see is what you get. It's unfashionable these days to be a decent person; it's maybe a bit uncool. He works with whoever he wants, going on to drum for Queens of the Stone Age, Killing Joke and forming Them Crooked Vultures with Josh Homme and John Paul Jones. He's a music lover and is now in the position which allows him to do his projects and work with whoever he wants to.

So Dave catches me watching his drumming. It's a drummer thing; if you know something you pass it on. It sounds a bit like 'Fool in the Rain' by Led Zeppelin – a nice shuffle but it sounds amazing. You look to see what the drummer is doing. Can you learn anything from them? You watch with greater attention, seeing if you can work out what they're doing. Dave's about to hand me the sticks to try, but Kurt's effects pedal starts to work and it's time for the drummer to get to work.

Watching Dave every night was certainly a unique and mind-blowing experience. Technically he's an outstanding drummer but like the best musicians, he plays for the band not himself. Often compared, especially by me, to Led Zeppelin's John Bonham, no mean feat. Sitting beside him live and at sound-checks, I keep trying to see what it is he's actually doing in the vain hope I could copy him. I wish I had the ability to draw a sketch that could capture him, like a Leonardo da Vinci drawing of a helicopter. I thought of taking the Kodak Instamatic 92 out and actually taking his photo but I wouldn't want to embarrass him, not with the camera that time forgot from the 1970s. Knowing Dave, he'd stop right there and come over and ask to see the curious little machine from the bygone era.

From a technical viewpoint I spend most of the tour and a huge section of the original diary trying to figure out what links Dave and John Bonham. Maybe it's the same thunderous drum sound in terms of tuning and set-up. Maybe it's the same effortless power and speed on the right foot and incredibly quick hands, allowing intricate triplets. In case there's any doubt with the comparison, he even has Bonzo's three-circle logo tattooed on his wrist. Whereas Led Zeppelin's Jimmy Page would encourage Bonham to do thunderous fills and incredible solos and he was given licence to go for it and show off when required, Dave had to keep it reined in.

The songs on *Nevermind* are mainly about dynamic, so Dave's role is crucial and his playing is as much about structure as if he were a songwriter using the drums to express and highlight specific parts of the song. Pivotal and powerful, his drumming almost has a structural cleverness to it. Perhaps to go back to the camera and photography comparison, it's about getting the most of the natural light, form and composition. Dave's a great drummer and deserves every bit of his success because he puts so much in and works his arse off.

Behind the scenes though, one thing I've noticed is that Dave is a bit distant from Kurt and Krist. When we're all around Dave is seldom part of it. He's usually away in his hotel room or on the bus with the crew. On stage the trio are a tight unit but in interviews he's reticent, if polite. I suppose Kurt and Krist have been through so much together from the start with the band, so it must be tough to come in and hit the ground running. I don't know if this is an accurate assessment, it's just my opinion from people-watching and seeing the band backstage in their more vulnerable, quieter moments.

It could also be that Dave is more than aware that Kurt banged around on the kit and was a frustrated drummer. He would also be aware of the previous difficulties they had finding the right drummer. Kurt's drumming ability was competent at best. The same thing happened with Paul McCartney, admittedly Ringo had temporarily left the band when Macca kept the beat on 'Dear Prudence' and 'Back in the USSR' and was on holiday when John and Paul hurriedly recorded 'The Ballad of John and Yoko'. But Kurt and Paul in my opinion were not great drummers. Honestly, I could give them a run for their money. Interestingly, a certain Jimi Hendrix was a fantastic drummer.

Dave, though, is one of the best drummers I've ever seen in my life, with a great ear for harmony, and should never have been worried about his ability. He is also an intuitive, sharp guy and I suspect (and this is only my opinion), from what he was witnessing every day, that Nirvana were never going to be a long-term career option – or if they were, there would be plenty of time in between albums for an outlet for all those Ace Frehley riffs. One of my favourite Nirvana B-sides is a Dave Grohl track called 'Marigold'. It's the B-side to the 1993 single 'Heart Shaped Box' and was originally released in 1992 on a cassette album called *Pocketwatch* under the pseudonym 'Late!' consisting of older demos and four newer songs recorded in 1991.

Since Gordon and I had arrived early at the venue, it meant a few extra hours seeing the crowds gather outside, the crew set up, barriers being erected and QM staff and security being briefed.

James arrives and we hang out with Shonen Knife and their tour manager Page. He sees us drinking a can of Irn-Bru and is keen to know about it. I call it ginger, that's what Scottish people (or at least people from Lanarkshire) call a carbonated soft drink; that, or 'juice'. He wonders if it's true that it has magical healing powers for a hangover. An American who lives in Japan asking me about a drink made in Glasgow while I'm on tour with a band from Seattle? They want to know if it has real ginger in it? No, just loads of sugar.

It's as popular here as Coke or Pepsi. I go on to explain that it's Scotland's other national drink but it gets too confusing, as they think that's whisky.

Eventually someone, possibly James, buys a couple of cans from a vending machine and we get some glasses and watch their faces and let them taste a normal and a Diet Irn-Bru. They think it's like liquid bubblegum.

Witnessing the build up, as well as briefly meeting the band as they were entering the hall to start a particularly long soundcheck, had got to me. By the time everyone arrived at the QM at around 6pm I was really nervous about the gig. About 6.45pm, I'd had enough and I went with Willie the roadie for a walk, as I needed to clear my head. At the front door we were met with the ubiquitous 'airport shot' of fans crushed up and battering against the window and squealing. I shat myself.

'Look, it's fucking Beatlemania, Willie.'

'Fuck me, they're shouting your name, big man.'

'Are they fuck!'

'Seriously.'

They were shouting my name but it wasn't adulation, they wanted something from me: they wanted in for free. It wasn't as far-fetched as it sounds. I saw Bryson and a few home town punks queuing up. When I approached the door to speak to them, Paul Cardow shouted: 'Andy, it's mental – you can't get out just now.'

He tried to open the door to let me and Willie out but this caused a stampede, then the movement at the start of the queue caused a ripple effect and the ones at the back were thinking the doors were open. So now Cardow and the venue's security were going crazy, but he was also laughing in an ecstatic, almost hysterical way, as only promoters with a sell-out show can. While holding back the surging, impatient masses at the front doors, I remember thinking it was probably the happiest I'd ever seen him.

'Fucking Andy Bollen, half of Airdrie's in here – you owe me a fortune!'

'Thanks, Paul. What's the hold-up?'

'Nirvana are still soundchecking, Andy – try the back door,' Cardow shouted, loving every bit of it.

At the mention of the band's name the crowd at the door went nuts. Due to the fact they'd taken so long to soundcheck, the venue had to wait until they'd finished and were holding back the crowd queuing outside, which was growing by the second and becoming more excitable.

Shonen Knife and ourselves were still waiting to sound-check once they'd finished. To this day I still don't remember soundchecking and there isn't a note in my diary of it happening. It may have been done in a perfunctory fashion with no drama and nothing to report, but it's more than likely we did have a very quick one and I was so nervous that I went through the motions. There was no chance of getting out via the front so we headed for the back door, but as we were going into the hall another almost theatrical vignette unfolded. We met Nirvana coming from their soundcheck so Willie and I stopped to chat to them, watched on by all the punters at the door. Kurt looked well, considering he was at death's door yesterday. Dave asked where I was last night, as I wasn't beside the kit.

'I sneaked off home. How was it?'

Dave shrugged and, diplomatic as ever, said, 'Well, we spent a lot of time on tonight's soundcheck.'

'You look better, Kurt. How's the throat?'

'Great, yeah. Weren't you at the show? It went well, considering.'

I just told Dave and I told you earlier I missed it. Aren't you listening? Maybe the prescription was kicking in, or maybe deafness.

'No, I couldn't watch you sing. Not after hearing what the doctor said.'

'You guys want anything from the shops?' asked Willie. 'Me and Andy are getting out of here for some fresh air.'

We waited for an answer. It seemed like a straightforward question. The windows now looked like they were going to give way and smash. You could see the glass almost change shape with the pressure. The time we spent standing and chatting seemed to make the crowd raise the noise a few more notches until they finally went berserk. Security and Cardow were squealing at me to get them upstairs. The band looked confused with our request. Dave decided it was time to scarper and ran off, waved and smiled and went upstairs to a massive swoon and cheer. I noticed the cheer sounded more high-pitched, one with more female squeals.

'Me and Willie are going out for a walk. I'm nervous, there's loads of people I know here tonight. We're going to the shops. Do you want anything?'

'Want some tobacco, Kurt?' asked Willie. 'What about yer Jacob's Creek, big man?' Willie was getting impatient and nervous as the venue's security people were starting to blame him for all the upheaval.

'You guys are going to get me tobacco? Wow. Yes, eh here…'

'You can square us up later,' I tried to suggest. I was getting a bit embarrassed now. Kurt started handing us money, far too much for what he wanted us to buy.

'No, here, take the money. I don't even like this shit. I don't want it. I want you and Willie to take it.' At the sight of Cobain handing over wads of notes and change falling everywhere, more bedlam ensued.

'It's OK. Stop giving us money, Kurt, for fuck's sake.'

'Shut up and pick up the cash.' Willie wasn't daft.

'It's Old Holborn,' Kurt said emotionally, as though someone was offering a kidney instead of something from the shop.

'Anything red by Jacob's Creek man, thank you,' Krist smiled, shaking his head.

'You guys are so fucking cool.' Kurt seemed moved. Then they both ambled off to the backstage area, which was four flights up. He waved to the fans at the door and continued to shake his head. I don't know why he was so touched by it.

Sometimes the little things can seem really profound. Kurt's reaction to a very small random gesture, let's face it, was a bit over the top. He couldn't get his head around someone just connecting directly with him without any bullshit. When we said we'd square up with him later we should've said, 'No, it's OK, thanks for letting us share your gear on the tour'. Then you remember they were surrounded by movers and shakers, and attending photo shoots, interviews, meetings, travelling, radio sessions and TV appearances. At every turn people who speak fluent bullshit, but then he had our lot who treated him like one of the gang, with no airs or graces – just a normal guy who you looked out for. Maybe it was just a small reminder that he was a humble guy who loved punk rock and smoking roll-ups and as the band's life seemed to be careering out of control, we had brought a moment or two of normality, which he genuinely appreciated.

I watched him go upstairs, smiling and shaking his head. As we crossed Lillybank Gardens and meandered up through Ashton Lane, heading for Byres Road, I said to Willie, 'I thought the tour was cancelled, he looked like death warmed up yesterday afternoon. Here, do you think he might be on something?'

Willie laughed. That was how we dealt with it, by not mentioning it. It wasn't our business. When people talk of the iconic suicide and self-destruction and guns and heroin and pain and the tortured artist, I keep that image of his smile and his pretend childlike clapping when he received his favourite tobacco and loads of change back. A genuinely happy guy touched at two dafties going to the shop for him.

Shonen Knife had given us T-shirts and mine was a bit small, so I remember giving it to Sharron's brother, Stephen. Then they saw me talking to someone wearing the new Shonen Knife T-shirt. They were so chuffed and took photos of him wearing their T-shirt. I didn't have the heart to say I had given him mine; they thought he was a fan and had bought it.

Our gig at the QM was very well received. Just as well – the place was full of family, friends and mates who'd blagged in for free. We played well and were tight, but I was nervous throughout. The drum riser seemed higher at the QM; I could see the distinctive, caricatured outline of Nirvana watching us from the mixing desk. I tried to maintain my concentration, always the biggest battle for me, despite the chaos all around. Things were happening all over the place; I could see my brother Gerard pished in the corner wondering what was happening around him, probably thinking he had parachuted into a scene from *Apocalypse Now*, but I had to block the distractions out and focus.

Kurt admitted after the show that Nirvana were incredibly nervous before the Glasgow gig too, because so many independent bands from here had influenced him, in particular The Vaselines, The Pastels and Teenage Fanclub, some of whom might have been in the audience watching them. I was amazed that he'd be nervous before taking to the stage but claimed that was why they'd gone down so well, because of peer pressure.

Eugene surprised everyone by dedicating a song to someone who had died that week. We thought it would be Freddie Mercury, but he dedicated it to the actor Klaus Kinski. Around that week we had been coming on stage, taking the piss out of Freddie and Queen by doing an ironic tribute of 'We Will Rock You', complete with the drum beat intro and with James doing a daft rap. It was another tight perfunctory performance, warmly received and over in what seemed like minutes. As I was coming off stage I threw both of Dave's drumsticks away and bizarrely I managed to hit the same guy, my pal Willie Watson, twice, with two different sticks. He didn't see the funny side. What are the odds of that happening? He claimed to be heading to the toilet straight after our gig and was angry at the indignity of me telling him he should've picked them up as Dave used great sticks and I was always needing spares. Sadly he is no longer with us. Hello to Emma, if she's reading this.

One of the better reasons for keeping a diary of gigs is the little surprises they can throw up. How many people at the QM, on 30 November 1991, will remember the song Nirvana came on stage to? The answer is 'L'Amour Est Un Oiseau Rebelle' from Bizet's *Carmen*. Nirvana liked to amble on stage and play a very bad version of the famous Bizet classic. There is a note beside the first song saying they've done a Les Dawson with Bizet's *Carmen*. Admittedly this is a very British reference but Dawson was a popular and clever TV comedian from the 1970s and early 80s, who used to play piano just out of tune. Actually quite a skill, as you have to learn it properly to deconstruct it badly.

The best part about watching the band come on stage in such a clueless goofball fashion, if you knew what was going to happen next, would be seeing the looks of sheer horror on those watching. Here they were, paying to see the best band of their generation, and they have a drummer out of time with a bassist playing out of sync with an out-of-tune guitarist playing – sorry, murdering – a famous piece. They shouldn't have worried; the band quickly exploded into 'Drain You' and the relief was palpable.

I didn't get a chance to really savour Nirvana play on my doorstep. I was somewhere between making sure that everyone I knew was OK and looking out for my brother who, by the look on his face, fuelled by free drink from his new-found kudos as friend of Nirvana, now thought that he was on a deadly mission in Cambodia to assassinate a Green Beret who'd set himself up as a God with a local tribe. The QM is a great venue and when it's packed and bulging at the seams, there are few places that can beat it. On 'Lithium', the third song in the set, the place went berserk. I remember seeing Krist, Dave and Kurt briefly glance at each other in disbelief at the reaction in the venue, as the packed crowd took it to another level, really going for it. In turn, of course, Nirvana were feeding off the vibe from the crowd and it was stimulating their performance.

Another fantastic show but it was difficult to relax as the crowd was just too crushed. Whether it was the heat, the excitement, the volume or the alcohol, I've never seen so many bodies passing out and being carefully handled overhead for the medical people to check over. I remember my pal Tom looking around at the chaos while out for some air and pointing at all the casualties.

'You OK?' I asked.

'It's like The Somme in here.'

As 'Smells Like Teen Spirit' was performed at its best in Glasgow, it might be a good time to reflect on the song. One of the many different titles for this book, a list that also included *In Bloom: Kurt, Comedy and Me,* or *Win a Lada Mrs Davies,* or *Smells Like Nirvana,* or *Bring on the Grunge Messiahs,* was *Anthem For Doomed Youth.* That was originally my title for a long treatise on the song itself. It was a detailed and even obsessive attempt to deconstruct and critique the song, to look at it in detail, to try and do a journalistic, highbrow piece on the power and impact it had and indeed still has.

At the time I was always dismissed by friends when I tried to frame 'Smells Like Teen Spirit' in the Top Ten list of best-ever singles. Now everyone's on side but then they weren't. At the time it was regarded as no more than a quirky, strange but catchy song that stood out from the crowd because of its different dynamic. There are a few things which make it different from the other Nirvana songs: for example, it was written by Kurt, Dave and Krist. Which implies it was worked through and all three had a significant part in the process of developing it.

But who saw it coming? Not their management or the

record company. That's the truth about 'Smells Like Teen Spirit'. The hit that changed Kurt, Krist and Dave's lives forever was so accidental it bordered on the absurd. From its inception, development and release then the inevitable implosion, the song could almost be used like a modern–day rock parable. As someone who was with them up close on tour, it was interesting for me to see the pressure a hit single placed on Nirvana and those around them. From a writing point of view, to be witnessing this at close hand was incredible.

In its F minor key, quiet verses and loud choruses, the dynamic of 'Smells Like Teen Spirit' is as intriguing as the sound of the record itself. Maybe like 'A Whiter Shade of Pale' by Procol Harum or 'Something in the Air' by Thunderclap Newman, or Talking Heads' 'Once in a Lifetime'. Songs you might not necessarily like but are almost destined to be hits because they stand out by sounding so different to their contemporaries in the charts.

As a pop fan and hanging out with musicians as they were having a hit single, I was obsessive about it. When I got the chance, it sounds now like I was bordering on being nosey, but honestly, it was natural at the time. But if I did come across like a demented irritating fan, Kurt never showed it. He was amongst the few people on tour who, purely by default, knew I was keeping a diary. I'd need somewhere quiet and sat in Nirvana's dressing room as he slept. If he couldn't sleep, he would chat. I wasn't scared or as deferential as everyone else about chatting to him. I wanted to be a writer, why not a music journalist? I almost saw it as my duty to ask questions like a journalist would. I never knew I would end up releasing this book. I was just a pop fan and couldn't believe my luck, chewing the fat with guys whose lives were rapidly changing. When I asked them about 'Smells Like Teen Spirit', the look on all their faces was one of incredulity. Anytime we'd hear of another milestone or more news about its success, Kurt especially seemed shocked at the world's reaction to the point of being embarrassed.

'Admit it's a modern classic?'

'Nah...' Lighting and exhaling, always a sign we're in for fun. 'It's a bit worrying when the experts issue it as a feeder, you know.' It's record industry policy (or indeed it was then – I'm out of it now, I write jokes and gags) to try and extend the life of an album as long as possible. Normally they would take a song that represented the band, a statement of intent, an introduction to the fans and radio stations. 'Smells Like Teen Spirit' was chosen as a calling card, to build up the following with the indie kids. 'Come As You Are', in fact, was deemed the better song and the one they felt would be the massive mainstream breakthrough hit for the band.

Kurt would doodle in his journal on the table in front of me, a kind of sick little cartoon, a distorted hardcore *Peanuts*-type thing. Elongated and unhappy and either involving a piss or a wank. Here was a guy who was a misfit, who learned about rock 'n' roll through listening to his family and friends' record collections and by the winter of 1991, was beginning to see it all come together. He wanted to make it but also wanted to do it with a punk rock ethos. I also have to say how dark his sense of humour was; you'd get the impression that he was a sociopath but quite a nice sociopath. At times he could be unkind to the same millions who would eventually make him the spokesperson of their generation. You'd imagine him to be more guarded and intensely private but he was quite relaxed and candid:

'Everyone knows now how much I fucking loved The Pixies right and it's true. I do love them. I came in one day with a mission. I just went in with this idea to write a pop song like The Pixies. It was shit. The band were unsure but honestly if people knew how accidental it all was they'd be shocked, maybe even pissed off or in fact feel like they'd just been duped. It was just before we went in to record the album so they were frustrated at having a new song to learn, I guess. We kept working on this tune then Krist seemed to get it, stopped everything, then told us to try and do it much slower. Then Dave slowed it down and they got into it. It really was so fucking stupid. By the time we got to actually record it, the song still wasn't finished. I was scribbling down lyrics, it's so outrageous for people to suggest that it was this great masterpiece, well executed from start to finish and delivered to the record company in a fucking jiffy bag marked hit single, no, sorry, Andy, *modern classic*.'

'What the fuck is it about anyway?' I tried to make him laugh.

'Fucked if I know.' He shrugged his shoulders and drank some Sprite, smiling with his eyes and puffing on his Embassy Tipped, shaking his head like some old codger on a park bench reminiscing some random moment of happiness and good luck, like the blow job from the hotel maid as a reward for winning the war in 1945 'cos you looked handsome in your uniform.

I tried to push him more and continued: 'It's confusion, frustration, The Beatles, 'Ticket to Ride'. It's anger 'cos a girl-friend pisses off with someone else.'

I could see I was getting at him. One side of me was getting a little scared. I didn't want to upset big famous rock star Kurt, but also I knew he wouldn't even enter into a conversation with someone who he didn't like and we were both sitting with our diaries out. It was like being back at school with your favourite English teacher, who everyone feared but you knew how far you could push in a debate. Kurt put his fag out, shaking his head, smoke exhaling... oh, here it comes.

'"Ticket to Ride"? That's a fucking classic by the best band. It's just fucking stupid to even make any comparison or have us in the same sentence as a Beatles song.'

He then looked a bit confused and slightly irritated and uncomfortable. I think he genuinely, at that exact moment, didn't know how good a song he and his band had written. It wasn't modesty or self-deprecation but a genuine refusal to accept how good it was.

'Fuck off, Andy.' Smiling that smile again. 'You're a fucking undercover impostor. Nice work.'

There's no doubt the band were bemused and bewildered by the song but as soon as it hit the airwaves and MTV started heavy rotation it had taken on a life of its own. Sometimes when songs like this come along, songs like 'Louie Louie' by the Kingsmen, 'Like a Rolling Stone' by Dylan, 'Telstar' by The Tornados, 'Rock Around The Clock' by Bill Haley and the Comets, 'My Generation' by The Who, '(I Can't Get No) Satisfaction' by The Rolling Stones, 'God Save the Queen' by The Sex Pistols, 'Tutti Frutti' by Little Richard, 'Strange Fruit' by Billie Holiday, they change the musical landscape and redefine the music scene of the time. When this happens, it's out of the group's hands. It's not only the song itself but also the impact it makes. Every so often it's about the way a group can capture the spirit of the time and seize the moment.

Nirvana's punk attitude was the very antithesis of a major label act and their self-deprecation and parodying of 'Smells Like Teen Spirit' in performance and interviews seemed to endear fans even more. It became like Monty Python's *Life of Brian*, you could imagine Kurt's mum standing at her window shouting, 'He's not the grunge messiah – he's a very naughty boy, now go away!' The more Nirvana said, 'You're fucking idiots, go away', the more the slacker generation said, 'Yup, but give us fucking more.'

The song had been in the hands of US radio stations in late August 1991 and released a few weeks later, but it was a slow burner and only gained momentum when alternative radio stations started playing it. I had always wondered as a kid what that must have been like. To write a song in your room, come up with some chords – and in Kurt's case, hurriedly come up with some lyrics at the last minute – and if all the elements take shape and it takes off, you have a hit single.

Gordon and I wondered what if they became as big as The Beatles. Their album was going crazy, their shows becoming the stuff of legend and now the single was really taking off. It was incredible to be around them at this point. The fans were reacting with the same intense level of hysteria. Their songs were brilliant. The only thing that made you rein the excitement in was that cool bands like Nirvana didn't get to the top of the US charts, did they? They were just like us, ordinary guys, not full of bullshit.

Looking back now, we got it wrong about them being as

big as The Beatles but they did get to Number 1 in the US album charts. Maybe instead of The Beatles we should look to The Kinks and use 'You Really Got Me' as the appropriate comparison to 'Smells Like Teen Spirit', exploding through the airwaves with a sound of a ripped speaker in an amp, an electrifying solo, a refreshing nod to blues, garage punk and the excitement of pop. I realised as I jotted down ideas that I no longer needed to imagine what it was like for bands to have a huge hit. I was sitting in the eye of a storm, somewhat protected, in a surreal place, capturing my thoughts and looking at a small skinny guy who just like me, was trying to think of what to write next.

Every band that goes on to scale the heights always has a defining moment. Of course talent comes into it but equally, timing, momentum and a huge slice of luck play a part. Take the example of 'I Want To Hold Your Hand' by The Beatles. In October 1963, when the group were still almost unknown in the USA, American TV host Ed Sullivan and his wife were travelling through Heathrow Airport and were caught up in a commotion with 1,500 screaming fans going crazy, despite the pouring rain, on the rooftop gardens of the Queen's Building. On hearing it was the band returning from a Swedish tour he famously said, 'Who the hell are the Beatles?' On witnessing first-hand the reaction from the kids, he knew there was something in the air and he promptly tried to book them on his TV show.

'I Want to Hold Your Hand' broke The Beatles in America early in 1964, changing the cultural landscape forever, and capturing the imagination of a country still in mourning from the death of President John F. Kennedy the previous

November. All down to a chance meeting at Heathrow. Similarly, even in Britain, it was one TV show – the primetime *Val Parnell's Sunday Night at the London Palladium* – that propelled them from chart-topping success to spectacular stardom. It was a level of fame that the *Daily Mail* called 'Beatlemania', and things would never be the same again.

It could be argued that Nirvana's own turning point had occurred on that cold and windy Friday afternoon at the Reading Festival in August 1991. Indeed, everyone has moments of luck, or that chance meeting, or people who try to help and nurture. For Nirvana, Sonic Youth were a primary influence. The New York band, formed in 1981, started out as a hardcore proto-punk outfit before becoming major players in the alternative rock scene. They had always been ahead of the musical curve and Nirvana were huge fans, who became close friends. They encouraged Nirvana to sign with their management company, Gold Mountain Management, and eventually to the Geffen alternative subsidiary, DGC. They were protective toward the band as they started to break through and even now, years after Kurt's death, are still very protective of his memory.

I also think, in terms of guidance and friendship, Buzz Osborne of The Melvins plays a crucial but underestimated role in the Nirvana story. Kurt looked up to his old high school pal, three years his senior, and Buzz kind of looked out for his friend, helping him play bass in his first band and project Fecal Matter. Kurt also helped the band move amps and equipment but you wouldn't go as far as to say he was a roadie; he was just keen to hang out with his friends in a cool band. It was Buzz who in 1990 introduced Krist and Kurt to a young drummer he knew, whose punk band Scream had disbanded in Washington DC. Dave joined Nirvana and then they recorded *Nevermind*.

At Glasgow QMU, 'Smells Like Teen Spirit' is played with respect and gusto, and probably the best performance at any of the dates so far. Previously on each night it has been perfunctory, played with a mild form of frustration and irritation. Maybe the band have felt a bit embarrassed by it or more likely just bored, but tonight the song that redefined a generation – or at least made them buy ripped jeans, Converse All Stars and steal their uncle's cardigan, is outstanding.

The title came from a line, spray-painted by Bikini Kill's Kathleen Hanna. She wrote that 'Kurt Smells Like Teen Spirit'. Not knowing that it was a female deodorant aimed at young women and that she actually meant he smelled of his girlfriend, Tobi Vail, Kurt liked it. He thought it sounded like a slogan, a punk rock call to arms, and wrote it down, or at least remembered it. There you have the brilliance of a writer or artist with an eye for detail, taking something, however flippant, and spinning it on its head.

In terms of structure, Kurt plays two notes over Krist's eight-note bass part. For the 16-bar solo, he plays a lead that reiterates the same notes as the vocal melody. With Dave propelling the song with thunderous drums, a nod to 'Louie Louie', Boston's 'More Than A Feeling' and a clear love of The Pixies, it was a perfect moment of so many different elements of luck and magic. It remains probably the strongest opening song to any of the Top 100 albums of all time.

The performance tonight is all the more remarkable because we know they are nervous and tired. Backstage, they seem jaded, almost splintered, yet on stage in that zone, Nirvana are exhilarating and full of intensity.

The next day, while I relaxed at home in Airdrie, after having two baths to help recover and ease my aches and pains, Nirvana did a charity gig at the Southern Bar, a pub in Edinburgh, with the Joyriders. They did it under the name Teen Spirit. Shonen Knife excitedly informed me of all the details. Apparently it wasn't very busy because the weather was terrible. Then the people who were there on the off-chance that Nirvana were going to play were told by the people in the Southern Bar that Nirvana were definitely not going to play, so loads left. Then Kurt and Dave showed up, played a few songs, one of which delighted my Japanese pals no end: a cover of their song, 'Twist Barbie'.

That's all I have in my diary about the night and it's second-hand from Shonen Knife. I've really tried to stick to things I witnessed myself, but it's a little bit of info and is in purely for the archivists and our fanoraks.

CHAPTER 12
LOST AT SEA

NEWCASTLE MAYFAIR, 2 December 1991

JESUS DOESN'T WANT ME FOR A SUNBEAM
DRAIN YOU
LITHIUM
FLOYD THE BARBER
SMELLS LIKE TEEN SPIRIT
ABOUT A GIRL
POLLY
BREED
SCHOOL
SLIVER
BEEN A SON
NEGATIVE CREEP
ON A PLAIN
BLEW

After the gig on 30 November at Glasgow University, we have a day off and meet up a bit worse for wear and head for Edinburgh and the coastal road to Newcastle. Maybe it was the small break in the routine from Saturday to Monday, the taste of normality, and a couple of nights in your own bed. Maybe it's because we're wearing and carrying clean clothes. Sometimes your jeans feel stiff and almost too clean and need to be worn for a few days to get dirty and comfy again.

Things seemed fuzzy and a bit out of focus as we approached Newcastle. Something just wasn't right. Everyone was the same, happy to be meeting up again but equally a little quiet. Personally, I felt really tired and jaded, both physically and mentally. God knows how Nirvana lifted themselves for shows every night but they did. Physically, I noticed by Newcastle I had new muscles coming out across my chest and shoulders and the previously mentioned toned fingers. Maybe they were muscles that had been in hiding. In fitness terms I was generally in good shape and capable of drumming each night without any difficulty, but the thing I noticed was how mentally draining it was. Maybe that's down to the nerves and adrenalin surge in the build up to a show, an anxiety just before it, then relief and euphoria after it's over. Doing this every day, travelling and keeping focused was tiring but I got round it by telling myself at least I wasn't working nightshifts in a factory or standing all day bored rigid in a record shop.

Speak to anyone on the tour that is still around and willing to talk and it's all a bit of a blur. The drug of choice at the time was grass and it was plentiful and if it was taken, it would be after the show or mostly on the bus in transit. But being working-class and Scottish we played up to every stereotype, and consumed every can of lager we could get our hands on. We were all drinkers and liked it that way. Bring it on. Once we got on stage we had, through nervous energy, probably sobered up a bit, apart from our – or at least my – biggest mistake: Newcastle.

The venue itself, Newcastle Mayfair, was like an old ballroom and function suite. It had those chairs you have at weddings stacked up everywhere at the sides. It was also underground as well, which seemed a bit strange. On hearing we were from Glasgow the promoter provided us with a rider consisting of the choice of the mental, hardcore Scottish drunk: Tennent's Super Lager. I should say I *now* know it's the tipple of the mental Scottish drunk; I didn't then. All day things seemed to be going slowly. Nirvana were recording a radio session and got caught in traffic, so instead of their usual show time start of 8.50pm, they were put back till 10pm.

Inside the venue, and I always remember this, we could hear the partying and noise from the street outside. Any time doors were opened to bring in amps or gear there seemed to be legions of half-naked women on a night out, defying the Baltic temperatures of early December. We managed somehow to last until early evening before we broke into the rider. At the time I wasn't aware of the mythical legend of Super Lager.

While hanging about drinking, a gorgeous girl with a beautiful smile kept waving and catching my eye from just outside the front door. At first I thought I knew her from somewhere, as she seemed to know me. By the second can I felt more confident. I went out to look for her as I thought, what if it's someone I do know? She'll think I'm being rude. I couldn't see her so headed for the toilet. When I eventually found the loo, to put it delicately, I needed to have a little sit-down. About a minute later she was in the next cubicle.

'Alright, drummer boy?'

'Aye alright, gorgeous. Nice to meet you.'

She was next door peeing. The chat was interrupted by a few deep movements and loud splashes, all of them emitting from me, as well as fits of laughter. As I wiped up and attended to cleaning matters, I looked up to see one of the most beautiful girls I've ever seen (but clearly a lunatic) look over and wave.

'Open up, bonnie lad.'

'Nah, yer alright.'

'I thought you Scots were game for anything?'

I said something strange like 'I've got a girlfriend', but even though I was immediately turned on by this stunning stranger, I walked away for some unknown reason, as if taken over by the Holy Spirit. Well, I had Super Lager.

'No, yer OK.'

'You what?' she said. 'I'm going to fuck whaur brains out.'

'Nah. But thanks like, you know.'

'Yer cock's fucking got more sense than you, pet.'

Jesus, I had been drinking Tennent's Super Lager for five minutes. I'd already said no to one offer and my cock looked like I'd taken five Viagra. I wondered if it was one of life's ironies that mad alcoholics couldn't get a woman but because of Super Lager, were all three-legged super shaggers. No wonder they were falling over all the time.

'Thanks for the offer. Yer a gorgeous-looking lassie.' Maybe it was the dumb expression on my face as I looked up but she shook her head and smiled, flushed and then disappeared. The women down here were horny as fuck and that made it twice as tough for me. They also seemed to have an open mind about using the gents because every time I went in, they came in behind me. On one occasion, on the way to the toilet I was followed by two girls who I assumed were in the wrong place; they looked more like they were heading for a night out clubbing. They didn't look like Nirvana types. Not that there was a specific 'Nirvana look' but even they didn't seem to fit the demographic. They followed me into the huge gents and instead of going to the urinals, I went to the cubicle to get away from them. They suggested I could have a quick fuck at them both if they could get to meet the band.

'How do you know I know the band?'

'Yer Access All Areas pass, pet.'

'Oh right. I couldn't do that. They're a wee bit post modern for groupies. Into feminism and that.'

'What makes you think we're groupies, bonnie lad?'

Their tits were nearly hanging out; both were wearing miniskirts, one a PVC plastic number, the other like a school-girl. Both were wearing white stilettos. The older one came in, sat down and started pishing.

'Well, get yer cock out for the lassies at least,' the one on the throne said as she lit a cigarette. The other one opened her handbag and took out a bottle of vodka. My base instincts were going mental. Who would ever find out? I'd let one amazing-looking woman pass. No, the guilt would kill me.

'Anyway, the band are going to be late. They're not around.'

'Let me sister suck yer cock, bonnie lad, she's good.'

'Oh aye, what's this here pet, eh?' She grabbed my crotch.

'Maybe later, girls. Aye thanks, eh, see you later.'

'You don't know what you're missing.'

'A fucking dose of it!' I said gallantly as I bolted.

I've always been too fussy. Honestly, to think what Virginia Woolf and Germaine Greer would've thought of the sisterhood.

By the start of the third can, Eugene sat beside me looking concerned and asked if I was OK drinking Super Lager.

'Yes, no sweat – elixir of life.'

I was always able to handle my drink. Not that this makes me anything special, I just didn't get drunk as quickly as everyone else. My grandfather was the same; he was a boxer, a British heavyweight champion, powerfully built and could take a scoop or two. That's who I look like physically and take after in terms of nature.

Eugene said that this particular range of beer was really strong. I suggested it was making the women all want to shag me, which got a nervous laugh. He thought I was making it up. I told him I was OK. Surely it's just normal lager but a bit stronger, like Red Stripe or Furstenberg? I did feel a wee bit tipsy and relaxed but at that point felt OK. It was only by my fifth can, when James came over and said that only mad Glasgow alcoholics drank Super Lager and that it was as strong as fuck, the message seemed to strike home because as he was telling me this, in his own inimitable way, the backstage area slowly started to feel like a cruise ship. He downed what was left, about half, and helped me up, calling me (as he always did), a big mad fucker. I remember looking out at the crowd going crazy as Shonen Knife took to the stage, and thinking I'd missed the gig.

Not only were Shonen Knife one of Japan's coolest and finest indie bands, they were very warm, tender and small people. We were all very protective of them but not as much as Page (James Page Porrazzo, 1953–2002), an American who lived in Japan and worked for Sony Publishing, who was looking after the girls on tour. An eccentric guy but an absolute music fan, he won us over with mono versions of The Beatles' *Revolver* and The Beach Boys' *Pet Sounds*.

On most of the tour we had played first, followed by Shonen Knife, then Nirvana, but for the Edinburgh, Glasgow and Newcastle shows Shonen Knife generously let us go on after them. So I hadn't missed the gig. Nirvana had still not shown up, so Shonen Knife were on. I noticed the sisters from the toilet wave via security from the backstage door of what now felt like a cruise ship at sea.

It was well after 9pm when we walked out to a crowd lusting for Nirvana but at this point any music would do. The heat, along with the feeling of 2,000 people all breathing in your air, was horrible. How could so many people get on this cruise ship? I'm not on a fucking cruise. I'm on stage supporting Nirvana. I didn't ever feel sick, only confused, disorientated, numb, but I kept managing to drift in and out of focus, through fear, shock and panic. The Newcastle gig was the closest we'd play to a full Nirvana house. The people were open, honest and were there to party. They could cope with another dodgy support band till Nirvana came on. But these weren't normal circumstances.

I don't know if Eugene, Gordon and James had been influenced by their drummer, but it seemed by the time we got the call to go on we were all half-cut. Eugene held up a can and said, 'God Bless Tennent's Super Lager' to a massive, tumultuous cheer. At this point I was negotiating how to climb the three-foot high drum riser. Normally it was a quick step and a hop but this time for safety, I was mounting it – pardon the expression – from the crawling position, pulling myself up slowly and sensibly and getting my knees up first. Then I was looking for the rope. You know, the rope and the ladder. For a brief second I thought I was Orson Welles as Father Mapple in *Moby Dick* assailing the ropes into the boat-shaped pulpit to do my sermon in the whale man's chapel.

'...And God prepared a great fish to swallow up Jonah.'

Thankfully some guardian angels passed. The next thing I remember I was being hauled up by the belt of my jeans by three passing strangers. The Super Lager wasn't making me drunk in the conventional way, it felt more opiate-based, like a painkiller. Maybe that's why it's Super? I could hear and see everything fine; it was just making me feel like rubber. The passing strangers were Willie, Michael and Alex. They were pissing themselves laughing and I heard one of them say, 'Oh, this'll be fucking good! I'm not missing this.'

I had made it to the sanctity of Dave's drum stool. I picked up a couple of sticks and did a quick fill. Snare, high tom, low tom, kick, but then I went for another drum that wasn't there and fell off. Forgetting that I sang backing vocals and the mic was on, I got up, dusted myself down and asked James and 2,000 mad Geordies, 'Who's fucking driving this ship?' James was pissing himself and applauding, while Gordon and Eugene fiddled about nervously with effects pedals. I poured a pint of ice water over my head, made four clicks and we kicked into 'God Bless Les Paul'. The crowd, either liking our pluckiness or newfound punk rock sound, went for it.

By the fourth song, through a horrible combination of fear,

sweat, adrenalin and confusion, I was starting to realise what was happening. I was playing drums to a lot of people and as I sobered up, I sensed that the gig could've been a turning point for us. They were up for it, a full house, and really responding to us even though we're this drunk; what would it have been like if we had been sober? It was a chance lost. A chance to show a full venue in the mood for some loud rock 'n' roll what we could do. It was my fault – I blew it.

Soon the gig was over, with Eugene informing the crowd, 'We were Stiff Little Fingers, goodnight.' To a large cheer and some chants growing louder for an encore, we headed backstage to be greeted by fucking Nirvana. I hoped they hadn't seen us. Dave jumped on me, with a happy big grin. I made my way carrying Dave on my back to a corner away from everyone and started kicking over chairs, and anything else around me that I could punch or kick. I was so angry and frustrated and without meaning to (perhaps detoxing rapidly through sweat and coming off the Super Lager) turned into a psychopath. Sweating and angry, I slumped in a corner and buried my head in my hands. I felt like I'd let everyone down.

We all sat at different bits of the big backstage area. Krist and Kurt sat beside me. Kurt said something which I can't remember exactly but it was something like, don't worry about it, everyone has shows like that.

Krist slouched down the wall very easily for a man his height, holding a bottle of Jacob's Creek and offering it said, 'Sometimes you gotta let off steam, Andy.' Krist continued, 'It wasn't actually that a bad show, what I saw of it.'

James came over too. 'SLF my arse, we were like the fucking

Dead Kennedys! Well played, big man, I didn't think you had it in you! Where's the drink? Haaaa!!!'

At that, Kurt jumped on James and started wrestling with him. Kurt did well for his size and height and had great wrestling technique. He was apparently on the school wrestling team. He did really well, had him on the floor, then Kurt kissed James. Krist picked up some food and started a food fight. Within 30 seconds chaos ensued, with food, beer and red wine everywhere. Kurt then climbed up a stack of 12 function suite chairs and dived off, bringing them all down. When he got up it was like something from the Charlie Chaplin film *Behind the Scenes* with all these chairs on his back. He was wearing a nice clean sweatshirt, either a Mudhoney or a Hole one – I was still too traumatised to look – and it was now covered in a red wine stain. Suddenly the three of them stopped and ran through the door and went on stage. I couldn't believe it. I thought they had another half-hour or so to go before they were due to go on, but on they went and delivered a brilliant gig to the fans in Newcastle. There's a photo of Kurt playing that gig and that red wine stain is clear to see.

Encoring with 'Blew', Kurt plays drums, Dave bass and Krist guitars. They go a bit crazy at the end, and basically demolish Dave's kit and smash up Kurt's guitar so they wouldn't have to come on again. I like to think we influenced them. Earlier, tonight's airing of 'On a Plain' is enlightening in two ways. Drained, I'm sobering up too quickly, but I suddenly hear the clarity and power of Dave's drum part in the song, with its intricate build-up work and the difficult harmony and how he maintains it. It's perfect. Delivered probably better than the version on *Nevermind*. I keep saying this but it's true. It makes me think of the thousands of bands I've seen who can't replicate the excitement of a record into a live show. Some can make a decent job of it, yet some bands like The Smiths, Killing Joke, Nick Cave in any of his guises, Teenage Fanclub and Nirvana are better live than on record.

As my addled brain meanders, Dave continues to sing and drum. We'd all be as well packing up and fucking off home, they are so far out of our league. Why even bother?

Three offers of sex, four-and-a-half cans of Super Lager and a food fight with Nirvana. Oh, and our soundman Murray got a speeding ticket the next morning right under the Tyne and Wear Bridge as we headed for Nottingham and our first sober gig of the tour.

CHAPTER 13
SURFER ROSA, SOBRIETY AND JAPANESE TV

NOTTINGHAM ROCK CITY, 3 December 1991

SIX PACK (BLACK FLAG)
DRAIN YOU
FLOYD THE BARBER
SMELLS LIKE TEEN SPIRIT
POLLY
LITHIUM
SLIVER
COME AS YOU ARE
BEEN A SON
ON A PLAIN
ALL APOLOGIES
SOMETHING IN THE WAY
TERRITORIAL PISSINGS

The December morning is crisp and clear, and we're in good spirits as we head for Nottingham. As always, the relative calm is slapped in the face by the East Midlands' answer to *Fawlty Towers*: the couple who ran our B&B were a tad eccentric. They would just walk in, using the master key, at any time, to check up on what was going on. They were like two *Scooby-Doo* baddies revealed at the end by the pesky kids. There was something in their *Hammer House of Horror* strange idiosyncratic behaviour we found funny in a slightly horrific way. They took great exception to being called a 'Bed and Breakfast' even though it said B&B at the front door. There was a slow, dramatic pace to their treatment of us. Maybe they were wary of having a rock group there. There had to be no drinking or smoking, or music of any kind. That clearly put paid to the endless coke-induced orgies each night of the tour.

I liked the drive to Nottingham; it was rural and tranquil. So our wacky landlords there must have inspired us, as we all agreed for one night only that we would stay sober. The shocker at Newcastle Mayfair had left its mark on our psyches and our livers. Our performance in Nottingham would be tight but nervous. I was actually too nervous there, not so much because I was going on stage sober, but because of the change of routine. It had become part of our tour tradition to have a few beers in a quiet place away from everyone and prepare with your mates, for 15 minutes or so, to get ready to face a new crowd and a new challenge, which helped you relax.

Murray, our tour manager and soundman, would record the Nottingham show on DAT. Remember that? DAT? Digital Audio Tape? It seemed so sophisticated in 1991. The mix coming through the onstage monitors, though, was terrible. All

I was getting was Eugene's rhythm guitar. In between songs I shouted for more bass, but kept getting a shrug. I liked loads of bass, Eugene's vocals, as I needed a guide to sing backing vocals and just some of Gordon's guitar. I knew the tunes and could play the middle section of the song 'Wow' in my sleep as we'd played it hundreds of times. As well as counting it in and prompts from each other, I still had no bass coming through my monitor at a part in the middle-eight that only featured the bass. In a mix of nerves and monitor problems I came in too early and fucked up with a fill. It was partly my fault, partly through not being able to hear James clearly on stage but the real problem was I was too nervous and too sharp and, dare I say it, too sober. Apart from that one small mistake we pulled it off 100 per cent sober and sounded, according to those present, really good. It was also duly noted that in future we would all be allowed at least two lagers before the show, if we so chose, to help, as clearly we were a bit too sharp and edgy instead of letting it flow.

During the day in Nottingham we split up and did our own thing – no walks to the local boozer as we were going on stage dry, and so stayed off the beer, at least till we had played. This meant I had time to get away and actually think about, take in and absorb everything that happened in Newcastle, and wanted to find a place away from everyone else to get working. While sneaking off, I saw the shape of Nirvana facing the opposite way in one of the venue's booths. I crept up from behind them and jumped up to give them a fright but stopped as I realised they were recording an interview for Japanese TV. If you Google 'Nirvana, Rock City, Japanese TV' you can see the footage on YouTube. There's an edit before they start talking about the underground scene and by coincidence Krist had just mentioned Captain America. While they stopped, he shouted, 'Hey! Speak of the devil, we just mentioned you guys on Japanese TV, man!'

It's good footage, the perfect memory for any of us on the tour or anyone who saw the band live at that time. The way they looked on that Japanese TV show clip is ingrained in my memory of the Nirvana I got to meet. Kurt always seemed to have this ability to transform dramatically, in Edinburgh he looked deathly but here looks great, Krist is thoughtful and Dave looks so young in his ponytail and nice little tie! But it's eight minutes with them, exactly as I knew them. It's heartbreaking too as Kurt looks so much like the guy I got to know and looks younger every year.

Later, we're sitting in a nondescript room in Nottingham. It's a heavy metal venue and the sexist unfunny rock graffiti on the walls reflects that. Those rock 'n' roll beasts with their super-strength turbo-boost hairspray, a walking Greek tragedy of ozone destroying parodies, worried about their cock size. It's a room devoid of hubris but not debris. There's no arrogance or high-handed haughtiness. The opposite in fact – there's a quiet, shuffling, chaos. A little bit of confusion. There's Nirvana. There's me and Gordon, there's Krist's wife at the time, Shelli. Dave picks up his ever-present electric guitar and sits on the floor in the corner subconsciously playing a Kiss solo, while he clearly thinks of something else. Ten out of ten for intricate fretwork, one out of ten for content. Thankfully, it's unplugged.

Kurt drags his feet around the worn, scorched, battle-scarred floor, a poster boy for bad posture, shaking his head, looking for something, perhaps his journal. The floor's messy and unkempt.

There are discarded raincoats and bags with airport tags from unfamiliar airlines from far-flung countries. There's the ubiquitous promoter or tour manager's metal case with Musicians' Union and PRS stickers. What's inside? Open it! Filthy cash, drugs and guns? No, looks like passports, visas, contracts and Optrex. It's now probably half-four but we occupy a world devoid of natural light.

Kurt finds his notebook, one of the many eventually published as a 'journal'. He still hasn't spoken. There's a side of me, the guy who buys records, who reads the music papers, who goes to gigs, who isn't enjoying being here. Don't cross the footlights. Where's the mystery in this quiet little piece of tranquil ordinariness? Where's the egotistical friction and tension? Where's the guns and smack and mayhem? Why is the patron saint of tortured angst pottering around like a forgetful pensioner trying to remember where he put his pack of seeds for the allotment? When do I get my excess? When will we share in the Dionysian spoils? No, it's just calm, and no, hold on, Dave and Kurt are having a cigarette, a small Embassy Tipped. Kurt has a pen and notebook and knows we're all watching him. Out of boredom he comically pretends to be searching for creative inspiration, before ignoring us and starting his work.

'It's fucking mental this tour, eh?' I suggest, looking on.

Gordon laughs. Krist smiles and nods his head sagely.

A bit later as everyone goes off, I bring out my own notebook and start writing. Kurt is clearly bored now. There is the standard brusque, churlish and surly image of him going through life like a truculent spoilt little rock star. Behind the complex and uptight façade, though, Kurt had a dark and sick sense of humour. Despite being a new man in terms of respecting women, hating sexism and worshipping feminism, Kurt informed me that he'd like to leave something ironic on the wall of the Rock City venue. He had the top off a black magic marker which Krist or Dave had left to write out the set list.

'Andy, I'm thinking of defacing this lovely wall. I need a revisionist statement.'

'If you have to think about it the moment's gone.'

'Yeah, it has to *seem* like I made it up on the hoof. Something about corporate rock.'

I should have said something like Picasso's 'Art is the lie that reveals the truth to us' but for some reason my head blurted out, 'Wake up you slacker cunts and smell my cheesy bell end!'

'You can't use the C-word, you sick child, not cheesy.' He was smiling, though. Then as he put the magic marker down, and laughed again. 'I can't beat that.'

He didn't use it. Maybe I should use it for a title for this book. It's something I felt the press overlooked, his sense of *fun*. Don't let the truth get in the way of a good story. It's hard to explain and justify when we eventually know how that other guy that I didn't get to meet – the other Kurt – the guy at the end of the spiral, killed himself. Cobain portrayed by the media as the 'gun-toting smack head rock star' when they reported his very public disintegration. It's the same with the title of the song, 'I Hate Myself and I Want To Die,' something that's very easy to manipulate and say again, 'What more proof do we need?'

'I Hate Myself and I Want To Die' was the initial title of *In Utero* but there's something about Kurt in that. That's a *piss-take*, that's his sense of humour right there. When people would ask

how he was doing he'd say, 'I hate myself and I want to die' –
part-parody, part-self-deprecation but mostly it would be him
hamming it up, as by this point the band were being taken so
seriously and he felt he had to burst the bubble. Every time I
read that I can hear him say it.

Nirvana were always portrayed as Kurt Cobain's band but
without Dave and Krist they would never have made it. One
of the things I'm most proud of, apart from all the great things
that occurred and meeting those decent, generous, sensitive
guys, was a discussion I had about the song 'Louie Louie' with
Krist and Kurt. Well, really it was mostly Krist, holding court
with a bottle of Jacob's Creek. He offered me a swig but I'm
being professional today, remember? Krist jokingly dismissed
'Smells Like Teen Spirit' as 'Boston's "More Than a Feeling"
meets "Louie Louie".'

'"Louie Louie" is the benchmark,' I confirmed.

'It's the prototype,' Krist nodded.

'Imagine a world where all the music was just garage punk?'

'Yeah, everybody has to sniff glue, take cough syrup and
sound like The Sonics.' Krist took a gulp and sat down,
enjoying the rap.

'Like Romilar D?'

'Hell, yeah, all the garage punk! How do you know about
Romilar?'

'I remember it from the sleeve notes of *Pebbles* compilations.
Mind altering cough syrup. Do you think the Ramones liked
the Kingsmen?'

'Hell, yeah.' Krist did his traditional hand greeting clasp and
high five, which involved an intricate pattern and finished off
with an imaginary puff at a doobie.

Kurt was lying in a bent, distorted foetal position on a very small, stained beige sofa – the sort of sofa that seems to be left in every dressing room large enough to hold them. I thought he was fed up, or getting bored or wanting me out of the way but then he smiled and said, 'Andy's right. It's all about "Louie Louie".'

Watching Krist Novoselic stroll or amble on stage each night of the *Nevermind* Tour is something of a privilege. When he picks up his bass – and believe me, they are heavy mothers – in his hands it looks like a ukulele. On stage he's the most relaxed of the three, a perfect foil to Dave and Kurt's guardedness. He shares their outgoing personality but has a special presence with his well-sculpted goatee beard and long hair, looking like a Viking planning to pillage and plunder, who ends up rather liking the enemy and sharing his red wine.

Once Krist starts playing though, he is the real deal: powerful and dominant, bringing intensity and structure, the corner-stone between Dave's drumming and Kurt's melody. Any three-piece band – Blue Cheer, Cream, The Jimi Hendrix Experience – all rely on great musicianship and collaboration. Krist seems to not only lock in with Dave's drumming as any bass player should, but also plays melodic hooks to strengthen Kurt's lead parts. I don't know if he knows how good a player he is. There's an eclectic mix of players you recognise when you watch him: elements of Peter Hook in his Joy Division days, Jean-Jacques Burnel of the Stranglers and Paul Simonon of The Clash. All three are bassists who stand out as individual musicians yet add to the band as well. There are also punk, pop and metal touches from Black Sabbath and pure pop McCartney-esque bass runs.

It's crucial to emphasise Krist's cleverness, sharp expressions, deftness of touch and the fact he plays a lot of high-octane stuff to enhance the melody and drive the song. This is underpinned with the collective aim and vision of the group being the priority, *not* the individual and Novoselic gets the balance right. Personally, I think Krist was one of the best bass players of the 1990s and not just because he was a fantastic natural musician but also because, unlike all those wanky musos on forums and in magazines chugging off to Mark King of Level 42's tablature to 'Lessons in Love', he was a fan of music. You can tell he listened to loads of records and like Kurt, just learned from listening to anything in their record collection. When you watch Krist play Nirvana's hits you can really see how he uses that enormous melodic hook. That comes from listening to good records and practising.

In between long periods of hanging around and waiting, punctuated by blips of activity, and while the others did their own thing, the best place to get peace and quiet was in Nirvana's dressing room. Kurt would either be sleeping, or doing his journal, or writing letters. He wrote a lot of letters on that tour. We were now a daily fixture in the dressing room, and we knew that if Kurt was sleeping, he'd be OK. Alex MacLeod and Ian Beveridge would look in, give us the thumbs up and run off to deal with an emergency with the bass amp or promoters, happy knowing that someone would be around. Apparently Kurt had a tendency to do heroin but I never saw it. The dressing room wasn't exclusive, and any of us or Shonen Knife were allowed in to chat or collect their thoughts, but Shonen Knife were rarely around during the day. I've subsequently realised they were very organised and professional and utilised their time productively by doing John Peel sessions and loads of interviews. Things we should've been doing if we could've been arsed.

Most of the time though, Kurt was sleeping, belying the crazed punk rock image of Nirvana. I'd have my Walkman on, playing tapes quietly while writing up notes and ideas from previous days. Normally if he wasn't in the mood, he'd be trying to sleep or be sulking in the corner, distant, petulant. Fair enough, he was under loads of pressure and the rigours of performing almost every day of 1991 (especially with his vocal style), were taking their toll.

Kurt needed space at times, and I was glad to give him it. When he was happy and started a chat it was always because he was interested. Once, he noticed I was rummaging in my bag and I pulled out a cassette of The Pixies' *Surfer Rosa*, which I had found in the compartment of the tour van and had claimed as my own. As I played it and started writing, he came over and looked at my tapes, mostly compilations for the tour, and picked up *Surfer Rosa*. I took it from the Walkman halfway through 'Bone Machine' and gave it to him.

'Here, take this. I need to catch up anyway.' I pointed to my notebook.

'Are you sure, Andy? Thanks, man. I love *Surfer Rosa*. What an awesome-sounding record!'

'*Nevermind*'s a fucking brilliant record! I bet The Pixies would rather have *Nevermind* than *Surfer Rosa*. They could never write "Smells Like Teen Spirit".'

'Ehhh, they could,' replied Kurt. '"Smells Like Teen Spirit" was me playing around with the way they wrote. The dynamic. Loud and quiet.'

I was about to tell him I know, you've told me already but I didn't want to be rude. Then I wondered if he even recalled speaking to me – there had been a few things he'd said and had repeated. I put it down to speaking to so many people. I also needed no interruptions and some peace to focus on my diary. In a funny fake music biz LA accent he said, 'Yeah, you know, like uggh, maybe we should get our people to hook up with their people and like swap careers?' He deliberately went up at the end of the sentence, like LA people and most of the world's youth do now. If only more people knew this side of him: a consummate master of self-deprecation. He placed the cassette into the Walkman and returned to the subject of The Pixies, specifically their bassist.

'Kim Deal should be singing more. I love "Gigantic" on this record. Did you hear *Pod*? I love her voice.' *Pod* was the first album by The Breeders, with whom Kim had sung. It was released on 4AD, and produced by Steve Albini on the cheap, up in Edinburgh.

'Isn't Frank Black King Pixie?' He couldn't hear me.

'I love the truncated production on *Pod* as much as the stuff on *Surfer Rosa*.'

Kurt continually went on about the production of *Nevermind*. It started to annoy me but one good thing in these private situations was how relaxed I could be with him. I could say what I wanted to him and on occasions he would be annoyed and fight his corner. I always felt that the image of him being this white-trash psycho punk was just lazy journalism. Everyone knows now he was a sensitive artist but in relaxed conversation, he *really* knew about music.

There was also the feeling on the tour, not circulated by him but by the others, that he was the big star and I felt sometimes he seemed genuinely lonely. He would just be left to sleep and rest, which suited me for writing purposes.

Krist and his then-wife Shelli were Kurt's closest allies on tour. Dave was always coming and going, hanging out, but would never stay for long. When Dave appeared, Kurt seemed happier: the group dynamic was back and it was time for some fun. It looked like Krist was his best friend. If Shelli and Krist were around he'd be a bit more polite and withdrawn as if they were his brother or sister, always a bit more sensible, listening to what they had to say. It's difficult to know what it must've been like, three normal guys from the independent under-ground scene who made a critically acclaimed album, which was now being embraced by the mainstream. Instead of taking Mudhoney's crown as kings of Sub Pop, they were on the verge of going global and we could all sense it. Thankfully, being the type of people they were, they didn't take any of the success too seriously. Their management and agents and 'people' were also adept at keeping it low-key and understated. The more I focused on trying to ignore Kurt and get down to my own work, the more he seemed to relax around me and sensed I wasn't one for showbiz or arse-licking. When he was on form I found Kurt really funny, sharp and sarcastic. I was brought up to be polite but to also have an opinion. To chat, converse, to listen.

Everyone read how open Kurt was about his drug use in the music press. I was guilty of burying my head in the sand; it wasn't any of my business. All I can say is that, in the many conversations we had, he seemed perfectly lucid and clean. Maybe he needed a prescription after talking to me. I asked

him why he was left on his own so much. Were they all scared
of him?

'No, I like sleeping, I guess. Maybe they're all scared of big
bad rock star Kurt.' He laughed heartily at the thought.
'Sometimes I just can't face people. I like you 'cos you've no
agenda other than the need to escape everyone else in case they
think you're a fucking homosexual for keeping a journal. But
if people have this perception, fuck them.' He was fast-
forwarding the tape in between chatting.

'People will start to change around you.'

'Well, already you're starting to ask questions like a fucking
journalist.'

'That's the nicest thing anyone's said to me on tour. People
are scared of approaching you and are warned not to get too
close as you like time to think.'

'That's fucking shit, Andy. Fuck them! You know what? I like
peace to think and write to my friends.' He held up a letter to
Calvin Johnson of Beat Happening with an address in
Olympia. 'It's all down to how we're perceived.'

'Why can't you enjoy it more?'

'It's not enjoyable anymore,' said Kurt. 'I get to hang out
with cool people and get to tell loads of people about bands
I like, but it's not like I'm dreaming of the car or the ranch in
fucking Arizona.'

'It's hard, back-breaking work on a ranch, long hours and
full of shit, like the record industry, see what I did there?' I was
chuffed with myself. Kurt was searching for a song on the
Walkman then he stopped, looked up and asked: 'Are you sure
you're not an undercover journalist or something? I feel like
I've been duped by a skilled investigator. That's what they do –

they get you relaxed, nudge you toward the cliff then watch as you fucking drive off.'

'Journalist? Nah, but right enough. I'm not even a fucking drummer. I don't know why I'm here. I can't concentrate long enough. I keep meandering off and daydreaming.'

'When you're actually playing? Cool.' Kurt seemed genuinely impressed.

'It's not cool, it's a pain. It must be really difficult if you're an artist to get what's in your head into someone else's. To try and get that album you want. Though that's where the magic comes in, the spaces in between.'

I was starting to talk shite now. That bit when you know you're losing someone in the conversation. Kurt lit a cigarette and shook his head.

'You should think about it. The best interviews are the ones that you don't notice you're having.'

I was saddened to think that someone who had worked so hard to write, rehearse and gig, who had made so many sacrifices to get his music out there, was so unhappy. It's not like today when you can record three songs in your room on a laptop, open a Facebook account and have a following in three hours. He knew Nirvana had made a commercial record and were on the verge of a major international breakthrough with *Nevermind* but once it became successful he felt he'd sold out. He was definitely unhappy with the sound of the album and seemed depressed about it.

As I listened to him, I felt genuinely concerned for this thin, straggly haired guy who was a few months younger than me. Someone who was happy at the little things people did for him, like let him listen to *Surfer Rosa* or buy him tobacco. The memories of the little conversations I shared with him taught me a lot: about humility, about generosity. I have since met loads of famous people in daft circumstances, some who are wankers, some great. But having met Kurt, I'm not intimidated by anyone.

I'm glad I trusted my instinct and spoke as candidly as possible at the time. It would be easy now to claim that I said to Kurt, 'Use Albini on the next record, make it as difficult as possible, challenging and only for true fans. Oh, and call it *In Utero*.' But the truth is I'd have said, 'Why not beg George Martin out of retirement or get Neil Young to produce you like a *Crazy Horse* album?' I'm not that cool. I like pop music. I thought Butch Vig did an incredible job and loved *Gish* by Smashing Pumpkins (an album I later got as payment for a gig at the Rough Trade store in Covent Garden).

Kurt stopped listening to the Walkman.

'Surely that's where the producer should come in?'

As I was preparing for some peace to write, I couldn't remember what he was talking about. Shit, that's right, we were discussing working with producers and how they should capture the magic. The gaps in between, whatever the fuck that means, explaining his vision to producers.

'I don't know, isn't the producer like a film director really?' I suggested. 'He has to bring what's in front of him together, reel it all in? Next time you'll be able to make the record you want. The bad news is, I think it's going to go nuts, a lot more than you think. You're too close to it.'

'I'm fearing the worst,' he drawled, smiling like he does when he's acting unhappy.

'The Pixies have critical acclaim but you've got the hit

record. Just because you're successful doesn't make you shite. The Beatles were successful and eventually received critical acclaim for *Revolver* and *Sgt. Pepper*. Look at R.E.M.? There's a cool, influential band. I remember when they started no one knew what Michael Stipe was singing. Now, they've had commercial success.'

I started writing up all the ideas I'd had. Like an annoying little brother he talked loudly over the tape.

'It's been ages since I heard this – thanks, Andy.'

There was so much truth in the Kurt I knew, and indeed the Kurt Cobain rock icon, that the world would sadly eventually know. He had a soft-spoken cleverness and razor-sharp wit, but also a punk rock attitude honed from a tortured past. He had been bullied and beaten, usually because of his sarcasm. At high school he had a homosexual friend and would be beaten by homophobes who assumed he must be gay too. Rather than run he would say something just to get a reaction. When 'Smells Like Teen Spirit' catapulted the band into the pop stratosphere, the equivalent would-be bullies of the next generation would be at the front of the audience, knowing all the words to all their pretty songs.

This is in effect what happened to the band. All the sensitive indie art school fans, all the good guys, the underground network of fanzines and record shops run by like-minded people across every state in America, who loved their early work, felt it was over when the normal jocks loved *Nevermind*. And they'd be right. Kurt knew he had made a record that was seen as too commercial by thousands of the early fans and I think it made a dent in his indie sensibility to be seen, especially by them, as selling out. The aftermath of the success of *Nevermind* on the band was an onerous one. Things would never be the same and I believe a less successful and more difficult record in 1991 may have given Nirvana longevity and have them gig to promote a new album for the next 20 years. That's why for *In Utero*, unlike most, I hoped that Nirvana would release an album that wasn't instantly accessible, something closer to what they really wanted to do. One that wasn't radio-friendly or commercial. One that was true to their early influences of The Melvins and Black Flag. I hoped if they were going to do something poppy it would be more like 'About a Girl' from *Bleach* or 'Sliver'. Maybe consolidate a bit, go back to simple straightforward pop music with an indie feel, like a decent Pixies album.

With regards to the production of *Nevermind* versus *In Utero*, I know bands who actually thought if they got Butch Vig as producer and Andy Wallace to mix, then a pile of shite demos would flourish into a worldwide smash. Nirvana worked on their songwriting and the years put in are evident on *Nevermind*. 'Come As You Are' and 'Smells Like Teen Spirit' are utopian pop singles. Quality songs would also be evident on *In Utero*: 'Heart Shaped Box', 'Serve the Servants', 'All Apologies' and 'Penny Royal Tea', the latter a song that sums up the horrific wretchedness of Kurt's suicide, as it was due to be released as a single and cancelled after he killed himself. When I hear that now it has the same resonance as John Lennon singing 'Imagine'. There are radical differences between *Nevermind* and *In Utero*. One is optimistic, powerful and full of energy; the other is fraught, insular and fragile, but both are great in different ways. I always remind people, in their rush to eulogise or demonise, to never forget their brilliant humour, especially with their videos.

'Kurt, why did you look so moody in the video for that shit Pixies song about deodorant?'

Kurt looked shocked at first but laughed at my cheek.

'Well, ND...' When Kurt called me Andy, it was prolonged and sounded more Southern, like the abbreviation ND. The others seemed to have a grasp of saying it, unlike Kurt's version, a camp Blanche DuBois from *A Streetcar Named Desire*.

'I wanted to be in charge,' Kurt continued. 'I'm a control freak. Hell, no! This set ain't big enough for the both of us. So I got blind drunk on bourbon.'

'Jack Daniels?'

'No, I'm not that clichéd. It would've been Jim Beam, I guess.'

He shrugged his shoulders, embarrassed by his rock 'n' roll strop. Every time I see the video I imagine him getting angry on JB. So next time you watch, remember this and I bet it'll make you smile.

In Utero reignites my passion for music as I always think it was recorded to be played as loud as possible. Kurt's oft-repeated claim that he didn't want to be bigger than Sonic Youth or The Pixies was true. Who knows, maybe if he hadn't been as successful, things might have been different. Maybe I'd have been listening to Kim Deal and Kurt do a Nancy Sinatra and Lee Hazlewood tribute album with the volume up to ten.

I continually tried to avoid being spotted with a diary or at least writing stuff in it. I don't know why, lack of self-esteem or confidence. It's ironic and maybe just sad to think the only place I could really get a chance to write was when Nirvana's dressing room became like a small library, when Kurt did his journal and I did my diary. Maybe it was just a quick five-minute chat and a brief scribble or maybe a half-hour here or there. At some point it became a familiar routine to Kurt. He became so relaxed about it and on a few occasions encouraged me to think about writing as a career.

On one occasion he asked what I was working on. I explained that, apart from keeping the diary entries 'in case you lot become the next Beatles', I had two ideas. The Lennon book was one, a dark comedy novel when he survived his shooting and realised how precious life was and like a man given a second chance shagged half of Hollywood, did all kinds of drugs, worked with Neil Young and exposed himself at Live Aid. The other was a James Thurber-type idea about a time travelling character called Dr Howard Smith. I later renamed him Dr Howie Paintgloss after the eternal optimist Doctor Pangloss in Voltaire's *Candide*, and made him a DIY painter and decorator. The pal who got me into *Candide* and also the Greek stuff was big Andra McKay, now an English teacher as well as a Killing Joke and Dead Kennedys fan, and another one who encouraged and nurtured my interest in writing.

Interestingly, till this point I hadn't told anyone about my ideas. I was so fearful it was something so far removed from being a drummer that it would be too difficult to do. Kurt loved both my ideas but seemed particularly keen on the Lennon one. I continually told him to tell me to fuck off if he was fed up or tired, or didn't feel like having company. It's a bit weird though, as I had seen him being quite moody and short-tempered with people when he couldn't be bothered doing something or being in company, and he just didn't want to be there. That look of sheer disdain for anyone who was boring him rigid or forcing him to be with people he didn't want to be around. Silent. Moody.

Thankfully it was never aimed at me or any of our party but when he was in a mood, or in a dark place, which to outsiders it probably looked like all the time, it was best to leave him. I can still see him with his raincoat on and fingerless gloves, with a busted bruised black nail, bemoaning the continual shit he had to deal with. He was always OK with me, though.

'Hey Andy.'

'Hi Kurt, is it OK?'

'Yeah, you strange boy! Why are you so paranoid?'

'I'm more embarrassed.' He looked tired and exhausted and was sketching, or doodling, not writing.

'I can't even think. What's the opposite of delighted?'

'Delighted?'

'Yeah.'

'Dismayed?'

I started work and within seconds Kurt is sleeping. I think of the pressure he's under and how I'd hate to have that. This articulate guy with the weight of the world on his shoulders, who is so fucked he can't even think? Is this what happens when you have success? Of course if Kurt had enough time to fake it, he'd pretend to be sleeping, so as not to get roped into shaking the hand of the local DJ or record plugger. Most times he'd be writing when I sneaked in to do some work, either writing or sleeping. When I asked what he was working on, he said: 'Kind of a journal, ideas, just thoughts. It's mostly random shit. Sometimes things come out and I develop songs. I get an idea and I'll start something. It's no big deal.'

We now know this became a big deal when those ideas,

thoughts and ramblings were posthumously published on 4 November 2002 as *Journals*. When I picked up a copy in Waterstones in Glasgow, it automatically opened at a letter that Kurt had written to Eugene. Coincidentally, at the exact same time, *Bleach* began playing from an adjacent staff room as some workers had their lunch. After looking around to see if a camera crew were filming me and trying to freak me out, I left the shop quickly. It was strange to think I'd chatted with the same guy while he actually did entries into his journal. I keep saying 'journal', I'm even becoming defined by the nuanced branding of the machine; it was just a notebook − a cheap, small, notebook.

Pete Townshend was asked to review *Journals* and there's a fantastic article in the *Observer* from around the time of its release, which is worth seeking out to read. Despite being the butt of one of Kurt's snipes, '*I hope I die before I become Pete Townshend*', which is actually a very smart reversal gag, its target refuses to gloat, and instead mourns his passing and berates the music industry's part in it:

It is desperately sad for me to sit here, 57 years old, and contemplate how often wasteful are the deaths of those in the rock industry. We find it so hard to save our own, but must take responsibility for the fact that the message such deaths as Cobain's sends to his fans is that it is in some way heroic to scream at the world, thrash a guitar, smash it up and then overdose.

If I'm asked, I always say it's important for fans to know that there was far more to Kurt than the 'random shit' − Kurt's words, not mine – published in 2002. What could be read as deluded, infantile or resentful would more than likely be Kurt taking the piss. A good case in point would be the 'I hate myself and I want to die' quip. If you read that in a diary it's deranged and psychotic. If you hear him hamming it up, it's farcical, funny, self-deprecating and in reality, closer to a Woody Allen quip. So that would be my argument: the way things are portrayed in print, it's about context. It doesn't pick up on Kurt's irony and dark humour.

I would feel hypocritical if I was too judgemental on the publication of *Journals*. By writing this book I could be perceived as being opportunistic and completely understand if Dave and Krist and anyone mentioned in it is upset by me doing it. That's not my intention, my aim is to try and tell a story to those who are interested when an extraordinary thing happens to an ordinary person. I'm not involved in bands anymore, and if I was, I wouldn't be writing this. My day job is a writer and I think it is a story worth trying to tell.

Anyway, Kurt wrote and doodled all the time. I always tell people he could've done anything, he had that distinct absurdist insight and eye you need to be a creative artist, painter, or a sculpture, a photographer, or even a cartoonist or filmmaker. However, I got a strong sense that he really wanted to write. He obviously wrote the songs and was more than capable of writing melodramatic lyrical vignettes but I think he could've been an excellent playwright or novelist, purely from his sensitivity and ability to express himself. That's just my opinion, born of the brief time I knew him and the amount of time, like writers do, he spent writing something, anything, down on paper. I don't think he'd have continued with Nirvana. Maybe another record after *In Utero*, then move on to something else.

'Why do you write, Andy?'

'I don't know why. I've never thought about it. I feel I have to – I don't feel like I have a choice.'

'Yeah,' he said nodding, and slowly broke into a smile. 'That's about right.'

'I'm looking over something I wrote after seeing you play for the first time, at the Astoria.'

'You guys and the Television Personalities, right?'

'After it, I go on about the first five songs on *Nevermind*. How they really come alive at the gigs, and if it keeps going like this, it's going to go crazy for you. I say it could be one of the greatest records I've ever heard, I haven't said to anyone else but now I'm saying to you and I sound like a fanny.'

'Is that a Scottish fanny or an American fanny?' replied Kurt. 'I think you're delusional. I'll call people to take you away. Do you know who I am? Look at me! I'm the king of adult-orientated rock. I'm the grunge messiah. I can have you removed from this tour.'

'Admit it's a fucking belter.'

'A what?'

'A great record!'

'I just can't see it now or ever being *Pet Sounds* or *Revolver*, or *Never Mind the Bollocks*. I mean, look at the Kinks, Creedence Clearwater…'

'*Face to Face* is one of my favourite albums,' I replied at the mention of the Kinks. 'I have a cassette somewhere.' I tried to find it as he continued.

'There's just so many groups and artists who totally exist on a different planet from us. The Stones, Black Sabbath, Bowie, The Stooges, The Clash, R.E.M., but thanks.'

'Mr Mister, Foreigner,' I suggest, but he's shaking his head.

He laughed again, warmly and shook his head. 'You're a funny guy.'

'Funny American or funny Scottish?'

'Funny, period.'

About half an hour before the doors open and therefore half an hour before we are on stage to an empty hall, I'm nervous, probably because I'm sober and sneak off out of Rock City for a walk and some fresh air. I can't believe how many people are outside the venue. They all seem so lost. It's like a scene from a war movie or a famine report on the BBC. A displaced grunge nation, so many people aimlessly wandering around looking for a ticket. No one had a ticket.

'Got a ticket, mate?'

Everyone wanted the same thing. Just to get in. So many fans just weren't able to get anywhere near the gigs. If getting a hold of the album just after its release was difficult, getting in to see them was just about impossible. On the tour, as the drummer on the third band on the bill, I am by definition the least important musician involved with the band who are the hottest ticket in town. Yet even if I walk out the front door of any of the venues my status instantly becomes elevated to someone with credibility. I'm someone who was in the building and now is nonchalantly leaving as thousands were doing anything to get in. Therefore I'm someone of merit.

Touts and fans don't care about me. All they want is a plus one. It could go to your head, especially when the pretty indie girls smile forlornly and look longingly at you with their gorgeous big sad eyes. Eyes you could dive into and fall in love with there and then. I have to shrug my shoulders and apologise: I can't help you, I'm only the drummer in the third band on the bill. Maybe they sense weakness or kindness, or maybe it's just your laminate and the merest chance that somehow you can get them in to see the show. I've been there and I know how it feels to be on the outside looking in.

I shove the laminate under my T-shirt and zip up my jacket against the cold. Many have given up; they walk around looking like they've just returned from battle to find their village burned down. Heads are down, spirits broken. I feel like saying, It's only a gig, for fuck's sake cheer up. As I continue, I see punks sitting on the roadside looking perturbed, as if they've survived a 30-car pile-up and are staring in disbelief at the carnage. Hundreds, probably closer to a thousand are facing the venue. Some have their heads in their hands. Some are still bobbing and weaving, desperately trying to get a ticket.

'Any tickets, mate?'

A few feet away from me, either a brave or stupid tout nods to one of the guys bobbing and weaving. I never heard what the price was but the transaction ended close to violence. The tout tells the guy to fuck off and goes about his business again. Within seconds a couple see what's going on, make eye contact and decide the price is worth it. The tout nods for them to follow and over in a quieter spot in a shop doorway, the transaction is completed, like a drug deal; done and dusted, with surreptitious looks over the shoulder, and they leave happy.

I see a foreign film crew, lights from a camera doing vox pops with happier-looking people, who clearly have tickets as they approach the queue. All this is going on under everyone's nose.

The misery continues, as fans are pleading to get inside the venue. I try hard to stop shaking my head at the torment and suffering. You feel like a UN humanitarian official witnessing the plight of the Grunge people. As it gets more packed and dense I'm forced to turn back. I see the tout again. Rejection, rejection, then a deal. He's off to the same doorway.

After about five minutes I realise that my quick relaxing walk is having an adverse effect. As I head back, I walk by the queue. Those in the queue look worried and they have a right to be. The ones without a ticket are all staring at the ones who are getting in. This is what it means to have a hit single and a sell-out show. The crowd gets tighter and more packed as more arrive to face the same disappointment. Wait till I tell Nirvana this. Maybe I shouldn't mention it. It's eerie, very quiet. Then because it's so quiet, when there's a squeal it sounds so desperate and tragic, like a crowd in shock at a terrible accident. There's an air of desperation, punctuated by the sound of females crying. I actually turned around and saw three female fans crying and being comforted as they wept.

Then, for a brief second, it flashed through my mind that maybe something had happened to the band? Surely not, I'd just left them a few minutes ago. They were wailing because they couldn't get in.

There are so many people that a nearby main road is blocked and traffic is being redirected. The fans have taken over. This is the cost of success. This isn't right. It's unfair. You'd be lucky, if out of all the people here tonight, one in five get to see the band. 20 per cent get inside; 80 per cent will be disappointed. I nudge and squeeze very slowly through the crowd and get to the back door with about five minutes to spare.

I notice how everyone has long hair, the same wavy curly Wonder Stuff hair. There's metal fans, Rock City being a bit of a metal venue, but there's punk indie and loads of happy mainstream music fans too. It's something I keep looking for, the demographic; maybe it's my record shop background. It's really noticeable how diverse and broad Nirvana's fanbase is. You can start to see the dilemma facing the band, and how they'll sell shit-loads of albums then I check myself for starting to sound like a corporate record company monkey.

It was becoming clear Nirvana had reached a tipping point. They felt disillusionment at the crossover appeal of *Nevermind*, and frustration and sheer incredulity at what was going on around them. They had become unwilling spokespeople for alternative *rawk* and had, despite their protestations, become a major commercial act. The music business is shallow and soulless and makes no bones about it. From the days of Tin Pan Alley and songs being churned out factory-style in the Brill Building right up to the *X Factor*, it's about making cash.

Nirvana's narrative is interesting as their story is one of being outsiders. They are always inaccurately described as being from Seattle. Kurt and Krist were in fact from Aberdeen, 83 miles north of Seattle, and a lifetime away. Dave, meanwhile, grew up in Springfield, Virginia, just outside of Washington DC. Kurt and Krist did move out of Aberdeen, though even then Kurt relocated to Olympia and Krist to Tacoma. So they were never truly accepted as part of the 'Seattle scene'.

Nirvana went from recording a record for $606.15 to releasing an album that knocked U2, Metallica and Michael Jackson off the top of the charts. The floodgates opened and the gold rush was on. There were bucks to be made on the latest trend from the Pacific Northwest and like lemmings, every A&R man made haste to Seattle – too late as ever and missing the point – for anyone with a delusional take on angst and a Marshall stack. The record industry couldn't get enough of this new cash cow, but how much did they really know, or more importantly have a feel for or care, about The Melvins or Mudhoney?

In and around the Seattle area, all the duff old local rockers had laughed at Nirvana's early gigs, when they were known as Ted Ed Fred, Skid Row, Pen Cap Chew or Bliss, gigs which had seen them drive round trips of 200 miles for a pointless opening slot. Now all these balding rockers were wearing hats, buying Neil Young's back catalogue – even the really bad albums – and changing their names to something more enigmatic. These once bitter and sarcastic local musicians began to be reverential. They stopped dreaming of a life of vacuous, sexist, misogynistic clichéd spandex and enigmatic bandana fame and started telling film crews from Texas to Timbuktu that Nirvana were incredible. How, even when they were starting out, they were destined for fame. Anything to get a deal. Suddenly, those who had hair didn't wash it. Those who didn't wore hats. The Levis were dragged around by their pick-up trucks to look old and jaded. And don't even start me on the music. Their uncle's old Blue Cheer albums were looked out, rifled through and the hurt, tortured frontman with angst in his pants was everywhere. The only thing missing was a band called 'Missing the Point'. Meanwhile, over in Milan and Paris, fashion houses launched the grunge look as this year's must-have. How fucking hilarious was this? 'Yeah, sorry sweetheart, you look too healthy. We want smack complexion, you know, the yellowish lifeless pockmarked look, yeah, heroin chic, darling. Sorry.'

Nirvana's best song tonight at Nottingham Rock City is 'Come As You Are'. It's played with a swagger, poise and the confidence of a band evidently, at least on the face of it, at the height of their powers. The Killing Joke-style melodic riff starts up, then Kurt's great vocal performance is as close to the accomplished version on *Nevermind* as I've heard on the whole tour. It leads into the simple but effective solo, building up to its catchy hook and blistering chorus. It has to be another well-structured pop hit. Dave's brilliant backing vocals embellish Kurt's at the chorus, building up a great rock dynamic, the foundations set brilliantly by Krist. The song even has a great coda. The only other unusual note is the encore, with the band switching instruments for what sounds like a bad Sonic Youth cover, with Krist chanting a mantra like a giant Maharishi on crack.

'Smells Like Teen Spirit', now at Number 7 in the British charts, continues to haunt and taunt Kurt, Krist and Dave. There's a bit of tension. Dave has had enough, gets up, stretches and goes off to do his own thing. Kurt says nothing. He looks pissed off, annoyed at the pressure being put on him. Krist is more patient but even his gregarious nature seems put out. It looks like someone has found out the band have a spare hour off and filled some free time with more interviews.

I'm sitting over in the corner with my Walkman on and my notebook out. Right in front of me the band have been asked about 'Smells Like Teen Spirit' and what it means by a rude long-haired guy, who looks like Robert Plant. He has too much curly hair for his 55–60-ish face, it's a wrong match. He's clearly an ex-frontman and a local legend perhaps in the 1970s and probably a presenter on some local radio channel. I don't know why they're even speaking to him. The guy's tone is despicable and he has such a bad attitude, but believe it or not, Kurt and Krist are too polite and probably too tired to tell him to fuck off.

I almost do it. I'm thinking of saying, 'For fuck sake, mate, that's no way to talk to people. Get a grip, show a bit of respect', when someone shouts from behind the door that the next person is here for an interview in five minutes and the chat comes to a natural halt. Then someone from France or Belgium comes in behind the rock-voiced DJ. They are more polite and sweet, but the first thing they ask is about the name of 'Smells Like Teen Spirit' and how it's a weird title – and so it goes on.

CHAPTER 14

BREAKING
POINT

MANCHESTER ACADEMY, 4 December 1991

JAM (KURT ON DRUMS/KRIST ON GUITAR/DAVE
ON BASS)
DRAIN YOU
ANEURYSM
SCHOOL
FLOYD THE BARBER
SMELLS LIKE TEEN SPIRIT
ABOUT A GIRL
POLLY (NORMAL VERSION/NEW WAVE)
COME AS YOU ARE
LITHIUM
SLIVER
BREED
BEEN A SON
NEGATIVE CREEP

ON A PLAIN
BLEW
JAM (UNKNOWN)
TERRITORIAL PISSINGS

This afternoon Kurt seems unusually healthy and clean. I hope he's not coming down with a dose of healthiness. It's strange to see him out of his old raincoat and looking energised and ready to work. I notice his small homemade tattoo on his left forearm. It's the K records logo; it looks homemade. I ask around about it. I'm told Dave helped him do it. It's mentioned in the song 'Lounge Act'. I finally get some confirmation on all the above from one of the crew later that day at dinner. Apparently he did it to impress an old girlfriend, Tobi Vail, from Bikini Kill, who were on K Records, to show his true indie credentials.

By the time we reach Manchester something else happens. I notice how 'Smells Like Teen Spirit' is starting to annoy me. Everywhere we go, the song is playing on the radio: in our hotel, on the bus, in pubs. Anytime you walk by a television set it's blaring from MTV. It's just on all the time, it's everywhere. Now I'm starting to agree with Nirvana's negativity toward the song, with the first tentative signs of criticism and disparagement in my notebook. The tone generally changes from loving the brilliant single to thinking it's not as good as 'Ticket to Ride'. I also suggest, rather haughtily, that Kurt's vocals are distinctive and tortured but Dennis Wilson can really do melancholic anguish and torment.

It's incredible to think, looking back, how we hung out with them at this crucial point in their career. At the time I remember thinking, *Well, I hope they have some time off, come back refreshed and keep writing and making interesting records. That way I might be on the guest list for the next ten years when they play The Barrowlands.* I knew they wouldn't last for seven or eight albums and that they'd want to do their own projects but hopefully would get back together every few years. The fans would always want to hear anything new they wanted to put out. There hadn't been a band like this since The Smiths, R.E.M., The Pixies, or The Stone Roses. Bands that had critical acclaim but crossover appeal and were writing songs that sounded great on radio. Even in the winter of 1991, though, the feeling in private from the band, particularly Kurt, was one of tremendous frustration. One of disappointment at the way they were achieving their success with radio-friendly, polished songs. They were starting to think *Nevermind* didn't truly represent them artistically.

It seemed the more the album sold, getting to Number 1 on the US *Billboard* charts in January 1992, the more the band's sense of frustration at *Nevermind* for being so commercial would surface. To be there at that precise time and to know what eventually happened to Kurt is as surreal as it is heart-breaking. From the winter of 1991 to spring of 1994, here was a guy who, through heroin addiction and mental fragility, declined to the point where he took his own life. To be that sick, in so much pain and in that dark a place just seems impossible to begin to comprehend. We didn't know what was ahead of us then, but for that exact moment, the good times, to be there was exciting, thrilling and never boring.

If I had to pick a city from the tour I felt most at home in it would be Manchester. Maybe it was the people, the buzz, the distinctive light when it's in between rain showers, the tranquil glow of a sun trying hard to get out then giving up, leaving a distinct grey. It just had a good, familiar feel to it. We arrived at 2pm and Murray drove ourselves and Shonen Knife toward the Britannia Hotel, a listed building on Portland Street and a beautiful sight, to drop off our Japanese friends. We stayed at the cheaper sister hotel across the road, though it was still posh for us. When it came to getting decent hotels Murray used his tour managing experience to great effect. We'd be staying in expensive hotels at reduced rates. In fact we'd have, on some occasions in big cities, fantastic rooms normally held back by staff, to make a few quid on the side. Maybe I'm wrong and it was all above board. Surely it's better to have rooms used on a quiet Wednesday? But there was definitely something going on.

People complain about travelling but I love airports and hotels. I can sit for hours at an airport. Just watch the world go by and take out a notebook and see waves of humanity in all its chaotic, muddled glory. The drama when a flight is cancelled? Not for me, get me a strong coffee, some chocolate, my notebook and I'm at my happiest. Hotels on the other hand are just about sleaze and sex. I can smell sex when I walk into a hotel. I love to walk in and take a deep breath and fill my lungs with sin. Sit at the bar of any hotel and within 20 minutes you could write a year's worth of material for any generic soap opera. There's lust, avidity, spite, regret, nostalgia, revenge, guilt, heartache, joy, cruelty. There are misdemeanours from minor drug transactions to major credit card fraud, gambling, prostitution. All the elements of the human condition and the dreaded writing cliché 'the journey' are here; just open your eyes and observe. It's all going on, right there, unbeknown to most, like rats in the garden at night.

James was excited about arriving in Manchester; he'd been to the Hacienda a few times and seemed a fitting tour guide for Gordon and me. We visit a cool indoor clothes market called Affleck's Palace, full of alternative fashion and vintage gear. I almost buy a really cool 1970s leather jacket but it's too pricey. While we amble around a record shop called Eastern Bloc, we get that magical feeling of seeing our own record, the *Captain America* EP, in a record shop for the first time. Maybe it's the love of music, vinyl and history, knowing that however cool and laid-back everyone else seems about it, I was excited to be a part of vinyl history.

I didn't act nonchalantly about recording and producing a record and having it out there. You never know who is going to hear it. The reason we were on tour with Nirvana was because Kurt heard The Vaselines on a college-based radio show on a station called KAOS in Olympia. Stephen Pastel had given Beat Happening's Calvin Johnson some of their records and he played them on his radio show. Kurt lived in Olympia at the time – a cool, artistic, vibrant college town – and fell in love with them. So thanks Stephen, Calvin, Frances, Eugene, Charlie, James and Kurt. Sometimes your record ends up in a charity shop, other times someone cool hears it and loves it.

In Eastern Bloc, I pick up *Pebbles Vol. 1* and the guy wouldn't take anything off me when he heard we were the support act for Nirvana. I got his name on the list for the Academy show, which he seemed a bit too cool about for my liking. Then we went to The Dry Bar, cool as fuck at the time, not sure what it's like now but then it was owned by Factory and felt like a place in Berlin. That whole area around Oldham Street's a cool bit of Manchester. It had a really long bar, decent enough in 1991. We were being chatted up – well, I say chatted up, we just entered into a friendly conversation but you know what men are like – by two hot art students and a trainee hairdresser-turned-Croatian supermodel. She was about six foot tall and all angles – angular hair, angular arms and legs, even angular Ziggy Stardust-era make-up. They were into my psychedelic punk compilation; they were into my chat. That pattern was developing again. They were hanging on to my every word. People who wouldn't normally give me a second look were starting to find my company compelling and most pleasurable. It's not that I haven't had my moments and made some pretty girls laugh but between us, I think my 20-foot Access All Areas pass was definitely working. Suffice to say all three worked their way on to the guest list too.

We arrived back at the venue after drinking most of the afternoon. There's a photo taken by Nirvana soundman Craig Montgomery and I'm just back from the pub, eating dinner, sitting with Eugene banging on about how cool Manchester is and the cracking girls, and how we'd just seen our record in the shops. I commented sarcastically on how crap life was on the road, getting a laugh from those at the table. After dinner I head off with my bag and notebook to watch Nirvana soundcheck yet again. Thanks to sales from Kurt advertising Captain America's T-shirt, we were starting to enjoy a good night's kip in decent B&Bs and hotels on the tour. Murray had even negotiated some on-tour catering. Now we shared with Nirvana's caterers.

So now I had a drum tech even though I used Dave's kit,

roadies and on-tour catering. Is this really happening? Someone's setting up my kit, even though my kit's in the van as back up, and making my dinner? I've made it, Johnny! On-tour catering involves being fed, as the headline band does their soundcheck. I used to have indigestion gulping down food so I could sneak off and witness Nirvana work through a new song. Everyone else, apart from Gordon, seemed quite blasé about Nirvana soundchecking, but we loved watching them, the way it almost became trance-like, playing the same song, locking in to this cavernous bass and guitar line. Like actors, rehearsing and repeating lines, each performance sounded more textured. Time constraints, because of TV and radio performances as well as interviews, meant they had to write on the road and work out songs while soundchecking. So while they were writing, arranging, rehearsing and working through this song, their sound engineer, Craig Montgomery, was checking levels for that evening's show.

Soundchecks are normally sacrosanct occasions. Most bands like to do them with no one there except the crew, who are genuinely all too busy to give the band a second look. I used to use the soundcheck to write stuff, away from everyone else, and it meant seeing the band in an intimate setting. On one occasion I proved useful by spotting a mystery surrounding Dave's snare, and ran round and plugged in a loose lead into a microphone, much to tour manager Alex MacLeod's hilarity. He had just had his tea and was in a good mood. As each night passed, I became a fixture at the Nirvana soundchecks.

'Well?' Kurt would ask, smiling sarcastically.

'Dave's not fucking loud enough.'

'I love the way Scottish people curse. It's so *fucking* poetic.'

Between Ian Beveridge (road manager/monitors and sound engineer), Alex MacLeod (tour manager), Captain America and our crew (Murray, Willie and Michael) it was particularly Scottish and very graphic in terms of industrial language.

In Manchester, I was convinced I'd just had Captain America kicked off the tour. I had about six ideas in my head: themes, the colours, the atmosphere of the band working in an empty hall and how crazy it would be in a few hours. Nirvana seemed so close after finishing their soundcheck, chatting and laughing. Krist was looking at his amp, adjusting the settings. Kurt sat on the drum riser and lit a cigarette, then lit Dave's too. They – Kurt and Dave – were looking over in my direction then got up, ending the soundcheck.

By now I had two notebooks out, the main one and the small one. I always carried, and still do, a small pocket notebook to catch up on ideas. It's handy if a good idea swirls through your head but when loads of things occur at once, which is most times in my head, it's best to have something at hand to scribble down ideas to prompt and remind you, usually of themes, later on in the day. The idea is to do this when it's appropriate and not, in hindsight, when you're privileged to be seeing one of the world's hottest groups working through a new song.

The new song sounds familiar. I recognise it and check the set lists. It was played at Wolverhampton, then it was dropped from the set as the band tried to work on it and tidy it up each night at the soundcheck. I was so caught up in earnestly jotting my thoughts down in the diary, scribbling down key words to describe loads of things that were going on, about how the band were working through a great new song that sounds a bit like Joy Division. I was trying to describe the scene in front of me. How I could smell the electricity, that smell of new gels on hot lights and the dust, about how the bass and guitar were so loud and Dave was locked in to a great groove. About how happy and relaxed they seemed.

I was so lost in writing I didn't realise the band had finished the soundcheck and had left the stage. Now Kurt and Dave were walking angrily toward me. Suddenly I realised how bad this looked. It looked like I was stealing lyrics or writing down chord changes, like some twat. I shat myself. I thought I was going to have us kicked out. I must've looked so guilty. What was I supposed to say? 'Oh sorry, I know it looks like I'm writing everything down like lyrics and the chord changes but I'm not. It's my diary – I don't want anyone in the band to see me doing it. I'm intrigued by the way you use your time at soundchecks to write a new song, that's all.'

Kurt nodded to ask what I thought. I held the diary open with 'Joy Division' circled. Dave smiled, Kurt said, 'Cool.' They went off and I tried to find, as my hands still shook, a sentence with an exact verb and an appropriate noun. I think that might've been what they were laughing at on stage, trying to wind me up. That song, meanwhile, later became 'All Apologies' on *In Utero*.

It was remarkable to see the care and attention to detail Kurt and his guitar tech, Earnie Bailey, took every night at soundchecks, to get the sound just right. The story behind that live guitar sound has a surprisingly punk rock and homemade aspect to it. When you think of the image most associated with Nirvana's frontman, it's one of Kurt at his peak, in full throttle with his very distinctive left-handed style as he swoops and flails with his favourite guitar, a Fender Mustang. The stooped slight frame in brown or green cardigan, with an indie band's T-shirt underneath as he kicks on an effects pedal while his flowing blond hair swings on the downbeat. You'd imagine there has to be more magical levers than the Wizard of Oz and more knobs and wizardry than NASA's mission control.

My memory from being a few feet away most nights was how fragile and makeshift and taped-up his effects pedals were. There was a board at his feet that poor Earnie kept functioning. I know nothing about guitars or effects pedals. I'm told by friends who play that it's an impressive fact to know such things. I only know because I scribbled down what was lying there on the stage as I heard their guitar tech and Kurt in deep conversation about the pedals one night, then realised this might be worth checking out as it's the thing which gives them their sound. From then on, I watched Kurt's deft footwork in between his power chords. To see the effects pedals with wires hanging out, all taped-down and on black makeshift wooden boards with extension plugs and leads, made the new grunge messiah seem like a mad inventor or a radio ham.

Whatever he was doing it was working. He was very fussy about the effects pedals and always tweaking and changing the levels in between songs to get it just right. Whatever the makeshift effects system at his feet was doing, it made a creative, original and distinctive sound. I loved it, the punk DIY aspect of it, but I'd imagine it would irritate the millions of guitar heroes who would later try everything to copy his sound. He had spent a lot of time getting the sound right.

For those interested here's what equipment was there. There's an Electro-Harmonix Small Clone EchoFlanger. An EchoFlanger? That sounds like it should be in an S&M

dungeon. Anyway, when he wants the sound of garage rock and fuzzy-sounding punk 1960s stuff – the thing guitarists call 'distortion' – he uses a BOSS DS-1 Turbo Distortion pedal, which Kurt calls 'the Roland' if it's not working. As in 'Hey, my Roland needs fixing, it's fucked.' When I asked why he attacked his Marshall stack most nights, he said he only beat up the Marshall as it represented the ultimate in rock 'n' roll cliché, and that his true choice of amp is an old knackered Fender Twin Reverb that sounds distorted and muddy, which he loves because it can perforate eardrums. Earnie has to fix that constantly. He also uses Messa Boogie pre-amps, which might mean something to some people – I hope it helps.

Like Krist Novoselic, the musicianship and skill that Kurt would bring to the band was honed from his early love of music. Friends and family would comment on his ability to learn any song quickly by ear and work out the chords and middle-eights and have it learned in a matter of hours. He didn't do guitar books, scales and muso stuff, just worked out chords and their natural progressions by listening to music and copying what he heard. Just like The Beatles did when they worked out Chuck Berry and Buddy Holly songs, Kurt was doing the same with everything from Aerosmith to The Sex Pistols, always learning about shape, solos and arrangement. It was no surprise then that the whole band would work this way, learning a new song through careful repetition and slight tweaking at soundchecks.

I don't think they caught the same drama or intensity in the studio version of 'All Apologies'. I still preferred the vast *Nevermind* feel soundman Craig Montgomery brought to fruition when they played live. The version on *In Utero* isn't as poppy or commercial and loose. This, however, answers the brief. Big Black's Steve Albini was brought in as Kurt loved his work on The Pixies' *Surfer Rosa*. To give Kurt an idea of what Pachyderm Studios in Minnesota sounded like, Albini sent him *Rid of Me* by PJ Harvey, which he'd just worked on. The band's aim was simple. Let's make a record that isn't *Nevermind*. Albini is famed for making records sound ferociously raw, abrasive and live, so why was everyone so surprised when they delivered the album to the record company? I couldn't understand what the fuss was all about; it wasn't as if they had called up Stock, Aitken Waterman.

Like every fan I was nervously waiting for *In Utero*'s release. I remember thinking, *Good, on the first listen it's challenging, so I know it's going to have some longevity*. Nirvana should be congratulated on digging their heels in. It's difficult to take a stance with your record company and management and to have the balls to go into the studio with a producer as sonically abrasive as Albini, and deliver a record that isn't too easy but sells well. But it befitted iconoclasts who were 'spokespeople' for disenfranchised youth.

There is a dry, live feel on *In Utero*, all down to Albini's approach. He uses very few overdubs, the vocals are always much lower in the mix; he puts loads of pressure on the rhythm section and always tries to get the feeling that the group are playing together in the one room. Once in that situation, microphone positioning will capture what feels like a strained and taut quality. It also creates a raw and powerful fragility.

The band and producer were doing it their way. Like everything else with bands, producers, labels and management there's always a stand-off between creativity and business. The band rattled out the record in two weeks. All the basic tracks were recorded in days. They did overdubs, mixed it and *In Utero* was recorded. The total cost; $24,000. Steve Albini doesn't accept points as he thinks it's immoral against the artists and took a flat fee of $100,000.

It's interesting to note that the band wanted to change sound and felt the success of *Nevermind* warranted that option so they went out on a limb and took a stance. Once *In Utero* was recorded, Kurt started to have doubts about the sound of the finished album. It must've been a nightmare for Dave and Krist going through this process. Kurt was becoming more and more difficult, and openly admitted at the time that after insisting on the choice of producer, once he got home and listened to the Albini mix, he felt that there was something not quite right.

By the autumn of 1993, when *In Utero* was released, fans were becoming bored with the saga of this third studio album. From a distance, there was a feeling that the intrusions into Kurt's personal life, the arguments, the rumours and speculation over the making of the album, appeared to be doing more harm than good. The difficulty of getting the record they wanted into the shops almost took the band to the brink. The desire for a less commercial sounding record which they craved had been satisfied, but Kurt felt it wasn't right. So Scott Litt, famed for his production on R.E.M.'s breakthrough albums, *Document, Green, Out of Time* and *Automatic for the People*, was brought in to work on the singles 'Heart-Shaped Box' and 'All Apologies'. Yet despite Kurt's spiralling drug addiction, his paranoia with the tabloids and the pressure of getting the work out there, the band delivered a great album.

After the Manchester soundcheck, I head to the dressing

room trying to get up to speed on writing the diary. Ten minutes later, Krist and Kurt come in, and they see me in the corner working. Dave isn't there. Both acknowledge my presence and smile politely. No words are spoken. Kurt falls back on his chair and Krist stares at his shoes then the wall, and drinks his water. I am at the very centre of planet Nirvana. I put my pen down and close the diary. I feel guilty being there, as it's their space but feel if I do move or speak to say my goodbyes it will be worse if I break the silence. It's frenzied and manic in the outside world – they've just entered the Top Ten of the *Billboard* charts. For them, it's a rollercoaster of travel, live shows, writing new songs on the road, and dealing with the music press, from fanzines to mainstream newspapers and TV, all asking the same dumb questions. Here in an idle moment in the sanitised, more modern backstage area of Manchester Academy, Kurt and Krist seem deflated and jaded. There is a strange tension. Kurt is quiet, while Krist seems more thoughtful.

The pair's demeanour and appearance seems so fragile, such a contrast to the way things are going outside. I know I'm fortunate to be here at such a unique point as it goes ballistic for them, but I'm trying to work out what makes them tick. How can they keep ploughing on with such intensity when the normality of the scene is telling me there's no great mystery? No one has anything to say. Or if they have, it can wait a few minutes. Sometimes words aren't needed. Sometimes the silence says it all.

Finally, Kurt wraps his coat tight around his thin frame and slides down the sofa. He briefly closes his eyes, then opens them and looks at me, smiles a bit, a slight acknowledgment, then he stares beyond me toward the table, which is draped in the usual finery of fruits and beer and water. Krist has his long legs stretched out and drinks again from the bottle of water. He thoughtfully flips the lid through his fingers like a poker chip. He's staring like you do, when deep in thought.

There's a brittle quietness and I'm fearful for anyone who comes in to the dressing room right now. This is what it's like. If anyone with ambition to be in the best band on the planet wants to know what it does to you, this is it. Isolation, confusion, disbelief, tiredness, frustration and concern for putting on a good show for the fans. Hard work, fragmented with adrenalin rushes, tremendous excitement followed by exhaustive lows, and on the better days, moments like this, when you're left to ponder and try and take things in. It's alarming and almost distressing to think something as positive as a hit single can do this to people. They look so sad, depressed, disappointed and dejected at a point in their lives when they should be happy. Kurt breaks the silence and heads for the rider.

'Fuck it, I'm getting drunk.'

'Yeah,' Krist agrees. 'Yeah, where's the corkscrew?'

I applaud their stress management skills and share a beer with them. Looking back, that was exactly what they needed; to release the stress and pressure. As the doors open, I'm called to the front door as someone's asking for me. I'd spoken to Kevin Dolan, an old school pal and Sharron's cousin, a few weeks previously in the pub in Airdrie. He attended Manchester University and I said I'd put him on the guest list for the gig. In all the excitement I'd forgotten, but suffice to say he and his lovely girlfriend both got in. I get a shout from Eugene and within a minute we are on stage, very happy and relaxed and have completed an incident-free and tight set, as good as the night in Wolverhampton. Though tonight my mind kept thinking about what I had for dinner. The meal tonight was Guinness stew and I'd never thought you could have Guinness in stew. I kept thinking, *If I play rubbish, I could blame it on the stew.* '*Yeah, sorry guys, too much Guinness stew you know, I was all over the place.*'

The Guinness didn't affect my playing and we were, despite my daydreaming, really confident on stage too. But as always when we were in the mood and playing well, hardly anyone was in the venue. It was always the way. When we were brilliant, no one was there and when we weren't, like Newcastle, everyone was. Like the scene in *Lost in Translation* when Bill Murray hits the perfect golf shot and looks around to see if anyone else has witnessed it. By the time we were finishing, though, the venue was filling up, and by the end of the set there were a few converts. As I left the stage, the girls from The Dry Bar were waving at me and whooping. Whooping in a half-empty venue has a certain embarrassing irony and pathos. It does sound like people, no matter how well-intentioned, are taking the piss. I waved but rushed off stage to meet Dave.

'Great set, Andy.'

'Thanks, Dave. The monitors on stage are brilliant,' I tell him as we walk back to the dressing room, 'Everything is clear as a bell.'

'You guys rocked tonight. Really confident, James and Andy... bang on the money.' Krist had his arm round me.

Kurt, though, was nowhere to be seen. We later found out that he got drunk watching us, got over-excited and then got into a fight with a bouncer who didn't know who he was and threw him out of the venue. I was so happy when I heard that. Later that evening in the hotel bar, James said to me, 'You know it's bad when you're on tour with Nirvana, you're on stage and you just don't want to be there.' Fucking hell. Earlier that night, one of the best rhythm sections in the last 30 years had paid him a massive compliment.

So for Nirvana it's another city and another gig. I don't know where they get the energy from. It can't all be adrenalin. Surely the body can only keep pulling so much from the well. The Americans call it epinephrine, a hormone from the adrenal gland in the kidney (from *nephros*, the Greek for kidney). That would be a useless fact if it didn't sound like the name of about four Nirvana songs or some never-made rarities and B-side compilation, what with Kurt being so enthused with organs, fluids and bodily functions. Whatever the source, they still dig deep and deliver for the fans, remembering each night that feeling they had when they too were fans and went to see their favourite band. They play another consistently great show in Manchester Academy, but tonight's show has a strange start. It may have been something as simple as the on-stage monitors being bang on but they also came on stage very relaxed and there was a slight change. I'm sitting by the drums with a few beers, one for Dave if he fancies it. Nice of me, eh? It is his beer after all. I look up and instead of Dave, see Kurt sitting behind the drums, Krist playing guitar and Dave singing.

'You're not Dave!'

'Hey, fella,' says Kurt. 'Great place you got here.'

I open a can of beer, pour it into a plastic glass filled with ice and offer it to the new drummer. So far on tour I'd rarely witnessed Kurt take a drink, never mind see him fairly drunk. He had a swig of lager but we should've been getting him a coffee.

'Thanks, ND.'

He takes another few sips and starts playing. The band launches into a shambolic jam. Eventually Kurt gets up, hands me the beer back, I quickly give him a plastic glass of water, hoping it might help sober him up. He winks, they switch back to familiar mode. Normal service is resumed and they launch into yet another staggering version of 'Drain You'.

The contrast from the opening shambolic jam to the power of the band when they start properly gets the crowd going. As ever, the crowd responded like they do every single night. The highlight for me, though, was 'Polly'. By far the most haunting and intense song on *Nevermind* and live tonight was incredible. The song's well-publicised and uncomfortable subject matter is clear as Kurt adopts a slightly more folkish approach. Most people know that it's based on a true story; an abductor raped and tortured his victim with razors and a blowtorch. In Kurt's version of events, in the song's narrative at least, she wins over the rapist's trust by flirting with him before managing to escape.

The song is like a modern melodramatic contemporary short story sung in a disaffected Woody Guthrie style. It was one of Kurt's earliest compositions, having been called at various times 'Hitchhiker' and then 'Cracker'. Originally written in 1988, Kurt felt it didn't fit with the rest of *Bleach* and it was left off though not forgotten. It was recorded in 1990 at the second Sub Pop sessions in Wisconsin, a year before the main May/June 1991 *Nevermind* sessions. The song was also performed in a fast powerful version called '(New Wave) Polly'.

As for us, we were just one day off the last night of the tour and somewhat ironically had started to find our feet musically. It just seems to be the way life in a band is. When things come together and start to click, you all feel and sense the project's really beginning to happen, it always goes wrong. People are responding kindly and enthusiastically to your band. Everyone individually is raising their game. You're part of a powerful, tight, indie band. After all the shite, the vans breaking down, going on stage pished, thinking you're on a cruise ship, you're finally becoming focused and everyone pulls together, and gets through. You dig deep, start to see and feel a positive groundswell and change of opinion. Then, just when there's that bit of clarity and purpose, James says he's leaving.

Even though I knew Gordon from Airdrie, I had grown close to James and loved being in the band with him. Sometimes it was volatile but that added to the tension and when he was in the mood, he had the ability to really drive the band along. As a drummer, it was brilliant for me to lock in and keep that momentum going.

After the show I was pissed off and just wanted away to get some work done, catch up with everything that had happened in case I forgot anything. I also wanted to have a bath and get a decent sleep in my posh hotel room. I left shortly after Nirvana came off stage and was driven back to the hotel by Murray for about 10.40. Since he had finished early, Murray was desperate to have a few pints and a chat so we arranged to meet in the hotel bar in ten minutes. I did a quick recap of the gig in my notebook – I knew because of the way Nirvana started with Kurt on drums that I had to get that down.

We discussed how good the gig was and Murray said it was one of the best shows he'd heard us playing. He also advised me to try and stop hitting the drums so hard and make my wrists do the work. I suggested my wrists were fine with the amount of drink I was consuming and raised my wrist to show an empty glass but I got them in. At the bar these two women, one in particular, were looking over and they struck up a conversation. The more drunk of the two said, 'We were just thinking, Wednesday night, rainy Manchester hotel, you must think we're a couple of old scrubbers.' They were in hysterics. The less-drunk one had short, cool hair and a voluptuous shape, but wore huge specs like Dennis Taylor. If she took off her glasses and teased her hair into a punk bob, she would have a look of Béatrice Dalle about her, with that pouting horniness and vulnerability in equal measure. That's if you can imagine Dalle as a frumpy sales rep living in a modern semi-detached bungalow outside Salford. She said, 'No, we're account managers on a conference.'

'Oh, that sounds a whole lot better.'

The more sober one laughed. The drunk one was intrigued by my exotic accent.

'Oh, what a lovely accent.'

'Thanks.' What a weird thing to say. We were hardly in a bar in a small Peruvian village at the foot of the Andes. It was Manchester, for fuck's sake. It was full of Scots.

I could tell the two were interested but I couldn't be arsed with all the drunken small talk, and headed back to the table and started chatting about the tour with Murray. Maybe I took him for granted, with all the shit he had to do, but he was being paid for doing the tour managing, the sound and the driving. The set-up was that Murray drove the band in a small mini-bus ten-seater carrier, while Michael and Willie travelled with the gear in a hired van. He was telling me about his life in Dundee working in Fat Sams and now he was doing this full-time. While he was speaking, Béatrice Dalle had taken her glasses off. She kept on smiling over from the bar. Then James arrived and told Murray that he wanted to leave the band. Gordon arrived and slowly the rest of the gang arrived, and then half the planet seemed to arrive.

It looked like another long session was starting but I wanted a bath and peace to catch up before everything in my head turned to mush. As our table and our corner got busier and spread out, I said my goodbyes and looked over to Béatrice and her pal to say goodbye but they'd gone. Probably just as well. I headed to the lift but when I got out, there they were, struggling to gain access to their room, which was directly across from mine. The less drunk one, Jenny, was trying to help her friend, Faith, into the room. She had already left some of her conference buffet on the carpet; the beige coloured pile now had a decadent Jackson Pollock-styled vomit pattern. How did I know their names? By now they had written each other's names on their foreheads in lipstick, which detracted from their overall appeal even more, it has to be said. Both looked smaller and younger with their heels off. Then Faith leaned against the wall and began to very slowly slide down it, like a cartoon drunk, before conking out.

'Do you need a hand there?'

'Oh hi! Eh, Faith here has had a few too many.'

'And you're completely sober.'

'I stopped hours ago – I'm driving first thing.' Fuck sake, remind me to stay away from her if we see her driving for London.

I helped carry Faith to their room and laid her on the bed

in the recovery position. As I left, Jenny was sitting on the toilet, peeing – quite the thing.

'Fancy a nightcap, what's your name?'

'What's-his-name is knackered. Goodnight, Jenny.'

'Oh, you're a sweetheart – and look, we're neighbours!!!'

I got to my room, scribbled some main points down in the diary, and started running the bath slowly. Ten minutes later I lowered myself into that sheer joyful exaltation of water just slightly too hot, slowly acclimatising myself. Just as I lowered in and sunk into perfection, someone rattled at the door.

'Fuck!!!'

The moment truly ruined. I had to get out, leaving wet footprints everywhere, and I opened it, expecting Gordon to have forgotten his key but it was Jenny, in a black thick winter coat, in heels, a red bra heaving under the forces of gravity, red panties, fresh make-up, not wearing her specs, with a small bottle of champagne and a huge joint.

'Right duck, you're not fucking me, no way. Here's my thing, I love wanking off in hotel rooms with strangers watching me. You got a light?'

'Knock yourself out.'

'Oh look, bubble marks, did I disturb your bath? Oh, I hate when you have a bath and the phone goes. Oh, you smell lovely and clean.'

'I'm going back in.'

'Oh yes please, you do that. You know, it's just my thing. No wanking, sucking or fucking?'

'Whatever floats your boat. I thought you were up early and driving in the morning?'

'No lighter, love?'

'It's a hotel room, there'll be matches somewhere.'

She was nice enough but talked too much. Fucking incessantly. Her thing was to have a wank in hotel rooms. Well, we live in enlightened times, it's the 1990s. It's not as if men haven't whacked one off in a hotel room. In fact the thought had crossed my mind to grab the unnameable as I ran the bath only to be stopped, ironically, by someone wanting to have one in front of me. She pulled her chair closer, found a light from somewhere, lit up and cracked open the mini bottle of champagne. While still talking, she went to work.

'Most men don't obey the rules, you're a good boy, nice and clean.' Weird noises. The most difficult thing to do at that moment was to not start laughing.

'You got a sweetheart back home?'

She made it sound as though I was in the Second World War helping to liberate Paris from the Nazis. My brain was cool with her rules but another part of my body didn't seem to have any control over the etiquette of the situation. I slid down into the bath so the bubbles would hide what was going on, but every so often there would be a twitch and she'd see what was going on. She pushed the chair closer to the bath and stared at what was under the water. It was bobbing and weaving, wondering whether it was coming or going.

'Don't touch it!' Jenny shouted. I obeyed. She was a sales rep and delighted in telling me she was recently separated and hadn't been near a man for seven months because she loved making money more than she loved her now ex-husband, and she had married too young anyway, no kids, just loved her career. Didn't like cock but loved wanking and making her own money. She might be gay, wasn't sure yet; she fancied Faith but she fancied me. I was touched. She was off cock but liked the idea of it. All in one big long sentence without breathing. I was in conversation, wait, no I'm not, a conversation involves two or more people. *You're the only one talking.* I was being spoken at, she proudly informed me, by the North West's salesperson of the year. She seemed so much older than her 27. Quite mature and obviously successful, she had a three-grand Patek Philippe watch, which she noticed I was looking at and informed me she had received it for being salesperson of the year, last year.

Even while smoking and drinking her champagne she still managed to keep on chattering and do her thing. How did she manage to breathe? I know I'm lucky, as I meander through life and all this shit, good, bad and strange seems to happen to me. I was looking at a stranger who was making all these weird noises, it was turning me on as she upped gears and began wanking herself into a coma but while she was doing it, she was talking all the time. She was speaking about the route she'd be taking as the traffic is terrible at that particular junction at that time in the morning. You can be there for 20 minutes and only move 20 feet, the kind of chat that people who drive must love.

Soon, though, she prattled on so much it was becoming painful. She was lovely-looking and a great shape but she was just so fucking boring and I had entered into the rules and couldn't do anything. It got so bad I slid under the water to get away from her talking. Even as I was doing this I could still hear her droning on incessantly, now about work and one of her bosses who won't promote women as he feels threatened. No wonder. I came up for air and she was still wanking off while talking about how in a day she out-sells her male colleagues twice over. I slid under the water again and started to count to see how long I could hold my breath for. The best way to describe her would be to imagine the two most boring bastards you know, then merge them into one and you have something close to how boring poor Jenny was. No wonder her husband left her. At one point, I never spoke for about 20 minutes and she never stopped. By this time my cock had given up on her through sheer boredom, too, and actually looked like it had hibernated for the winter doing its best impersonation of a tortoise eating a Walnut Whip, shaking its head at me on its way back in and asking for some Tennent's Super Lager.

I knew I was here for a while so I used my left foot to turn on the hot tap. Then I started laughing really hysterically. It was like listening to Vera Duckworth having a wank: 'Oh duck, oh yes!' What the fuck is happening in my life? Why am I here in Manchester in a huge hot bath with the North West's saleswomen of the year rubbing her fanny like a magic lantern and now wailing like a banshee. When I see that advert on TV now, with Churchill the dog saying 'Oh yes', I'm reminded of her in heated rapture but perversely she was still talking about directions on the route she'd be taking tomorrow. That was her hardcore stuff, roads and directions. Is there such a thing as traffic porn?

It's strange how you spend your adolescent life imagining this kind of thing happening and when it does you act as if it's an everyday occurrence and you can afford to be fussy. Now, if the chance came, we'd be breaking her rules in the blink of an eye because we get old. We become less attractive and less interesting. We don't get that moment back.

She finished off the job but it took her some time. I tried to keep my face straight as she continued with the crazy noises. She stayed for about 45 minutes and as I dried off, I topped up the bath with some bubble stuff and she jumped in. Leaving shiny and clean, and not speaking for 30 seconds she seemed really attractive again. As she left, she asked if I'd mind knocking her up in the morning. Woman are magic, especially when they're quiet and clean.

A few minutes later, as I tidied up, Gordon came in. He looked at the floor and the soapy wet footmarks across the carpet and then looked very suspiciously at me.

'What?'

'What's been going on in here?'

'If I told you, you'd never believe me.'

'Someone's been smoking in here.'

'You are.' He looked down, squinting at a lit Silk Cut.

'Oh, so I am.'

In 1991, Nirvana's attitudes, especially on the treatment of women, were similar to those of bands like Sonic Youth and Beat Happening. Feminism was good, and groupies and hedonism clichéd and uncool. The tour was so evangelical that if there were any conquests, like in my diary, they'd have to be hidden as it wasn't cool to treat women as objects. Even dirty ones who begged you to treat them like an object and do all kinds of dirty stuff that dirty girls want you to do to them so they can feel like an object. It was all about loving the ones we were with and treating them with respect, or at least trying to. So there were no salacious backstage antics or hedonistic orgies. No, basically we got pished and Nirvana found the strength to get to the next venue to make the next show for the fans.

CHAPTER 15

DRUMMING WITH DAVE, T-SHIRTS, NIRVANA'S TOUR BUS AND TOAST

LONDON KILBURN NATIONAL, 5 December 1991

DRAIN YOU
ANEURYSM
SCHOOL
FLOYD THE BARBER
SMELLS LIKE TEEN SPIRIT
ABOUT A GIRL
POLLY
L'AMOUR EST UN OISEAU REBELLE (CARMEN)
SLIVER
LITHIUM
BREED
BEEN A SON
NEGATIVE CREEP
ON A PLAIN
BLEW

MOLLY'S LIPS (FEAT KELLY AND BOLLEN)
TERRITORIAL PISSINGS

We arrive in North-West London with plenty of time to spare before the gig. I go for a quick stroll down Kilburn High Road. I always like going for a wander, to look for the local record shops wherever I travel, but even this brief walk was a magnificent multicultural education. Afro-Caribbean and Irish families live side by side with a warmth borne out of hardship and mutual respect but even the food stores and newspaper shops catered for people from Somalia, Pakistan, India and Bangladesh.

On return, everyone seems excited. We have reached the end of the UK tour. Everyone is demob happy, Kurt especially, asking our roadies Willie and Michael to dress in white boiler suits and wear mad professor glasses, and encouraging them to walk on stage intermittently during the set, with yellow and orange feather dusters to clean the microphones to make them sound better.

There is a feeling of happiness, fun and madcap zaniness. Alex MacLeod jumps into the dressing room struggling with a bucket full of water and throws it toward Gordon and me. It was all planned. Someone took a photo showing me in an unflattering camp-faced squeal at what I could see coming. Considering my size, I managed to avoid it quite skilfully, only to realise the bucket was empty. I later hug and kiss the sweetest band of all time, Shonen Knife, and they write 'Andy Bollen' for me in Japanese. Or at least I think that's what they've written. As I still marvel at the incredible neatness of their handwriting, they thank me for protecting them. Kurt shouts me over.

'Andy, why can't I spend this money down here?' He's holding a Scottish one pound note and looks confused.

'Not sure, most of the shopkeepers down here don't even know Scotland exists.'

'It's the UK, right?'

'It is indeed. In fact you're right: it's wrong. I'm just used to it. Normally it's with bigger notes, they just won't touch them.'

'But when we stopped at a service station yesterday, I bought some gum and cigarette papers, they wouldn't take the 20 as it was Scottish.'

'Sometimes if you're not spending enough they'll say, "Got nuffing smaller, mate?"'

'"Got nuffing smaller, matey."' He tried to copy me doing a bad Cockney. 'No, it was because it was Scottish. I found change and threw it at him in a hissy fit 'cos I am a rock star now.'

'Did he know you?'

'No,' he laughed. 'I don't think he fitted our demographic.'

'I swapped English for Scottish with Alex. If I have to pay taxes, can I pay in Scottish money? Get your camera out, Andy,' Kurt suggested, before lighting a cigarette, smiling that mischievous smile and had me take a photo as he gestured to burn the Scottish note. 'It's fucking useless anyway, right?'

'When you came into Scotland with English money did you have any problems?' I asked.

'No fucking problems in Scotland, man, but Scotland's a cool place.'

'We'll take anyone's money.'

We played a blistering, confident set but with a mixture of elation and sadness at James, who told us he'd play the remaining gigs at the Rough Trade shop and the sold-out gig at the Camden Underworld but was then leaving the band. When I talk it through with him, I'm not surprised as out of us all, he's the most cynical about the Captain America project. I make a point of enjoying the gig and locking in with James at Kilburn. The sound on stage is incredible, one of the best of the tour.

I was hopeful that once we were back in Glasgow and things calmed down that James would come round again. But to be fair to him, he never did and stuck to his decision.

Krist was sitting writing Nirvana's set list for that night. It was hilarious watching him pretending to sniff the black magic marker and get the set list written down. It was also unusual as Dave normally wrote out the set lists. Afterwards, I checked the list to remind me of the show, as though Nirvana always went on stage with an organised set list, it was usually rearranged slightly. Kurt would judge the crowd, gauging how receptive they were and adjusting the set accordingly.

I'm in the middle of the crowd. I need to get this right. I need to feel it, sense it, digest and take this in. It's my last night; I need to be part of it. I'm looking around at the legions, all in grunge uniform. The heat, the power, a small framed, stooping, pale, left-handed guitarist squeals out 24 years' worth of psychoanalysis and vents his spleen to a crowd so caught up in the overall event that they don't care about the singer's shit, just how it all sounds. Imagine a huge moth asleep on a cold light bulb. Then the light is switched on. Seeing Nirvana is like a moth on speed inside a lampshade. The sound washing over like a stereo tsunami and a hurricane, bouncing off the four walls and drowning the audience, all so sick of bullshit, in a new-wave postmodern wall of sound. Fuck grace and brushstrokes, just wash us free of this apathy. The singer dives into the crowd. Gets back on stage, and continues the set. I don't know what the three of them are doing up there but it has got this cynical, opinionated pop fan transfixed. I keep saying it but this reminds me of a Killing Joke gig: powerful, celebratory, exciting, hypnotic and visceral.

At the core the singer isn't happy. There's something bleak about the soundtrack, yet something uplifting and truthful about it. Nirvana deliver the manifesto: say no to homophobia, no to sexism, no to racism. Fuck the corporate machine. They want to share. They don't feel special. Punk at its most altruistic; there's the repetition of the Dead Kennedys, the simplicity of the Ramones. I get it. But then there's a deluge of everything I love in music: loud guitars, drums, bass, punk rock, indie sensibility and great pop songs; truth and honesty.

Having nearly had my head kicked off by stage divers, I quickly make my way to our dressing room for some beer and catch the eye of music journalist Everett True, hand him a lager and head backstage to sit in my usual place at the side of the kit. I take my camera out and try to take some photos of Dave and then Willie and Michael as they walk on stage to dust Kurt's mic. Most of the photos didn't work out. One of my favourites is a grainy image of Kurt, with his left hand straightening the mic stand, as he addresses the faithful. You can see the fans look up at him, in his cardigan, and from their vantage point they are wide-eyed, hanging on his every word. From my point of view I see a stooping, unsure thin little guy.

I like it as it reminds me of the place I spent the majority of the tour, looking out at Kurt. As I open my beer to settle down beside Dave for the last time, I try to take that in too. Watching Dave Grohl drumming at such close proximity, how lucky am I?

Michael and Willie wander on stage again with their dusters. The crowd still don't get it. Kurt plays it straight, acting deadpan to the crowd, but when he turns around he thinks it's hilarious. Dave drives the band on. He is totally focused and powerful. He looks over at me nodding and smiling, and smiles back while he batters the kit into submission, taking the dynamic up and down and coursing the good ship Nirvana through another show. I leave Dave and stand beside Eugene as Nirvana come off to a rapturous ovation. Eugene offers me one of his cans, from Nirvana's supply. The band return and within seconds they launch into a version of 'Molly's Lips'. Dave signals for us both to come on stage. I look at Eugene.

'You're scared too.' He's thinking about it.

'You fancy it, Andy?'

I nod. 'Aye.'

Within seconds we both run on stage to Nirvana's delight; Eugene is dancing and throwing himself around, trying to do his trademark handstands which turn into drunken forward rolls. I jump on to the riser and Dave nods, smiling as I pick up two of his sticks, careful not to grab the sides that give the poisoned splinters, even though I'm pished.

I try to keep up with Dave, who is playing at an alarming rate. I stand to his right and play the floor tom of his kit, hoping not to put him off. You really shouldn't play drums when drunk, honestly. But, despite all the distractions, I make it over the finishing line, just. So, on 5 December 1991, I played drums with Dave Grohl on stage at a Nirvana gig in Kilburn. All in all, a great day and everyone for once truly happy. Our Nirvana tour is over.

Nirvana's set tonight is up there in terms of energy. The goofball *Carmen* jam, 'L'Amour Est Un Oiseau Rebelle' happened around mid-set, eight songs in. After the small interlude they ignite the place with a run of 'Sliver', 'Lithium', 'Breed', 'Been A Son' and 'Negative Creep'. All knockout blows. Say what you want about Nirvana, they know how to end a set. After Eugene and I join in with 'Molly's Lips', they end with 'Territorial Pissings'.

By this point, Kurt's guitar is literally in bits and giving the kids what they want. Tonight the equipment is attacked then it becomes GBH, then destruction and carnage. The crowd go nuts. Dave gets up from behind his kit and takes the drums with him. He physically picks up the bass drum and places it over his head; the high-tom is still attached. The snare rolls from the drum riser, caught in a mesh of cymbals, stands and mic leads. Kurt then rattles his guitar off the drum as it's balanced over Dave's head. The busiest guy on the tour is Earnie, the guitar tech.

I get the feeling, garnered from their previous live shows, that some of the fans are just here to see Nirvana trash their gear. Don't get me wrong, it can be viewed existentially as some form of hardcore punk and an artistic statement. I don't like seeing them trash their gear and breaking equipment. I don't see it as the ultimate in rock 'n' roll cliché, I see despair, angst and desperation and above all, an anger and frustration at the situation they're in. For the band the destruction of the gear was as much about saying, 'OK, that's it, show's over'. You have no idea unless you were there how much damage they did. Of course there are far easier ways to end a show, like 'Thanks for coming, goodnight!' but this is the real punk rock side of Nirvana – not the glittery, shiny 'Smells Like Teen Spirit' and MTV image, but the explosive, impulsive, can't take your eyes off, impossible to ignore, fuck-you Nirvana.

I suppose it's the last night of the tour and there'll be time to fix things. I think the audience see it as part of the fun; I am worried. After amps and drums and guitars splintered and cracked, the stage looks like a scene from an electrical musical murder show: *CSI: Rock Carnage*.

The show and the tour, for us at least, is over. For Nirvana, in terms of promotion, it's job done. 'Smells Like Teen Spirit' is in the Top 10 and as well as an onslaught in the music press and radio, there are memorable TV performances in between the sold-out shows. The appearances on *The Word, Top of the Pops* and *Tonight with Jonathan Ross* have subsequently all passed into the legendary status of TV folklore.

This is just the UK leg of the European tour. The same momentum was picking up across the rest of Europe. Kurt has jumped from indie fanzine hero of the underground to classic tabloid material and the music press are eulogising *Nevermind* and the tour as one of the most significant moments in the UK music scene since The Sex Pistols.

I suppose coming off stage with Nirvana is cool enough but when Krist walked in seconds later with two bottles of champagne and a gift for everyone in a big brown box, things couldn't get much better. The band had a special tour T-shirt made, a limited edition run made up for all the people on tour, and flowers and Ferrero Rocher for Shonen Knife.

I suggest we all put on our Nirvana T-shirts for one big picture, a team line-up, which I'm not in. The photos are taken on the Kodak Instamatic 92. Nirvana, their crew, Captain America, our crew, Shonen Knife, Dave Barker of Paperhouse all hang around. A few years later, while visiting my friend John 'Sherry' Sheridan, who is working at Great Ormond Street, I went for a walk and saw signs for a record fair at the TUC building on Great Russell Street. While there, around six different people approached me and asked about my T-shirt. One in particular asked if I was part of the tour. I explained I was in one of the support bands. He asked if I'd just slept in it and I said yes. He revealed he worked for the company who made them; they were a limited edition run of about 20 and would probably be worth thousands. I still have mine lying around somewhere – it's good for doublechecking the tour dates.

It's a great atmosphere after the Kilburn show; the beers are going down well with Krist's champers. As we all loiter around the stairs before heading to a free bar across the road, as we are all together, all the crew, both ours and Nirvana's, it occurs to me I should say a few words about Shonen Knife and Nirvana and their crew, but I'm too shy and don't say anything, just lead a round of applause and a wolf whistle. Everyone is so happy. A perfect moment, the last time we are all together.

Across the road in the bar I start chatting with a pony-tailed guy called Ian, who introduces me to his wife, J'aimee. I marvel at the amount of hair both have and the colour of

J'aimee's eyes. We speak about the gig we're playing at Camden Underworld the next evening and I invite them on the guest list.

From the photos I have, it's interesting to see how happy, healthy and content Kurt is. In the ones taken in the dressing room, he looks alive and full of the joys and is smiling. Subsequent publications have focused on his heroin addiction and his ill health and the *Nevermind* Tour of 1991 is generally given what is in my opinion an insufficient couple of pages in the band's history. Kurt is often described as being incapacitated by pain in London leading to the subsequent cancellation of six Scandinavian dates. Of course he may have been on an extreme painkiller but if you're going to make dramatic sweeping claims, have the decency to be there.

Kurt and Courtney Love are spending the time apart by sending really darkly funny faxes to each other. He shows us one he's particularly proud of and as we know by now, Kurt has a very dark sense of humour but Courtney is his match: she is far more literate, better read and much funnier. They seem genuinely into this (love, not rude faxes). However, in my opinion it is noticeable that when Courtney's around, there seems to be a different atmosphere and the Nirvana people divide into two camps, the Kurt and Courtney group and the rest. It hasn't happened much as Hole are touring and Courtney's only been around a few times. That's the third time I've been sitting around in a backstage area in her company.

When I first met Courtney she was touring with Mudhoney and she was more famous than Kurt. Now Kurt is more famous than her. He could sit back and watch her demolish anyone who fancied a verbal fight. On one of the occasions when she was in town, spirits were high, and I heard her argue with four or five guests. I didn't know who they were, maybe journalists or guests of the record company, having a beer in the dressing room and arguing about music. It all started highbrow and ended in a debate about, of all things, the Bay City Rollers and how big they'd be if they were American. Much bigger than Cheap Trick. She knew her subject. What is it about Kurt and Courtney and the Bay City Rollers? As the debate got louder and louder I was one of the few who laughed and nodded from under my biker's jacket, on back to front, like a cover, in case I got a chance to dose off. Like a big sister, she ruffled my hair as she left the dressing room, knowing I was on her side.

Meanwhile back at the end of tour proceedings, after we leave the pub, I find myself on Nirvana's tour bus as we head for a club called Syndrome. On the way there, maybe because of the champagne or the free beer, I was upset and had a dose of the drunken emotional shit that seems to come with the Scottish genes. Nirvana must've thought we were basket cases. As the tour was ending, I was in bits.

Maybe it was the accumulation of hopes, dreams and two weeks of solid drinking but it was also that James was leaving. I got on well with him and sensed my position in the group was weakened without him in my corner. He was also a great, instinctive bass player. At the heart of this chaos lay a sensitivity which was hard to dislike and out of everyone in the band, James is the one that I still keep in touch with. He helped me out on early demos with Boomerang along with Murray Webster and the engineers and everyone around couldn't believe how intuitive and creative a bass player he was. I'd say in Captain America he was a powerful bass player and commanding presence: a presence like Vesuvius is to the natives of Naples.

I knew it was ending, I knew then it was special. Krist sat beside me. 'It's just messing about in bands, Andy. You're too smart to take all this shit too seriously.' Then he put his arm around me as we drove through London. Krist made me feel ten feet tall.

'This fucking bus is a horrendous colour!' It being a melted chocolate shade of brown shit. 'Who the fuck allowed the saviours of rock 'n' roll to drive around in this jobby-mobile?'

'What the fuck is a jobby?' Kurt asked. (For the uninitiated, a 'jobby' is a Scots word for a shit, a turd, or a crap or all of the above.) It was even funnier when Kurt deliberately pronounced it in a thick Scottish brogue, mocking me saying it like 'jaw-bay'.

'I've grown to love it so,' mocked Kurt, looking out the window and flipping the bird to people outside. 'Can people definitely not see me from outside?'

As I left their tour bus I made a point of saying something and if I remember rightly, they were the last words I ever said to Kurt.

'Thanks for asking us on tour. It's been amazing.'

'Thanks for coming with us; keep working the diary, man.'

I could never dream looking back that those would indeed be the last words I'd speak to Kurt or him to me, but sadly they were. At that point he seemed happy after the Kilburn show, and they all were. He looked tired but also on top of his game and I clearly remember him mingling, signing autographs in a slightly embarrassed way, and shaking hands with people in the club. He accepted demos and records from them too. He was always happy to speak to the true indie fans.

As we all ambled into the club, I had a second wind and noticed once again that, with Krist's arm around my shoulder and Kurt on the other side, I seemed to become really interesting and more attractive to girls and even to loads of navel-gazing boys. When the rarefied atmosphere of the club got a bit much I headed out for some air. There was no one around so I took out my small notebook and wrote down some prompts for later. I knew I was drunk so scribbled down, *'Played on stage with Dave, T-shirts, Nirvana tour bus and club called Syndrome.'*

A girl with a cool, short, feathered bob approached. I know, at this point, the more observant amongst you will be thinking just about all these women are punky and wearing fishnets and no doubt looking for mad sex. Well, not all of them were like that; sometimes we were just kindred spirits. It was like that in 1991. The gigs still included the fringes of the punk scene, those who were into Mudhoney, garage bands and The Cramps. People were friendlier and less selfish and you could, by and large, connect really quickly as you felt you were both on a shared path and not like everyone else. (Though while I'm here, can I just salute the fishnet-wearing punk and all she stands for?)

The girl had beautiful white teeth and luscious lips and was so stylish. She was intelligent and very funny and had this amazing mix of sexuality and vulnerability. I know her name and what she does now but won't embarrass her. I wonder if she remembers me? She better had.

'Just as well you're writing that down, you probably won't

remember in the morning. What was that like, playing on stage with Nirvana?'

'Weird. You like them?'

She put a silly face on as if to say, 'Of course, what a daft question.'

'You want to meet them?'

'No, I'm off home. I'm only five minutes away and some of us are working in the morning. You better get back in, it's freezing out here but thanks again. That was nice of you.'

Then she looked at me, smiled and then said the daftest yet sweetest thing I'd heard on the whole tour: 'You fancy a bit of toast?'

'Seriously? I'd love a fucking bit of toast. But I could be a mad axeman...'

'You're too sweet-natured and gormless-looking to be an axe murderer. Come on, that's my taxi. And it's just toast – I do need to be up for work.'

She laughed a bit nervously as if realising what she'd just done. We were at her flat in minutes and as if to try and make it clear she was safe, I said I was seeing someone and wouldn't cheat on her, no matter how easy it would be to get away with it. She smiled and started making coffee and the best toast I'd tasted in months. We chatted and laughed and time flew by.

She said, 'Don't take this the wrong way but I'm getting into my pyjamas.'

While she was gone I checked her bookcase. It was full of the usual stuff: *Ulysses* by James Joyce, dear old Leopold Bloom, walking through Dublin. As I sit in a gorgeous stranger's house, I'm like Stephen Dedalus, the guy in *Ulysses* who is based on Telemachus, who in Greek mythology was the son of Penelope and Odysseus in Homer's *Odyssey*, far from battle in the Trojan Wars. I realise my brain is like a scarred battlefield that can't switch off. Then I spot Voltaire's *Candide*, with all that Leibnizian optimism, Huxley's *Brave New World* and Orwell's *1984*, which I hadn't read. *Of Mice and Men* and *The Grapes of Wrath* by Steinbeck, two crackers I had read. Nathaniel Hawthorne's *The Scarlet Letter*, which I'd never read and only knew that it had been banned. Heller's *Catch-22*, which I had started trying to read about seven times but became too confused with the number of characters. *The Crucible* by Arthur Miller and *Uncle Tom's Cabin* by Harriet Beecher Stowe, the clichéd *Catcher in the Rye* by J.D. Salinger, and *Slaughterhouse-Five* by Kurt Vonnegut, which I hadn't read either but everyone always went on about how good a read it was.

It always puts me off if everyone tells me I should read something. Worse still, if movies become a cultural phenomenon like *Star Wars* – I don't want to be like people who love *Star Wars*. I've never seen it. I've never read Tolkien, never seen any of the movies or read the books; it doesn't make me better but it makes me unlike you. This is what happens when you treat 'I'm Not Like Everybody Else' by The Kinks as a mission statement, not a great pop song.

She came in all snug in a housecoat and pyjamas and cuddled into me as if we'd known each other for years, and her clean smell wasted everything and gave me this urge to fuck her but the dynamic had changed. I tried to think about the books again. Then it occurred to me, they all had something in common: they'd all been banned. I must've still been drunk because I remember at one point thinking if she could pack up and leave her exciting job in the throbbing metropolis and come back to Airdrie, who knows? She could've worked in the local library and would've loved Garfields (that's the defunct Coatbridge indie hot spot of the day, not the comic strip creation of Jim Davis).

She was out of my league. She smiled and yawned, and said stuff about hoping to find a guy like me who wouldn't cheat on them when toast was offered. How she thought I was funny and sharp, and a great guy with good morals. That's right, that's me, good old reliable Andy. Everyone else in the world is fucking around and shagging everything and breaking hearts and being unfaithful but not good old solid moralistic Andy. I've been far from perfect on this journey but there is a line and I always try not to cross it. I'm sitting beside her right now and she wants to meet someone like me one day? She moved me big style and I think she liked me too. She called a taxi and as I left, I got the biggest smile of the night.

'Those books are all banned.'

'Clever boy, now piss off.'

She kissed me on the cheek and with that I was off into the night thinking how beautiful and kind yet confusing the world was.

Just over an hour later, I returned and would like to say I was badly missed. James asked where I'd been but I got away with it. We got back, knackered, to our hotel – The Embassy, in Knightsbridge – at 6.30am. Another great place, with almost palatial rooms; with four or five beds in each room, we only needed two rooms for the whole gang. Michael, our roadie, sleepwalked and jumped into bed with me. I crawled out and went to sleep in his bed instead. Then at 9am we were awoken in a numb state of panic as the hotel's fire alarm had gone off. By the time we got back in, I couldn't sleep, had a bath, then actually went back to bed and dosed off till 1pm.

As we headed to play our gig at Camden Underworld, before briefly dropping by the record company office, Nirvana were heading to do *Tonight with Jonathan Ross* on Channel 4. They were supposed to play 'Smells Like Teen Spirit' or 'Lithium' but did 'Territorial Pissings' and stormed off stage with minutes to spare, just leaving feedback. I was missing them already, missing them and the routine – chatting with them, watching them soundcheck and seeing them play. Was that it over? I also found it strange how Jonathan Ross's show seemed to top and tail my story. I had been watching it in August when I was asked to come in and help Captain America in the QM in Glasgow, and now near the end of my journey, Nirvana were heading off to do the very same show.

I remember feeling nonchalant about yet another interview, this time with Michael Bonner for *Melody Maker*. Our friend Helen had been backstage at Kilburn with Andy Ross, the boss of Food EMI, and came to see us again that evening at the Underworld. Helen had previously put us up at her place on 5 October. Remember the small tidy room way upstairs and her flatmate Dave from Blur with the bad record collection?

The Kilburn gig had gone really well. We were so relaxed and happy and by this time surprisingly on top of our game. J'aimee and Ian thought we were brilliant and the reaction from the crowd was warm and friendly, with two encores. Backstage, Ian gave us T-shirts of a friend's band. They were called Anna and had a single out called 'Masonic Youth'. I got on well with Ian and J'aimee and they invited me back for a drink and an offer of a bed in the spare room. I clearly remember J'aimee went to bed early. Ian and I listened to music, and got pished and blethered into the night. Thanks to them, I had a great sleep and was made to feel at home, even if I was sharing a bed with a big fat cat who did actually look like Garfield (the comic strip created by Jim Davis, not the indie nightspot in Coatbridge).

The next morning J'aimee, Ian and I headed across the road to the location of our last gig. The rest of the band were looking nervous, wondering if I'd been abducted and if I would ever show up again. We gathered with Shonen Knife to play the Rough Trade shop in Covent Garden. On the way there, I spotted a famous London blue plaque, which commemorates someone famous once living or working there. I was excited to find out it was the offices of *Monty Python*, or at least two of them. Terry Gilliam and Michael Palin had bought the offices and used them as recording studios and editing suites. I loved that little corner of Covent Garden, called Neal's Yard.

The shop was mobbed. What was going on here? We played then signed, yes *signed* autographs on the EP. We were paid by being able to pick two albums each. I chose Smashing Pumpkins *Gish* on the Caroline label and Velvet Crush's *In The Presence of Beauty* on Creation with a cracking sleeve with a cool fish. Thanks again to Ian and J'aimee, they were great people.

We headed back home from the Nirvana tour. Quietly ending something special in a very normal and natural way. I was back home in Airdrie for 8.30pm and arranged to go out with Sherry; busy end to a busy day. Somewhere in a big box full of memories there's a photo of a relaxed 24-year-old man who was fast becoming a rather reluctant rock icon, smiling with a Scottish pound note that he couldn't spend in London. There's a memory of a guy who seems so happy, relaxed and without a care in the world.

CHAPTER 16

'YOU CAN'T PUT YOUR ARMS AROUND A MEMORY.'

So sang Johnny Thunders, who died in New Orleans in April 1991. I agreed with Johnny's sentiment: it would eventually be time to realise it was over and move on. I would've preferred if it were my choice, but fate had decreed that with Captain America, it would be over and it would be time to move from drumming to the equally precarious world of comedy.

After the Nirvana tour finished in early December 1991, Captain America were back in Scotland, still working hard. I was still a pivotal part. We started work on our second single on Wednesday, 18 December. The songs 'Flame On', 'Butter Milk' and a cover of Beat Happening's 'Indian Summer' were recorded with Jamie Watson, and with Joe McAlinden from Superstar temporarily helping us out on bass. We played Glasgow Tech on 21 December, now Glasgow Caledonian University but there was little or no advertising or posters around. Maybe it was too close to Christmas but it wasn't packed. Very goth and punky audience and well paid though all the money went back into clearing our Nirvana tour costs. Merry Christmas! Sharron's brother Stephen taped it on VHS and we headed off home to watch it.

1992 begins with the mixing of the EP from Monday, 6 January, to the Thursday. The sky is clear and blue as we hear news of dates in Norway. We will play seven days there – five gigs with accommodation and a possibility of a gig supporting Nirvana in Oslo on my birthday on 16 March (though this gig is later cancelled due to Nirvana's rapidly increasing world domination).

On Tuesday, 14 January, Alistair McKay interviews us for *Scotland on Sunday*. On Wednesday, 22 January, we audition for bass players. A small, curly-haired confident chap from Largs who we liked called Mark Guthrie tried out. He later went on to find success with The Supernaturals. The other was Sean Jackson from 18 Wheeler, who played more like a guitarist than a bass player though does well. After rehearsals and auditions we head to The Variety Bar to meet Roddie McKenna from Silvertone Records. Following our meeting we head to The Griffin for a post-meeting meeting about the meeting and agree it doesn't feel right. We stay out and head to Club X in Royal Exchange Square. We end up staying in Sinclair Drive in Battlefield, where Eugene's brother has a nursery and he helps as some ad hoc mild mannered janitor-meets-security-guard and we stay above it, in the coldest flat known to man.

On Thursday, we head for yet another record company meeting, this time with Gordon Charlton of Epic. He takes us for an Indian and seems very nice. He pays for one of the best lunches I've ever had, amazing fish pakora and promises to come see us play in London the following Friday at New Cross. On Sunday, grumpy and hungover, we have another bass player audition, this time with Richard, one of Eugene's flatmates. Richard is honest and admits he hasn't really learned the songs so we decide to give him another try later. Joe from Superstar continues to help us out during rehearsals in Glasgow's Berkeley Street.

On Friday, 31 January, we leave at 10am to play a gig at London's New Cross Venue and arrive two hours late at 7.50pm, again a mixture of busy Friday traffic and dense fog. The doors are already open, and we don't have a soundcheck. Our producer Jamie Watson is doing the sound and we start out ropey, but soon kick in once we level out and take it up a gear and the place goes crazy. We're very aware there are loads of A&R people from record companies, publishers and booking agents there. The one we all seem most eager to impress is Andy Ross of Food EMI.

I was glad to be playing the support band's kit as it was all set up and on other people's drums I always play better. I remember that night was probably one of my best Captain America performances. Everything just seemed to fit in and feel right and my monitors had a great mix and I could really hear everything. I think Joe was also a calming, reassuring influence and smiled all the time. My concentration was good. The crowd embrace us and we get two encores. Before we knew it, we had headlined New Cross Venue and it was over. Friends from Airdrie, Elaine and Julie, were on the guest list and are suitably impressed. We went down really well at New Cross and Eugene, looking back, was strangely very complimentary about how well I played.

I meet the Norwegian promoter and his wife who are putting us up on the Norway dates and she excitedly says we are like a mini-Pixies. So for me it's time off as Eugene and Gordon are going to Japan with the BMX Bandits, but not before we're on the guest list to see Teenage Fanclub, Redd Kross and the BMX Bandits play the Town and Country Club in Kentish Town the following day. We meet Teenage Fanclub about 2.30pm and I have the bizarre experience of playing football with drummer Brendan O'Hare in the empty former art deco cinema venue. Afterwards I head for a walk with my old pal Mark Hughes, who is guitar tech for the BMX Bandits, and have a relaxing afternoon in a boozer, with a few pints watching England beat Ireland at rugby. When we arrive back, Teenage Fanclub's Norman Blake generously gives us all a copy of 'What You Do To Me'.

Later that evening Redd Kross were exceptional. Teenage Fanclub's performance, a more than two-hour set, was probably the best I've ever seen them play. I manage to get some cool photos and at the bar afterwards hang out with an American called Bettina from a record company who really likes the band.

On the drive home in a bus we shared with the BMX Bandits, I feel a weird vibe from Eugene when I brought up some business, but just put it down to tiredness and a long weekend. Conversations are perfunctory without the usual fun and warmth.

A few weeks passed, there was still regular chat on the phone, checking in with the odd call and more talk of gigs in

Norway and Japan to look forward to. There was a possible problem looming with Marvel Comics, as they had taken none too kindly to the name of their registered character Captain America being used by a Scottish beat combo, and the band were forced to change name and became Eugenius. There was also a legal issue with the C&A chain over the use of their logo for the artwork for 'Flame On'. I found it amusing, but the phrase publicity stunt did spring to mind.

When I got a call to meet in the chosen pub of the time, The Staging Post in Airdrie, I knew from Gordon's nervous tone what it was about. I didn't even bother to go down to meet them. I kept it neat, purely a phone call. At the time I was really annoyed but I was always just a stop gap, helping them out but then it got quite exciting and I felt I had earned the right to stay. We've all been dumped by someone who was a great ride and that was about the extent of it for me. I knew from the way it was handled that they felt guilty – I suppose it was awkward for them as well as I knew they liked me.

Looking back now the most exciting time was when James was there. There was more power, it was punkier, and we may not have been as good musically but there was an energy, excitement and fragility where gigs could either be a nightmare or amazing. With Joe McAlinden, a very talented musician who I like a lot, in for the second Captain America single, the music was more stable, more professional and not as chaotic. Probably the way it should be.

I tried to ignore everything despite the rumours that were coming back to me on a daily basis and tried to keep it as dignified as possible and get on with something new. I kept trying to work out what the problem was. If it was the drumming, then why were the same two guys so chuffed for me when I was mentioned in a review for the first EP of being able to understudy Crazy Horse's drummer? In the phone call, Gordon asked if I'd like to come over to Norway and Japan and hang out with them as a mate and maybe be a drum tech and roadie a bit. I'm sure his intentions were heartfelt but that's when I hung up. My drumming was suffering from lack of concentration or focus.

I do bore easily. Sometimes singers and guitarists just like working with the drummer they're used to. I know singers and guitarists who only like working with me. It's weird and it's about the aesthetic involved and the feel, which may sound strange if you aren't in a band but if you are, your instinct is everything. It really can be that simple.

Maybe they didn't want to hurt my feelings. It was all clumsy and awkward and much as I still like Eugene and Gordon, I felt let down by them. Eugene has since apologised for the way I was treated and I've told him I forgive him and I do. They're good guys and it wasn't personal, just business and aesthetic. I'm sure looking back now when James and I were there, it may have been mental as fuck but that's what music is about – energy, mayhem and excitement.

There's an interesting addendum to this. I bumped into Eugene on 30 September 2011, and ended up going to the pub for a pleasant catch-up. He wanted to tell me, after 20 years, about his decision, to clear it up and get it out of the way so we could enjoy the rest of the day. He explained they were concerned at the time I was taking to get the songs recorded and was fearful of having to go in and record an album with greater financial constraints. He was used to having the drum tracks banged out really quickly. Ironically, I was used to banging out garage punk drum tracks most of my drumming life, and doing five or six tracks a day was nothing. For once, I thought I had the luxury of being able to take my time: I was making a fucking record, Paperhouse were paying for it. I almost thought it was your duty *not* to care about the financial constraints and the budget to record the songs. I was taking my time to get it right. I was in the studio, wrote up the drum sections for each part and wanted it to sound and feel right. I should've been told but they were maybe too nice to say, 'Come on Andy, pick up the pace'. The only sign of any tension was watching Gordon, who was playing some guide guitar but had this fixed stare that added to the tension. Concentration or lack of it fucked it up for me – after 40 seconds my mind starts to wander.

In 2010, my friends Garry John Kane and Andy Gardner asked me to play drums on a garage punk song called 'Midnight Stroll' for their Mod and soul project, Button Up. I was great at the start, did a nice bit in the middle but the same problem happened again: my mind wandered. On that session I was thinking it would be funny if you were the best drummer in the world but couldn't come in on time, you were terrible at starting but once you got going were unstoppable.

So maybe Eugene had a point: I might've been in the wrong job. There's a small line in the diary from around the time of Captain America's first EP that may hold the key. It says, '*Love playing live but hate the studio, I can't concentrate and it's so long and boring. On "God Bless Les Paul" the drumming is done quickly and there's a live feel to it".*'

So I had played my part in the small piece of pop history

that was Captain America. We released a debut four-track EP, then a second 12-inch with three tracks. All the songs I play on apart from 'God Bless Les Paul' were released on Atlantic in America. There was a second album in 1993, after Captain America changed their name to Eugenius, before they called it a day in 1995. There were also a few songs on indie compilations. I've never heard the Atlantic album let alone seen a copy. Again I never said anything. The upside? The band didn't become The Beatles and leave me with a Pete Best scenario. I played drums on an album on Atlantic, the same label as Led Zeppelin and Aretha Franklin, and toured with and got to know Nirvana.

Like Doctor Pangloss in *Candide*, I kept telling myself everything was for the best. Everything happens for a reason. Maybe it was the kick start I needed to really try and be a writer. I always remember, when I got my first sketch on a BBC Scotland show called *Only an Excuse?*, that I was more elated than I ever was playing on stage with Nirvana. What I do miss is the banter and the chat. I missed the 'meetings' in The Griffin and Equis Cafe. It felt like the rest of the world had to go to work in an office or a factory and there we were, skint, almost kidding on we were a band but happy. There really was a feeling we were just fannying about at being in a band and at that point it really was great fun. Honestly, no hard feelings, no regrets.

Actually that isn't strictly true. I do have regrets. You get no reward for loyalty and being faithful. Ultimately you come into this world on your own and leave it on your own and if you're lucky, you have a good time in between. It's not very politically correct but I now wish I'd fucked the brains out of everyone who wanted me to, instead of being a good guy because ultimately everyone lets you down.

It took me a long time to shake off the Nirvana tour. Anytime I remembered something, anything, any dialogue, I'd write it down. I loved music too much to walk away from it. Looking back, it was my brother Peter's fault. He had a friend at school called John Heaney who played drums and gave him a set of old sticks. I'd pick them up and dream I was Micky Dolenz, Ringo or Clem Burke but I would rattle them off every cabinet, wardrobe and table till my mum thought it cheaper to buy me a snare drum to save the furniture.

Back to 1980, a time when I was preoccupied by two singles. One on Island, a hit record from 1977 by Eddie and the Hot Rods called 'Do Anything You Want To Do'; the other was a single on Virgin in 1979 by XTC, called 'Making Plans For Nigel'. As soon as the house was empty I would play along to these songs and an album by The Rolling Stones called *Some Girls* constantly. If any of the neighbours are reading, I'm sorry.

Being the youngest of five, I grew up with loads of albums lying around: The Stones, Hendrix, Roxy Music, The Beatles, Captain Beefheart, David Bowie, Led Zeppelin, Free, Blondie, Simple Minds, Talking Heads, Joy Division, The Undertones, Neil Young, Ian Dury, The Police, Aerosmith, Queen, Orange Juice, Rainbow, Deep Purple, Japan and Black Sabbath. Add to this my sister's records: Bay City Rollers, David Essex, Bee Gees, Abba, The Carpenters, The Osmonds, loads of disco and soul stuff. There was always something new for me to find when the house was empty. I'd try and work out the drums to everything from Motörhead to Josef K. I would listen to my brother Stephen's punk and new wave records. There was 'Transmission' by Joy Division, and Simple Minds at this point were a cool art school band with songs like 'I Travel' and 'Changeling' – all great to drum to. When it came to drummers, I really liked Steve Jansen of Japan and Clem Burke of Blondie. I remember thinking that Clem must be some kind of six-armed super freak and marvelled at his separation on 'Heart Of Glass' only to find out years later, on a BBC4 documentary about *Parallel Lines*, that producer Mike Chapman made Clem drum every part of 'Heart Of Glass' separately.

I remember 'borrowing' three albums in 1982 for about six years from my then-girlfriend Patricia, which I drummed to relentlessly. They were *Boy* by U2, a Monkees greatest hits double album and an incredible double album by The Kinks called *Lola, Percy & The Apeman Come Face To Face With The Village Preservation Society...Something Else*. They belonged to Tom Roche, her older brother and my friend, who I'd later be in bands with; a country-folk project called The Rembrandts, years before the guys who wrote the *Friends* theme and better. He would then join me in Boomerang, and I'd help him out in his band, Monkeyfinger.

Looking back, I was very lucky to be surrounded by so many talented musicians. My brother Stephen, despite loving Yes and Rush, was a great bass player and folk guitarist; we had the Dave Grohl of Rochsoles Drive next door: Billy Gilchrist, a great drummer and an even better blues guitarist. We had guys like Joe Pearson, Bob Merry and bassist Campbell 'Cumba' Stewart. My pals growing up, Paul Hawthorne and Mark McDermott, were all great natural musicians, playing trumpet and coronet. We should've started a bluesy punk rock jazz ensemble. Creatively, I got on best with Mark Leslie who, like

Tom, had a diverse record collection, from 1960s pop to punk to jazz and blues, and understood what I was trying to do. He was an excellent guitarist and bass player with a great feel for the structure of a song.

Actually Mark was a like a young Kurt, a bad boy punk who was obsessed with Bowie and misunderstood. He would spend hours working out songs and getting his guitar sound just right. Lyrically and artistically, he also had the same dark sense of humour. Mark would push me; we would get set up in living rooms in council houses and play until we would be physically assaulted by neighbours because of the noise, so he'd hire out classrooms and we'd have the loudest jams, always working out different rhythms and time signatures. Eventually he managed to get a Fine Arts degree from Glasgow School of Art. He would always encourage me to listen to early Hendrix, the mid-era Berlin trilogy of Bowie albums (*Low, Heroes, Lodger*), The Stooges, MC5 and Iggy Pop.

I had songs, even though I couldn't play guitar. I had the words and the tunes in my head, and I had the attitude. I hooked up with Eddie Butler at high school, who helped get the tunes out of my head. I liked Echo and the Bunnymen's drummer, Pete de Freitas, and even had my matching haircut and second-hand Crombie from Oxfam. At school the cool common room chat was about Stiff Little Fingers, The Ramones, The Clash and The Undertones. I caught on quickly that the girls liked Big Country, Simple Minds, U2, Duran Duran and Culture Club. My pal Mick Lambe and I spent most of our sixth year dogging Higher Chemistry to discuss a new band called The Smiths and *Chronic Town*, R.E.M.'s first EP.

Much to the irritation of some of my family and the fears of fellow band members, I was so obsessed with music that at 18, I quit a job after nine months: a secure job in the Civil Service with a pension. As soon as I saved enough for my next drum kit and decent cymbals, I'd be off and wondering why everyone else wasn't as committed. I also went through a weird folk-rock period. Probably a mixture of Neil Young's folkier moments and because a girl I loved at the time was into Tim Buckley and Nick Drake – aren't they always?

By the age of 22, I went to America and did the Greyhound thing, my Jack Kerouac period of trying to find myself. A visit to Graceland, Sun Studios and Nashville gave me a new love for country and folk Americana. I went through a mad period of listening to Gram Parsons and The Flying Burrito Brothers, and Tom gave me *Sweethearts of the Rodeo*, The Byrds' country-rock album, which I was hooked on. We'd try and do cover versions of The Left Banke's 'I've Got Something On My Mind' though our version was closer to The Buckle on the Pebbles compilation *Highs in the Mid Sixties, Volume 12 (Texas Part 2)*. During this period I was also obsessed with Scott Walker and one song in particular, his cover of Tim Hardin's 'Lady Came From Baltimore'.

I put this eclectic dip into most genres to some good use by working at Our Price, a record shop in Cumbernauld. There, the manager, Mathew Cassan, encouraged and helped, and allowed you to play stuff you liked. Bands like Dinosaur Jr., The Replacements, Hüsker Dü, Big Star but also Nick Drake and surprisingly, 'Like a Virgin' by Madonna were always on the shop turntable. He would always listen to anything on Geffen as if it was a benchmark for decent music, the same way Faber and Faber or Bloomsbury or John Blake, obviously, are treated by readers as a home for the discerning writer. Around five o'clock, I used to play Sonic Youth's *Evol* and *Sister*, and a colleague called Chris would play Frank Zappa stuff. The idea was to get the shop emptied so I wouldn't miss the bus home but it didn't work that way. Instead we'd end up selling loads of Sonic Youth and Frank Zappa.

Eventually I learned some chords from watching friends and playing along with records on a Fender acoustic borrowed from my brother Stephen years ago and did more projects with Ben Mullen and Tom. Then I worried that I'd never do anything and had to get out of Airdrie or do something else, possibly writing or hairdressing. I didn't know it at that time but all these influences and experiences were aligning; all the rehearsals, gigs and hard work were leading up to the moment when I met Gordon, and ended up in Captain America touring with Nirvana.

After Captain America ended, I formed Boomerang. I went into the studio and recorded ten songs in a day with help from Mark Leslie, Tom Roche and Stuart MacLeod engineering. Murray Webster and James Seenan came out to help. I made a few calls and managed to get, via a nice piece of kindness from Paul Cardow, our first gig: supporting the Screaming Trees at the Cathouse in Glasgow. The first line-up had Nicky McQuillan on bass, Tom Roche on guitar, and I played drums and sang. Boomerang evolved into a steady line-up of Tom, Ross Clark on bass and Mark Elliot on drums and I eventually played guitar and sang.

Around this time, I was sneaking on to the campus of Stirling University by day to write the Lennon novel on Sharron's word processor, while at night Boomerang rehearsed and gigged. We played constantly at King Tut's, Nice 'N' Sleazy, and at the 13th Note, run by a dapper Alex Kapranos, who used to phone and book us regularly and later went on to form Franz Ferdinand. Our hard work culminated in playing T in the Park in July 1996, where I noticed Dave Grohl, then at the start of his Foo Fighters career, doing a TV interview. Dave spotted me and ran over while recording and jumped on me, then asked when we were playing to see if he could play on stage with us. We were selected to play by the festival director, Geoff Ellis, who liked the band from booking us for King Tut's. Dave Barker at Paperhouse really liked my very first demos though he may have been just being a good guy and supportive but he along with Justine Sullivan (who was at Nude Records before moving to Too Pure) wanted us to play some gigs in London before taking it any further.

We were offered a deal with a major: they loved the songs, wanted me as frontman and songwriter, but it involved sacking two of my mates. At that point, I realised I hated the music industry; I wouldn't stab people in the back to get a record deal. I'd had enough and this just confirmed it. Having worked tirelessly to make something happen, the nearest I got to being even close to a break was when I was the drummer in Captain America. But that was it. All my hard work from 15 to 25 finally was rewarded; I was proud to be keeping the beat for the third band on the bill on the Nirvana tour. I was on stage at King Tut's on my 30th birthday pretending to be 24 when I decided I'd had enough. I didn't say to anyone, I just let it come to a halt, really slowly.

After finishing the fictional what-if account about John Lennon that would probably set a benchmark in the libel laws and therefore never be published, I was playing drums with Tom in a studio connected to a library. We were asked to turn the noise down because the creator of *Rab C Nesbitt*, Ian Pattison, was a guest at the library's writers' group. I spoke to him about the book and he went on to mention it to his colleague, Philip Differ. Together they encouraged me to write comedy and opened doors for me at the BBC.

Pattison used my first sketch on a BBC Network comedy pilot called *Pulp Video*. I was delighted as before my sketch, two of my favourite DJs, Mark Radcliffe and Marc Riley (also known as Mark and Lard), had a sketch on. I had been a fan of Mark Radcliffe since his BBC Radio 1 show on a Monday called *Out on Blue Six* from 1991. My *Pulp Video* sketch was mentioned in a review by the *Independent* on 19 August 1995 by critic Jasper Rees as one of the show's better sketches: '*A sophisticated* Reservoir Dogs *spoof in which the Michael Madsen character lops off his own ears, not his victim's, as Danny Baker babbles over "Stuck in the Middle with You".*'

I knew if I channelled the same energy into comedy writing as I had with bands, I might have a chance. Highlights included a sketch show called *Sabotage*, for BBC Scotland for Nick Low's Demus Productions which, after a generous email invite from writing pal Gerry McDade, Norman Ferguson and I quite literally sabotaged, as well as festive shows for Radio Five Live produced by the Comedy Unit.

The next logical step would be to see if I could write a slightly different book from the diary, and write about my time on the road with Nirvana. As well as working for TV and radio, I had a brief spell with a column in Scotland's biggest-selling Sunday newspaper, the *Sunday Mail*. The editor at the time,

Allan Rennie, had me in for a chat and the subject of the Nirvana tour came up. Allan is an experienced journalist, knows about the human condition and I was keen to gauge his response. When I explained that I hoped to write something with a similar feel and tone to *Almost Famous,* the Cameron Crowe movie from 2000, his reaction was very positive and encouraging. From then, the summer of 2008, I concentrated on shaping up this book. What would it be like to have a drummer write the story? Someone who was lucky enough to be there at this moment when for a few weeks in Nirvana's life, things went crazy. I would be there in the wings, full of excitement, just like the six-year-old who loved his Aunt Ellen's records, and who was moved by the storylines in the lyrics on those 45s. The same person who was obsessed with The Monkees, The Banana Splits and *Bilko*, and went around for most of his childhood, adolescence and adulthood daydreaming about music, drumming and comedy.

Looking back at my time on the road with Nirvana, I realise that the events of 1991 and meeting these three gentle guys from Seattle had a monumental effect in shaping my life. Ironically, touring with Nirvana had made me want to write.

EPILOGUE

I was lucky to get to meet Kurt, lucky on two levels. I was fortunate to have met a guy who subsequently made a tremendous cultural impact in a short, troubled life; lucky in the sense that my inclusion in the band really happened by chance. Maybe because of the unintentional and accidental nature of the way I became the drummer, I went for it, enjoyed myself but for some reason kept a diary in case anything exciting happened. At times we saw the relentless pressure placed on the band, all on top of Kurt's chronic stomach complaints and his heroin addiction. Ask anyone who witnessed any of the shows if he let the fans down on the 1991 *Nevermind* Tour and the answer would be no. Apart from mentioning Kurt being laconic, another adjective seldom used to describe him was courageous. For such a small guy he was brave, fearless, unafraid of upsetting people who were racist and homophobic. He would stand up to people who were bullies.

He would scale PA systems and leave crowds captivated (though maybe that's just stupid rather than brave) before diving in. At Nottingham, he stopped the gig when he saw an over-enthusiastic bouncer scuffling with a fan. I was close enough to see him, to see that ugly incident all unfold. That bouncer was a massive fucker.

In terms of Kurt's health whatever your opinion over his drug use, none of us have the right to tell people what's right or wrong. It was up to him to sort himself out, no one else's business. In Edinburgh, even when he was ill, like the show at Calton Studios that I couldn't watch, I saw the doctor examine him and tell him he was too sick to perform, but he did anyway. One of the things that really impressed me, apart from their modesty, warmth and skill as musicians was how each night, no matter how drained and tired they'd be, Nirvana made the show. I saw them so many times and thought, *These guys are fucked.* You'd be fearful, as they'd be so weak with sheer exhaustion, jaded with nothing left, yet each night they dug deep and performed as they felt they owed it to the fans.

So for me, the band was over but for Nirvana, it just went stratospheric. It was chaotic. In the week after Christmas 1991, *Nevermind* sold 373,520 copies in the States and the following week, in January 1992, went to Number 1 on the *Billboard* album charts. It would eventually go on to sell over 26 million copies globally.

I find it hilarious and surreal in equal measure. How can this be happening to these three unpretentious guys, all this crazy adulation? One minute they were a punk band on Sub Pop with a skinny singer with a rock 'n' roll scream, the next they've become a phenomenon. Suddenly they go from the Nirvana I briefly knew, no longer competing with The Pixies or Sonic Youth but instead mentioned in the same breath as Bruce Springsteen, Neil Young, Tom Petty and the Heartbreakers, Bob Dylan, Jimi Hendrix and The Doors. If Petty, Dylan or Young were the literary equivalent of Steinbeck, Mailer or Bellow, Nirvana are like the gonzo bastard child of Charlie Brown and Hunter S Thompson. We haven't even mentioned the best album polls and greatest-ever band surveys.

I knew from the brief time I spent with them that success on this scale wouldn't rest easy on the group's shoulders, particularly Kurt's. I knew Dave and Krist would be fine but we were all a bit fearful of what the future held for Kurt. None of Nirvana would accept the responsibility of being anyone's spokesman and couldn't care less what their music was doing for a disenfranchised generation. Kurt just wasn't strong enough to keep it stable.

If there's anything to be gleaned from Kurt's story, then the end of his life shouldn't be shrouded in rock 'n' roll heroism but viewed as a tragedy. Here was a creative soul who just couldn't, and in fact didn't want, to handle it. Someone who is gone, someone who was sick and who you'd hope, in the correct frame of mind, would still be with us.

I was shocked but not surprised to hear that Kurt took his own life. As Tony Parsons, an exquisite commentator of modern culture, put it so brilliantly in the *Daily Telegraph* of 14 April 1994, 'We mourn Kurt Cobain not because his death comes as a surprise but because it feels inevitable.' I thought he was too cool a guy for the oldest of all the hackneyed, lazy clichés: a rock 'n' roll suicide. But the signs were there; it's really hard work maintaining a heroin habit and takes loads of key skills like dedication, application and deception.

In 1993 Kurt 'overdosed' six times. In Rome on 4 March 1994, he took 60 Rohypnol, leaving a suicide note. His management and record company, family and friends could only do so much. There was an extremely protective veil thrown over the last year of Cobain's life when his overdoses and fragility were spiralling out of control. Maybe they were being responsible to the millions of vulnerable young fans who worshiped Kurt to the end and think dying as he did at 27 was clever, heroic, poetic and iconoclastic. If there's a line that sums up Kurt's suicide and encapsulates the sense of waste and futility, and the feelings of a mother losing her son, then Wendy O'Connor's quote is profoundly poignant: 'Now he's gone and joined that stupid club, I told him not to join that stupid club.' She, like the rest of us, must have hoped and prayed he'd get through this.

Kurt died like a sick drug addict and the only tragedy is that's what he wanted. I like to remember the self-effacing, funny guy, the genuine fan of pop music and punk rock I met in the winter of 1991. Maybe I was lucky to get to know him at his best. There were subsequent flickers of hope that maybe it was going to be OK for Nirvana. It happened with Kurt's performance on a French TV show on 4 February 1994. It's one of the best performances I've ever seen of 'Drain You'. They look fantastic, Krist has his hair cropped, they're all in white shirts and black tie, Dave is on the money and Pat Smear beefs out the sound terrifically. At one point during the performance Kurt's guitar fails so he throws it off and grabs the microphone stand like Iggy Pop, and gives the most haunting, piercing scream he's ever delivered of 'Drain You'.

It's tough for me to be critical, but at the time he seemed hell-bent on fulfilling his destiny as a clichéd junkie icon. In the last few months of his life, despite all that success, he seemed to become more and more self-obsessed and bounced it all back on to everyone else – always the victim. It seemed to drag on so long that you started to lose any sympathy for him and only a matter of time before you put on the TV and saw his face, and the dates of his birth and death underneath. In his final days, it's now clear he was looking into the abyss. Some can look into that void and walk away, others get sucked in.

It's different for those who met and knew Kurt, however briefly, to witness his descent into disillusion and desperation. Stars, celestial ones, generate light and energy then explode because they run out of fuel. That's how I like to remember Kurt: a little skinny force of nature, who expressed himself with incredible power, who lit up the world with his music. I'm glad I wasn't close to the tortured soul at the end of his life; the addict at the end would probably tell me to fuck off if I met him. It's hard to connect that this is the guy I knew in 1991. I can't say I cried when I heard he had taken his own life; I was upset and shocked but more angry than anything. I'm sorry to have to admit this but it was a selfish anger: I liked the band, I wanted to see them play again. What really upset me, though, were the more subtle things. Sometimes it could be as tenuous as that final photo and seeing that hand lying dead, that same one you held and shook. The one that held up the Scottish bank note, or waved at you, or flipped you the bird, or went through your tapes and annoyed you as you tried to concentrate; the same hand so full of life, warmth, blood and creativity. When you see the name Converse and you see that same shoe. That very same shoe twisted in desolation and splayed in unnatural wretchedness. A cadaverous decaying glimpse left for the world to gawk and gape and scrutinise.

The tortured, sick and frail addict is the lasting image the world got to know. Kurt's spiral and inevitable demise has been well documented but Captain America were fortunate to know the band just at the start of their global breakthrough when they were in bloom. I only knew him briefly and Kurt's death, though not unexpected, had a profound effect on me so it's impossible to gauge the loss experienced by his family. We were all just old colleagues and fans that you'd hope if you bumped into 20 years later he'd maybe remember you, and it was hard to take, but it's difficult to imagine how Dave and Krist got through. They did though, with a lot of good old-fashioned class and good manners. Clearly Courtney took it badly and in some way is still probably trying to cope with Kurt's death. I hope she stays strong.

When we knew the band, they were bemused at the incredible reaction to 'Smells Like Teen Spirit'. They were friendly, warm, affectionate and kind, far away from the public image of guns and drugs and breakdowns. When I watched them awkwardly shamble on stage each night I felt so concerned and worried that they wouldn't pull it off. I couldn't believe they had the energy, power or skill to transform into a rock 'n' roll juggernaut but they did, and something magical happened. Chemistry? Adrenalin? Kurt's prescription painkillers? The three of them may have been knackered and worn out, yet when they went on stage, they seemed to be fuelled by the love and energy from the crowd.

When I see winter skies at dusk I always think of the Nirvana tour. Looking out of the van travelling across the UK, as it kept breaking down. Looking out at that distinctive late afternoon light as it fades, and as November slumbers into December. I still see those glorious winter afternoons and think of 1991, just as the sun is low in the sky, as the crepuscular rays of light flicker through the trees, the sun almost gone, radiating from a single point in the sky. There's a delicious luminosity to the smouldering winter dusk. A distinctive tranquillity and glow as the sun travels along the ecliptic and is farthest south of the celestial equator. Its journey, like mine, is almost over and about to turn back.

At a set of lights somewhere in deepest darkest England, the scene is like something from the Dutch landscape artist Aelbert Cuyp. A cow surveys all before her, so full of bearing, stands impressively beside a flowing stream, the orange and dark blue tones reflect and diffract distinctive lights, which shimmer and light up the cow's udder, the veins are pumping and the universe is connected. The stream moves swiftly, heading toward the sea. In the sky Mother Nature takes care of business, heading toward the winter solstice as the weary world celebrates Christmas, lighting up her winter skies so beautifully with her own illuminations. Soon again returning, when the flowers will be in bloom, seasons change and we are all as one.

There I was, connecting with the universe, at one with

nature and hanging out with the hottest band in the world as they lit up and connected with the planet. Life, for us at least, goes on.